Empty Seats

Empty Seats

by

Michael White

Hamish Hamilton London

To Joshua, Liberty and Sasha

First published in Great Britain 1984
by Hamish Hamilton Ltd
Garden House, 57–59 Long Acre, London WC2E 9JZ

Copyright © 1984 by Michael White

British Library Cataloguing in Publication Data
White, Michael
    Empty seats.
    1. White, Michael   2. Theatrical producers and
    directors – Great Britain – Biography
    I. Title
    792'.0232'0924   PN2598.W4/

    ISBN 0-241-11348-2

Photoset by Rowland Phototypesetting Ltd
Bury St Edmunds, Suffolk
Printed in Great Britain by
St Edmundsbury Press, Bury St Edmunds, Suffolk

Contents

Illustrations

1. *Loot!*
2. Michael White, Lyndall and children in 1974
3. On the roof of Duke Street in 1968 (*left to right*): Michael White, Sarah White, Pauline Fordham, Gala Mitchell and David Hockney
4. At Sadlers Wells in 1963 (*left to right*): John Cage, Merce Cunningham, Robert Rauschenberg and Michael White (© *Douglas H. Jeffery*)
5. During rehearsals for *Any Wednesday* at the Apollo Theatre in 1964
6 & 7. Two faces of the reaction to *Oh! Calcutta!* when it first appeared in 1969 (© *Marc Boxer*, and © *Sir Osbert Lancaster; from a* Daily Express *Pocket Cartoon by Osbert Lancaster*)
8. A restaurant in Rome in the late Sixties: Peter Daubeny (*left*), with whom Michael White spent 'five happy years of apprenticeship', and Federico Fellini
9. Kenneth Tynan, critic, friend and co-presenter of *Oh! Calcutta!* (© *Donald Cooper/Camera Press Ltd*)
10. An invitation to Harold Wilson to attend a performance of *Soldiers* received a dusty answer
11. But the *Daily Express* had to apologise for misrepresenting another of Michael White's shows
12. Hewison's *Loot!* cartoon
13. A card from Willie Rushton
14. Programme montage
15. 1970 – *The Dirtiest Show in Town*
16. 1973 – during filming for *The Rocky Horror Picture Show*
17. 1976 – *A Chorus Line* directed by Michael Bennett at the Theatre Royal, Drury Lane (© *Zoë Dominic*)
18. The Young Vic production of *Cato Street* with Vanessa Redgrave
19. Spike Milligan and Marjie Lawrence in the 1963 production of *Son of Oblomov* (Daily Mirror *photograph*)
20. Tony Richardson at the first night of *The Threepenny Opera*
21. Clive Goodwin, key Sixties literary agent
22. American glamour in Earls Court: Diana Vreeland and Jack Nicholson with Michael White at a Bob Dylan concert
23. The Comic Strip: Rik Mayall, Nigel Planer, Jennifer Saunders, Adrian Edmondson, Dawn French and Peter Richardson line up (*left to right*) in *A Fistful of Traveller's Cheques* (© *Channel Four*)

CHAPTER ONE

From the Lighthouse to the White Barn

In 1956, at the age of twenty-one, I was sitting in a lighthouse in Connecticut about to start work on my first novel.

As a child I had daydreamed, read extensively and watched a lot of films. Confined to my bed over quite long periods, I had developed a vivid imagination. Right now, I was happily engrossed in my fantasy of becoming a bestselling novelist. Then, as if in one of Hollywood's sillier movies, the telephone rang.

'Michael?'

'Yes.'

'This is Mr Cugat.' (He was the owner of the lighthouse.) 'How would you like to work in a theatre for a month and help out my sister Lucille?'

'Well . . .'

'It wouldn't be for long and it's a very interesting theatre nearby in Westport . . . I would be most obliged. . . .'

Having just chucked my coveted job as a messenger boy on the floor of the New York Stock Exchange in order to concentrate on my first novel I rather guiltily thought: 'But what about my book, what about that publisher climbing the steep stairs of the lighthouse to admire my manuscript, and what about my new-found solitude on the edge of a beautiful blue sea glinting through the narrow windows?'

Instead I said, 'That sounds fun. When?'

'Be in Manhattan tomorrow and Lucille's husband will drive you to Westport.'

So, by that one conversation, my career as a writer was over (even though I did finish the novel and indeed wrote four more – all unpublished) and I embarked instead on a stop-gap job in the theatre which has lasted ever since.

Most summer theatres in America are given over to local re-run versions of hit Broadway or West End shows but the White Barn Theatre was very different. With a mere 130 seats it existed as a try-out for the adventurous and the new. And Lucille Lortel, who ran the theatre, generously insisted that admission be free. I soon discovered that she could afford to be generous. Her theatre was fully subsidised, ad infinitum, by the local equivalent of the Arts Council – her very rich and indulgent husband, Lou Schweitzer. A penniless émigré from Russia at the turn of the century, Lou had become enormously wealthy through the manufacture of cigarette papers.

Lucille, who had started her theatrical career in Berlin, had come to Hollywood in the Twenties and starred in several movies but, after meeting and marrying Lou, agreed to retire as an actress. To reward her, he not only bought her the beautiful Theatre de Lys, one of the first off-Broadway theatres, but also built the White Barn Theatre actually on their Westport estate.

My friends in New York were understandably surprised to see me back quite so soon. (I must confess I had only been working on the Great Novel for three days.) We decided to celebrate this new twist of fate and hit the Renaissance bar on 49th Street. Rather more sophisticated and smart than any London pub, it was the hangout for many young people with European backgrounds. In those days it was much more glamorous to be English than it is now. This was pre-jet set, when people rarely travelled abroad and, if they did, usually by boat, to Europe. The USA was still somewhat uncharted territory and Americans were consequently more than hospitable to anyone with an English accent.

I fitted the bill. And, in addition, I had acquired something of a European gloss because of my distinctly peripatetic childhood. It was happy enough, but complicated by extremely bad asthma, which I contracted at the age of six and which lasted for seven or eight years. The doctors blamed Scotland's damp conditions and suggested I be sent to the Swiss Alps until completely cured. Although this seemed a drastic solution, the attacks were so violent and unpleasant that I was prepared to try anything to cure the dreadful wheeze.

The first school I went to in Switzerland was 'interesting' since out of sixty pupils, I was the only British one; no one spoke any English and I certainly didn't know a word of French. To begin with, I was lonely and miserable, but it is extraordinary how quickly human beings adapt when necessary, for within four months I spoke French fluently, albeit with a slight accent.

Unfortunately, although I was now bilingual, my asthma was just as bad and it was decided that Villars was not at a high enough altitude. So off I went to the Engadine which was 6,000 feet up and to a school where everyone spoke German. At least there were half a dozen other Brits there, all of whom were asthmatics like myself, but German was harder to learn and less rewarding. Also it was difficult being at a school were there were so many Germans only a few years after the war.

Almost everything has its good side, however, and in this case I was able to devour all the books I could lay my hands on as I languished in bed. By the time my asthma started to improve I was more than au fait with English and French literature; it was useful education for later life, even though my slightly snobbish intellectualism often involved me in furious arguments with Hollywood studio executives over what they termed badly written scripts.

I decided to stay abroad when the time came to go to University. I started off in Italy at Pisa and ended up at the Sorbonne in Paris, which was not nearly as amusing or romantic as it might sound and, I suspect, much more demanding than a British university. At the end of all this moving around my father decided that I was ready for a career in the City and, although by this point he had gone from considerable wealth to relative penury, he still had connections. And so I became a messenger boy on the New York Stock Exchange.

Again I was something of a rarity – being British and working on the actual floor of the 'big board' – but, although I soon realised I was not suited to the world of finance, I did meet some highly amusing characters amongst the brokers. There was one ancient man of ninety who, once he heard that I had studied in Paris, would sit on a stool in the corner and insist on discussing the different merits of the French Impressionists. There were many others who, having been stationed in Europe during the war, enjoyed a chat about Mayfair and surrounding areas. Unfortunately I knew nothing about any of this as I had hardly set foot in London since I was a small child. Still, they were all very friendly and generous, and the ones I met seemed to have made enough money not to have to do very much work. I did, however, see them leaping around on one extraordinary day when Eisenhower had his first heart attack and panic struck the market. It was the biggest single drop in one day since the Depression.

But it was after-hours New York that intrigued me. In sharp contrast to the drabness of post-war Britain, it was alive and seething with energy and prosperity. As a messenger boy I was making a pittance but I found a room in brownstone marvellously situated opposite the Morgan Library.

And as it was eight flights up with no lift – something most Americans wouldn't consider – it was very cheap.

As a bonus to the convenience and the view, I encountered my first serious American writer, Robert Hoig. He had arrived in New York from Nebraska and was determined to write his first novel and track down the contemporary writers he admired, in particular Hemingway, on whom he had a serious crush.

When I first moved in next door to Robert, he was flat broke and hadn't eaten for a couple of days. I took him to Horn and Hardart's famous self-serve cafeteria for a slap-up dinner. This perked him up so much that we set off on a tour of the Third Avenue bars that Hemingway frequented and sure enough found him somewhat under the weather, but in a very friendly mood, on an Irish bar stool. That night he certainly lived up to his reputation as a great storyteller and amazing company.

Through my Sorbonne friends, I began to meet a very wide range of people. New York, then, worked on the domino theory: once one door opened, lots of others followed. Although hard-up, I still had my good London suits and ties to go with them, and being a European in New York really was a considerable social asset. One of my friends, Lenny Ladin, had an uncle who was fortunate in possessing a box in the Golden Horseshoe at the Metropolitan Opera House. The uncle, who also happened to be the most decorated civilian in America, was very generous and offered us the unlimited use of his box. Miraculously from my point of view, it was the year when Callas was starting to make a major impact on American audiences.

Then there was the Renaissance bar – introduced to me by friends from Paris, the Kossokowskis, who were good-looking, glamorous and witty. The Renaissance had its own little clique of regulars and, although dining there was prohibitively expensive, the bar (and this is one of New York's pleasant and more curious customs) was no higher priced than any other in town. Perhaps it was part of the American democratic process.

This was the decade B.D. (Before Drugs) and the night life, in retrospect, was safe, perhaps even a trifle middle class – but a quick trip down to the Village and you were in Bohemia. My favourite spot was the Cedar Street Bar where the painters hung out and which I discovered by accident as I had a girlfriend who lived across the street. (This was the girl who much later told me that in between seeing me and others she had also been dating James Dean.) Of course hindsight is the easiest course. When Jackson Pollock walked into the Cedar Street it didn't cause a ripple.

All this was fun but I truly believed I wanted to write and I knew I would never do so in New York. Every night there was another temptation and the day was far too busy even to think about writing, as, in my uniform and brown shoes, I was kept running around between the brokers for hours.

Finally I found that fatal summer job as a sitter for the lighthouse – which led to my turning up at Lou Schweitzer's office on a very hot May morning with the temperature at over forty degrees centigrade and the humidity touching a hundred . . . a typical New York summer day. The heat, coupled with my Renaissance hangover, caused me to faint while I waited in the garage of the office building for Lou to arrive and give me a lift back to Westport. Lou found me being splashed with water by the attendant, but he was kind and friendly and suggested a whiff of oxygen at a nearby drugstore. At last we headed off and he told me a bit about how the theatre operated and how this year the famous American actress Eva Le Gallienne, daughter of the English poet and the actress who had done much to popularise Chekhov and Ibsen for American audiences, would be organising a summer school with about thirty students, some of whom would also help around the theatre.

The basic plan for that summer was eight productions, each running for the weekend only. Some of the high-profile Westport residents were expected to take season tickets and make a donation towards the costs. The true cost, though, was subsidised by Lou. He himself was not that excited about theatre. His personal hobby was radio and in the vast grounds of the estate, which was adjacent to that of the Ira Gershwins, he had built a highly sophisticated radio receiver and transmitter from where he conducted dialogues with enthusiasts all over the globe. All the year round Westport had a high proportion of writers and actors living there, as well as advertising types with artistic pretentions. It was only about an hour from New York City. It was also a high income area and supported the Theatre Guild's famous Westport Playhouse which was run more along the lines of an English rep theatre. It was, therefore, an ideal place to try out the original and the avant garde. Arthur Miller and Marilyn Monroe were sometimes in the audience, and, as I was to discover, Lucille's visitors' book looked like a Who's Who of the American Theatre.

We swept in through the gates leading to the estate. It had a marvellous lake, immaculate lawns and flowers. The theatre was white and gleaming and the Schweitzers' beautiful house lay just behind the trees. There was also a natural amphitheatre built around a small hill for outdoor performances. Then there was the accommodation for the students, a large swimming pool and lots of garages filled with all kinds of exotic motor cars.

After a pleasant lunch with Lou and Lucille I quickly found out why there was an extreme staff shortage, for easy going as Lou was, Lucille was the exact opposite. She was friendly but terribly finicky and hard to please. But, by being thrown in at the deepest end without warning, I learned more about theatre in a couple of months than if I had spent three years at drama school. Firstly, because of the staff shortage soon every detail of the day-to-day running came across my desk – from auditioning to building scenery and manning the box office. At the same time I was in constant touch with the students, the girls outnumbering the boys by at least two to one. Then, the new manager never quite materialised and, although I had the odd title of executive secretary, I found myself quite happily working from nine in the morning until midnight or later. It was exciting and fun and, as each weekend brought a new production, there was never a moment to get bored or indeed to question too closely the quality of the work being done. But somehow I found time to write some articles and dance reviews for the local newspaper. All good experience, but it was still out of the question to consider working on my novel. After a few weeks Lucille asked me if I would stay through the season and of course I was by now hooked. I had to learn more. My love of the theatre had actually begun in Paris when, although I could only afford the wooden benches at the Comédie Française, I went several times a week. And before that even, during holidays in London, I would squeeze in every West End matinée I could.

One of the earliest lessons I learned in the theatre was that there were as many dramas off-stage as on ... and the first example was not long in coming. One day I was talking to Lou about Russia and about my grandfather also being Russian. I casually mentioned that, through my friends the Kossokowskis, I had briefly met the current Soviet Ambassador to the United Nations, who was something of a celebrity. Lou was impressed and begged me to invite my friends and the Ambassador up to Westport. I passed this on to the Kossokowskis, who were keen to see where I was working – and soon a Sunday lunch date was arranged.

It was another of those incredibly hot days and Lou had prepared a barbecue by the swimming pool with, unfortunately as it turned out, lots of Bloody Marys and iced vodka. During the time I had been at the theatre Lou always seemed at one remove from the perpetual hysteria and drama. He ambled around, usually with a cigarette dangling from the corner of his mouth, a funny round hat rather like a bee-keeper's perched on his head and the oldest of grey flannels. Often he seemed more like the caretaker than an enlightened patron of the arts. This Sunday, however, was different. Although Lou had spent all his adult life in America, like all Russians he still felt strongly the pull of Mother Russia and he had turned up immaculately dressed and in a state of high excitement.

After lunch the Ambassador and Lou began to argue about the respective merits of the Marxist and capitalist systems. The vodka flowed and somehow the excitement for this poor émigré who had become a multi-millionaire became overwhelming. In the middle of a speech extolling the virtues of the American system he clutched his chest and had to be rushed to the nearest hospital suffering from a heart attack. Fortunately it turned out to be of the mildest kind. Lou soon recovered and obviously bore no grudges for when, much later, I finally finished my novel, he insisted on treating me to a professional typist. He was unfortunately not repaid since the Boston publisher rejected the book. On a Calcium Terrace, as I called it, was never published. It was nearly accepted by Victor Gollancz years later, but on the condition that I would do some rewrites. However by that time I was totally immersed in working for Peter Daubeny.

Meanwhile the season at Westport was drawing to a close. I still clearly remember the students doing *The Seagull* and one in particular attacking what must be one of the most difficult scenes for any young actress. (Much later I saw Vanessa Redgrave render it as I had always imagined and hoped it could be done.) There were other dramas that summer – but of a more conventional kind. There was the drama coach who imagined that I was having an affair with his girl, which was not completely untrue, and who, on a hot and steamy night, attacked me with a bread knife. Fortunately he left soon afterwards.

I returned to New York where I took a smooth and undemanding job in an art gallery. It was run by two elderly spinsters – both leading lights of the Daughters of the American revolution – and specialised in portraits. Most of my time was spent showing chairmen of major American companies selections of the artists the gallery represented so they could make a choice for their boardrooms. Among these were two highly regarded English artists, Gerald Brocklehurst and Simon Elwes, and I later became friends with the latter's son, Dominic.

Rather to my surprise I seemed to fit rather well into this milieu and, when I decided that after two years in New York it was perhaps time to return to London, the ladies made much fuss and pleaded with me to stay. It would have been a pleasant but extremely placid life but, after my experiences of the summer, I wanted to be involved in a more theatrical environment.

In the Renaissance one night with a girl from the White Barn Theatre, I started talking to a man who turned out to be Charlie Feldman, then the top talent agent. I told him what I had been doing and that I wanted to be a writer. 'You ought to be in Hollywood,' he said, as though he were advising someone who was looking for smoked salmon that they should try Zabar's. From his office a few days later he telephoned Hal Wallis on the Coast. 'Why don't you give this English boy a job on your next movie?' His next movie, I recall, was an Elvis Presley picture.

Nothing could have been easier, it seemed. People liked to do favours for Feldman. Everything about him – the gleaming office, the limousine, the pink Park Avenue apartment where the girl and I had ended up drinking brandy with him that first night – reeked of achievement. This was a vastly different world from the White Barn – for all the latter's air of wealth and comfort. This was Show Business and it alarmed me. I did not want to go to Hollywood. I was no longer as certain as I once had been, even though I was well embarked on my second weighty novel, that I wanted to be a writer. But I was not yet aware, in the flurry of different experiences, of how securely I had been hooked by the theatre.

A few days later I told Feldman thanks, but no thanks. I was going back to Europe to explore Lou Schweitzer's radio plans (he had bought some stations and seemed to think I might be helpful in some undefined way). 'You look a bit starved,' Feldman said, shaking my hand and stuffing some bills into my top pocket. When I got outside I saw that they amounted to about $300, ten weeks' wages at the White Barn. But perhaps he was happy to see the last of me. The girl I had been with that first night we met was going out with him now.

CHAPTER TWO

An International Guide to the Theatre

'My help in ages past,' wrote Sir Peter Daubeny, on the flyleaf of his autobiography – kindly referring to me. 'My hope in years to come.' And if, in the theatre, I have fulfilled the hope of anyone at all, including myself, it is due more than anything to the apprenticeship I served with him.

Peter was then easily the most exceptional of all Britain's impresarios. As an actor at Liverpool Rep he was a contemporary of Rex Harrison and Ivor Novello. Noël Coward and Vivien Leigh were among his friends when his career was interrupted by World War II.

Although he had already begun to consider becoming a manager, the decision was made for him by a German mortar bomb, which, in the battle of Salerno during the 1943 Italian campaign, removed his left arm. He was still wearing the uniform of a major in the Coldstream Guards when he set out to plan the first new production to be staged in London after the war in Europe had ended. It was called *The Gay Pavilion* and, despite being received ecstatically by theatre-starved Londoners, it only ran four weeks. This gave him good reason to believe the first part of one of Novello's admonitions to him that he was fond of quoting. 'The theatre is the most exciting profession in the world. It is also a very dangerous and treacherous one.' But he must have had his doubts about the second part. He was particularly anxious to impress upon me: 'Never mind what other people think. Follow your own judgement and no one else's.' Actually, that was something I did not need telling.

I came under Peter's sway as inadvertently as I had found my way to the White Barn. By the time I had settled myself in London again, the European radio plan was off. An American playwright I had met on the return crossing suggested that I might get some career guidance from his agent, Aubrey Blackburn. I still planned, of course, to be a novelist. But Blackburn, a kindly Edwardian gentleman, urged me to try for something creative where my languages, my knowledge of Europe and America and my theatrical experience would all be useful. That rather narrowed the field. Narrowed it right down, in fact, to Covent Garden where Blackburn thought there might be something, or to Peter Daubeny.

Peter was already firmly set on the path that was to make his reputation as an adventurous and steel-nerved importer of the best that the world's theatre could offer to Britain. Since 1951, when he opened a season of international ballet at the Cambridge Theatre with the celebrated brother and sister flamenco dancers Antonio and Rosario, he had been engrossed with dancing – all kinds of dancing. He had brought to London Katharine Dunham, Ram Gopal, Roland Petit, Martha Graham, and a score more foreign companies and soloists.

But he had not turned his back on drama. At that moment he had the Chinese Classical Theatre from Formosa booked into Drury Lane. And, as I soon found out, Peter had been responsible for the only event that could make me wish I had spent the previous year in London rather than America. Under his management the legendary Berliner Ensemble of East Berlin had staged several items from their repertoire of Brecht at the Palace Theatre. I regarded Brecht, whom I had read extensively in German, as the finest contemporary playwright.

As well as impeccable taste, Peter had other advantages. For a start he was ready to give me a job. To this day I do not really know why. Like all successful entrepreneurs he would get five or six letters a week from young 'hopefuls' seeking work. For eighteen months he had refused to see anyone. But my letter – succinct and typed, I regret to say, in green, apparently impressed him. He agreed to see me. We got on well and he offered me a job – as his assistant at £6 a week – on the spot. I was not sure quite what this entailed but eagerly accepted, not even bothering to go for an interview at Covent Garden.

The next company he planned to import was the Moscow Arts Theatre – a hugely impressive event and a major coup. Numerous attempts to lure them had been made but Peter was the first to meet with any success. Meanwhile, there was always something to be done at Drury Lane where, because of their inability to communicate with the Chinese company, the theatre staff were somewhat confused.

There was certainly something to be done the first night I reported to the English company manager. 'Thank God,' he said when he saw my occidental features. 'You do The Corner.'

The gesture that brushed aside the Chinese stagehand I was to replace indicated that I was to operate the curtain and scenery change signals on cues from Tsai Chin, the girl compère. Tsai Chin was the only member of the company who spoke any English. She had come to England after the Revolution and was the daughter of China's greatest actor. Fittingly, for the sister of Michael Chow, the restaurateur, she was also an amazing cook.

Because of my White Barn experience, I was not completely intimidated by the task I had been given. But the White Barn had been a 130-seat theatre. The Lane held almost twenty times as many (2,400, to be precise) and the mechanisms were proportionately complicated and daunting.

The performance seemed to last for two days rather than two hours, and I prayed for it to be over. When Tsai Chin eventually gave me the cue to lower the final curtain I discovered, to my horror, that high above us the flymen had gone to sleep. I can still feel the tension rising like a thermometer as the audience clapped and clapped while the actors, inscrutable as ever, took encore after encore after encore and the whining, plunking Chinese orchestra played on and on and on.

The welcome I received from Peter was echoed less than faithfully by his staff. Although there was a secretary who was as wonderful to me as she was to everyone, there was also a production manager of many years standing who had fallen victim to a malady that seems to strike at every generation of theatre craftsmen. It is the conviction that since things were always done successfully in one particular way then that is the only way they should be done subsequently and forever. What I like is someone who says: We've done it that way for the last twenty years, let's see if we can't do it better this time.

The third member of the entourage was Duncan Melvin – Peter's publicist. At the first opportunity he swept me across the road to the tea shop opposite the Drury Lane Theatre where he suspiciously grilled me as to who I was, what I knew, how I'd got the job and what exactly I was supposed to be doing. He was obviously afraid that I might intrude on his territory. Matters never really improved with Duncan, partly, I suppose, because I adopted the defence that is still habitual to me if anyone is unpleasant. I just turn away and ignore them, having as little to do with them as possible. And I regret it in this instance because, although exceedingly camp, he was really very engaging and gregarious. I first encountered Roman Polanski and many other celebrities at Duncan's house. He loved the ballet and curiously co-authored a book on bullfighting with Kenneth Tynan. If we had met in different circumstances we would probably have become fast friends.

19

It would be impossible to exaggerate the value of my experience with Peter. A few years later he was to develop his World Theatre Season in partnership with the Royal Shakespeare Company and finally achieve some financial security together with the recognition he had so resolutely earned. But, at the time, my £6 a week had to be found on top of the cost of the next production. And the commercial West End was sewn up, to a point that hardly anyone today remembers, by the notorious Hugh Beaumont.

'Binkie', as he was invariably known, was the managing director of H. M. Tennent and on the board of Stoll, who together controlled – and still control – dozens of theatres. He signed up every speck of talent that floated into London – or banished it forever. No one has ever had such power in the theatre before or since. So established a character was he on both sides of the footlights that many revues had a song with his name in it, which always got a laugh. He had all the stars, all the plays, and access to all the theatres. He also had the backing of Prince Littler, who in turn controlled Stoll.

Binkie had the West End in his pocket, but that was not enough – he wanted everything and without competition. I swung into his orbit much later on and he was always very nice to me. But Peter had told me stories about Beaumont trying to hinder him from establishing the Daubeny Management. Fresh from the battlefields, he described Binkie in his own autobiography as more dangerous than the Germans.

Peter financed everything himself at terrific risk, borrowing money from moneylenders at killing rates and getting into the most appalling tight corners. There was never enough money. Indeed he was generally in the red.

He had a wonderful Russian associate, Dimitri Spount, a fascinating figure of a kind not seen today, always impeccably dressed in double-breasted suits. Whenever we went to Paris, Dimitri would head for the expensive Russian nightclubs and gypsy violins. He fixed loans for Peter, with hideous interest rates, but they often saved the production.

Peter was not a businessman. He was a creative person with a great instinctive feeling for acting. He loved the big performance – the great singer, the star. We once sat in a theatre in Paris and he whispered: 'He's not a good actor – look at the way he's putting his hands in his pockets – it's awkward. I would sew them up if he worked for me!' His hero and model was the great entrepreneur C. B. Cochrane.

He had total confidence in his own taste and judgement and an extraordinary ability to get on with people. At the same time he was terribly dependent on others – particularly on his wife Molly who was the solid rock in his life, on his secretary Ann, on me. He had very, very low energy. In the middle of the day he would say, 'I've got to go to bed.' He went to endless doctors but only just before he died after twelve years of misery was it discovered that he had a brain tumour.

There was never enough money for the simple reason that the only big foreign companies that Peter wanted to bring in needed such huge amounts to make the trip – just to cover the expenses. Profit was usually out of the question beyond a small management fee. It would not be possible to sell enough seats to cover the costs of a large company. So, although Peter would take the risk initially by offering a guarantee, he would have to try to get whichever country the company represented to subsidise its visit.

Thus many of the actors I met when I was with Peter were foreign. In London they were greatly sought after and we therefore had a non-stop social life, some of it very trying. The actors would be on their best behaviour: they were keenly aware of representing their troupe, their country, and usually very appreciative of appearing in the London theatre. Once they came to trust us, those from the Iron Curtain countries would sometimes unburden themselves in the small hours and we would get a glimpse of the unhappiness that restriction, even with the considerable privileges most of them enjoyed, means to an artist.

All this time, I was discovering London. Peter lived and had his office in a beautiful house in Chester Square. Right up the main staircase stretched a marvellous mural of all the great theatrical figures he had presented. I was lucky to find a flat in Chester Street nearby belonging to Harry Miller who ran the Redfern Gallery. It had been magnificently decorated by his friend and compatriot, Loudon Sainthill, the stage designer. (Much of my life seems to have been lived alongside Australians – my long-term girl friend Lyndall Hobbs, Richard O'Brien, the creator of *The Rocky Horror Show*, and Jim Sharman, its director; but Harry and Loudon were the first I met.) New York had convinced me that, whenever possible, one should live within walking distance of work.

Just down the road, in Sloane Square, was the Royal Court Theatre. The Court was then enjoying a peak period, forging ahead with the momentum provided by the success of John Osborne's *Look Back in Anger*. In command was George Devine, himself surrounded by young and brilliant disciples such as Tony Richardson, John Dexter and William Gaskill. These directors and the playwrights with whom they collaborated on so many major breakthroughs fascinated me more than the actors did.

In the early days of its tenancy the English Stage Company used to try out plays at the Court as Sunday night productions without scenery or costumes. These productions, new-born and full of promise as it were, drew keen audiences of the bright and aspiring.

I would often go with Michael Hastings, a young rising star of a playwright with whom I became friends soon after my return from New York. One night there was the first performance of a play by Stuart Holroyd, the philosopher, which had attracted much excitement and anticipation. In Act 2 there was an exceedingly unpleasant torture scene, which seemed to many perverse and right-wing.

Christopher Logue, the poet, sitting with Ken Tynan and his wife Elaine Dundy, took exception. 'Rubbish,' he pronounced in splendidly projected tones that completely silenced the actor who was speaking at the time, Robert Shaw.

Ann Hastings, Michael's wife, rose and yelled, 'Christopher Logue – get out of this theatre!' Logue and Elaine Tynan swept out on a gale of boos, applause and laughter and went next door to the pub.

It was not long before the play ended. The doors burst open and in swept the avengers headed by Ann and Michael and, among others, Colin Wilson, author of *The Outsider* and one of the angrier of the angry young men. Ann hurled herself on Christopher with the unlikely threat, 'I'll crush you with my Daimler.' (The Hastings had actually just bought an old Daimler. I had chauffeured them in it to Wales on their honeymoon as neither of them could drive.) As they wrestled on the beer-stained floor Elaine Tynan shouted, 'Don't worry about the women-folk, Christopher! We can look after ourselves.' She took off her shoe and laid about her. Finally the combatants were separated.

Ken Tynan, more amused than affronted, demanded of Colin, 'Why don't you get out of our lives?'

Replied Colin, shaping up like a Western gunslinger, 'There's not room for both of us in this town.'

Another pub which played a part in my life and in that of many others was equally theatrical in its own way. This was the Markham Arms in the Kings Road, headquarters of that gossip columnist's labour exchange, rumour bazaar and faithful stand-by, the Chelsea Set – although the nickname was yet to be invented.

Opposite the Markham was an old-fashioned 'café' which served English breakfasts, bubble and squeak and other traditional fare. It was cheap and well frequented. By chance one of the *Daily Mail* diary writers, who was often there, became interested in this well-heeled group and the attractive young ladies who went between the café and the pub. He coined the phrase 'The Chelsea Set' and it was taken up with enthusiasm by the rest of Fleet Street.

The regulars would meet around drinks time to find out where that night's party was taking place. Then, armed with bottles of wine, the group would set off. One memorable party took place at a house in Edith Grove. It was to be demolished and the party set out to beat the wreckers to it. By the time the police arrived the staircase had been ripped out, but half the guests were still having a tremendous time on the upper floor.

I was with this group rather than one of them, since my foreign schooling had not been quite the same thing as their sturdy English public schools. Also, for the most part they were slightly older than me. But we got on well enough, rendezvousing at the Arms and tumbling out of Esmeralda's Barn at dawn. But the defiant splendours of hippy gear still lay ahead. In the Kings Road I was sneered at for wearing a seersucker suit – the one contribution America had made to my wardrobe. London was really extremely staid, save for the Chelsea Arts Ball on New Year's Eve.

Meanwhile my theatrical education continued; indeed my work with Peter was the equivalent of a tutorial in the theatre every day.

The lore of the theatre can be as instructive as actual experience. And Peter, as one of its more eccentric masters, had some marvellous stories to impart. In 1956, for instance, he had put on one of his major commercial successes, a thriller called *The House by the Lake*, by Hugh Mills. One of the main characters was a girl of twenty-five, but Peter was looking for a part for Flora Robson whom he greatly admired. Flora was then in her fifties. He sent her the script, inking out any reference to age. She agreed to do the play, but at first it did not do well. Peter was about to put up the Notice when on the Saturday of the sixth week the house sold out. *The House by the Lake* then ran for some eighteen months.

That story made a deep impression on me on two counts. If an actor or actress is good, there is no limit to what they can do. Age need not matter, unless the plot totally hinges on it. Secondly, if you bother to produce a play in the first place you must give it enough time to find its audience in spite of what the critics may have said, as the real test is the word of mouth of the audience which can take months to spread. Although, as every producer knows, the easy way to go broke is to believe that, if only you pump enough money in to cover the losses, advertise and keep the show on, one day the tide will turn and the flop will become a hit. The list is lengthy of those who have lost all their money by believing in the theory of 'if only we stay put'. On Broadway this rarely occurs as the costs are so astronomical. Hence the one-night production which eliminates this very tricky decision which often involves the producer dipping into his own funds, or indeed running up a heavy overdraft.

Peter had been characteristically astute about Flora's appeal. One fan indeed found it quite irresistible. Later, when we did a season of Ibsen's *Ghosts* at the Shaftesbury with Flora playing the mother, a very ordinary-looking woman, also in her fifties, came to see it every night.

Monday and Tuesday she would sit in the back stalls, Wednesday in the upper circle, Thursday in the gallery, Friday – payday, presumably – she was in the *front row* of the stalls. Saturday also. She would stand by the stage door every night. The company were all soon aware of her. Flora lived in Gerrards Cross, driving to and fro in an old-fashioned Daimler. One night as she arrived home she and her chauffeur heard a noise. The woman had hidden herself in the car's luggage compartment.

*

First nights come about last on my list of favourite occasions, even today and even when they are triumphant, enriching and reeking with acclaim. Only the theatre is judged on the effect of a single nerve-racking exposure.

My distaste may go back to 1960 when Roland Petit and Zizi Jeanmaire – whose work was among Peter's passions – brought their dance troupe to the new Royalty Theatre under his management. Stories abound of shows that seem mysteriously cursed. Despite the prestige and appeal of the principal duo this surely seemed to be so fated.

In the middle of one of the ballets there was a very simple cue. A dancer stepped to an old-fashioned gramophone, lifted the arm on to the record and the music started. Or it was supposed to. A man backstage had to press a button, that was all. Even in rehearsal they could not get it right – to the point where everybody became hysterical.

In Peter's box on opening night was his friend Gilbert Harding, an early television celebrity with a reputation for irascibility. (Actually, like many others, he was very different off screen, when he was warm and sympathetic and most enthusiastic about the theatre.) The first act did not go well. And, at the beginning of the second act, which contained the unnerving gramophone sequence, the curtain would not rise.

Michel Legrand, then unknown outside France, was the conductor– today he would have filled the theatre by himself. He kept the orchestra playing. But after about fifteen minutes of this extended overture, the audience began to express its impatience. A baying audience is an ugly sound and always strikes terror into my heart. But those were inveterate theatre-goers of the old school out for their money's worth. The Gallery First-Nighters' Club, they called themselves, and they were as merciless as the mob in the Roman Coliseum.

Peter jumped on a chair in his box and yelled encouragement to everyone behind the curtain. With only one arm, he did not have a very good sense of balance and we had to grab his coat to stop him toppling over into the stalls. Gilbert Harding was so upset that he seemed on the verge of apoplexy. And, of course, when the second act did get under way they failed to get the cue right with the gramophone. It was a night to forget.

It took a while for me to understand the extent to which Peter's – and therefore my – future in the theatre had been staked without reservation on the first adventure in which I was completely involved. If acting were a religion, one of its most hallowed shrines would be the Moscow Arts Theatre, home of Anton Chekhov and the great teacher-sage Konstantin Stanislavsky. The company had not played outside the Soviet Union since the Second World War. It had never visited Britain.

It was a measure of Peter's determination that after five years of delicate and tantalising negotiations with the Russians – to whom the very concept of an entrepreneur was bewildering – they were finally signed to mount a Chekhov season in London on the sixtieth anniversary of their formation. But it was typical of the indifference and complacency of the British stage at this time that no theatre could be found where this unique and illustrious company might perform, as theatre-owners wanted long runs and did not like the idea of the one-month season.

Apart from the prestige and the size of the company – over fifty actors and technicians – a sizeable theatre was essential. The 'get-out' (one of the most crucial terms in my new vocabulary, meaning the amount that must be taken at the box office in order to cover expenses) was more than £6,000 a week, which Peter, his nerve as firm as his beliefs, had guaranteed. The average West End play at that time ran to about £2,000 a week, so this was three times higher and in Russian!

Every one of London's omnipotent theatre-owners claimed to have a better use to which to put their stages. And in those days it was the bricks and mortar, as they were called, who ran the West End. Even if a producer could raise the money to rent a theatre, he still had to launch a play in the provinces and wait patiently and nervously for one of the bricks and mortar to pay it a visit. With magisterial indulgence the landlord might then agree to take it into London when some current show in one of his theatres ran out of steam.

Nor were the ticket-brokers, whose support was also essential, at all enthusiastic. Peter Cadbury, the head of Keith Prowse, was blunt. 'Chekhov? In *Russian?* We might sell £10 worth of stalls.'

Finally, the only theatre available in London was Sadler's Wells, a subsidised house and mainly associated with dance. And there Peter was finally forced to turn, guided by one of the friends from the Establishment who came to his aid. From his army days Peter maintained these friends and sometimes they asked him to give them a hand. Once, when we were preparing for a trip together on the other side of the Iron Curtain, he requested me to arrange to be out of the office, while he entertained a visitor. By then I knew him well enough to ask why.

He was embarrassed. 'It's the head of MI5,' he eventually explained. 'And he does not want to be seen. I expect they just want me to keep an eye open while we're there.'

In Peter's early skirmishings with Russian bureaucracy it had been Christopher Soames, then Winston Churchill's private secretary, who had engineered a crucial meeting. Now it was Peter Thorneycroft, Chancellor of the Exchequer, who turned him in the direction of the British Council, a body as mysterious in its way then as it is now. The Council graciously consented to make Sadler's Wells available, though not to become investors. However, they said blandly, they would expect to share the honour of being billed as co-presenters.

Almost as soon as the box office opened it was clear that the Council had muscled its way into an historic triumph. By opening night the Moscow Arts season was a sell-out. The three main plays, *The Cherry Orchard*, *The Three Sisters* and *Uncle Vanya* were luminous testaments to a Chekhov whose true nature had barely been suspected in the English theatre.

The production, the actual nuts and bolts with which I had become involved, since I was billed as production manager, was of a dimension to which London was simply not accustomed. Storm effects for an English play usually meant a lone assistant stage manager banging away at a muffled gong, or a pre-recorded tape being used on the sound system. For the storm scene in *Vanya* a ten-piece sound effects 'orchestra' appeared backstage complete with conductor. They produced light rain, heavy rain, thunder, lightning, banging doors – all perfectly synchronised to the dialogue on stage. It would be hard to produce a better example of the advantages of a large state subsidy.

Above all, there was, of course, the acting, nourished by a devotion to Stanislavsky's spirit that I found infinitely more enlightening than the morose dedication to Method acting that I had come across in America.

The virtue of collective work free from constant financial pressure shone out.

That Method worship came vividly to mind when I watched the venerable actor Gribov who played the old servant Firs in *The Cherry Orchard*, the one who is shortly going to be put out to pasture after a lifetime in the service of the family and the estate. It is a sad role and very difficult. Gribov's preparation was to stand around backstage making jokes. Then he would go on stage and instantly be amazing in the part. This was precisely the reverse of everything Lee Strasberg and the Method people had made of Stanislavsky. Gribov showed – the only other actor I have seen capable of transporting herself so insouciantly from life into art is Maggie Smith – that it was an actor's *ability* that mattered. Working as a waiter for a year will not necessarily make an actor appear any better as a stage waiter.

There is not much doubt that the Moscow Arts season encouraged the idea of subsidised theatre in Britain. In a way a commercial management like Peter's had helped its opposition.

In Paris where, flushed from the brilliant London success, we confidently booked the Sarah Bernhardt Theatre, we were doomed to lose everything we had gained in London. The theatre belonged to the city of Paris. No one had told us that members of the City Council, and officials of all branches of the civil service, were entitled to free seats every night. Thus instead of having, say, 1,000 seats to sell at each performance we were left with only 700 – not enough to cover the high costs.

So I was very parsimonious with our own comps. But I had met the poets Alan Ginsberg and Gregory Corso in a bar near the Odéon frequented by American writers. They were staying in the Rue Gît le Coeur where I had lived myself as a student. I gave them tickets for a Wednesday matinee. The curtain was delayed for some reason and they asked, 'Why don't we go on and read some of our work?' The vision of this particular matinee audience, many of whom were elderly Russian émigrés being hit with a burst of Ginsberg's masterpiece *Howl!* still makes me laugh. I wish I had had the nerve to let them go on.

At least, though, it was on that particular visit to Paris that I attended my first happening. With great solemnity William Burroughs, watched adoringly by Ginsberg, Coso and myself, fried his radio in his hotel room. I did not realise that it was an historic moment.

Ginsberg would not tolerate too many dull moments. Standing on a street corner, I was looking at a pretty girl in front of us. He turned on me fiercely: 'Don't waste your time looking at women, you should be thinking about how we're going to change the world.' For him, homosexuality was a political issue. In the British theatre of the 1950s I had discovered it was – as it had been for decades – a distinct professional asset. With certain significant exceptions, the West End scene, from Binkie Beaumont to the chorus boys, was gay. Or at any rate if actors wanted frequent work they were gay. Not until the Royal Court got into its stride did the mould break. After *Look Back in Anger* it was all working class and straight. Too much so in terms of class. Not until *Chariots of Fire* did educated voices really come back into fashion. The pendulum swings violently with fashion and against minorities.

After a while with Peter I was almost ready to write an International Guide to the Theatre. Following the Moscow Arts tour he brought over an extraordinary company of superb quality, the Comédie Française. Peter had first been promised this national treasure by the French government in compensation for the financial losses incurred over the Moscow Arts Season in Paris. But the decision had been mysteriously reversed, and only by the most amazing campaign of personal lobbying among the great names of French theatre did he finally get his way.

The Comédie Française gave us a far more nerve-racking few days before their opening than the Moscow Arts simply because of their sheer insouciance. They did not arrive at the Princes Theatre in London until the day before the opening night, a Sunday. Yet by Monday evening the scenery was in place and everything polished to perfection.

The get-in was a staggering performance in itself, all the more so since the most popular of the four plays they had brought to London was *Le Dindon* (*The Turkey*), one of those farces by Georges Feydeau constructed like an expensive watch. The play depended almost wholly on the precision and delivery of each cue. Every door must open at the precise moment, and during the course of the play there were many such cues. The stars were Robert Hirsch and the great Jacques Charon and they were wondrous to watch.

The happy fact that we did so much business with the French theatre gave me the opportunity to demonstrate my usefulness. By any standards I was well-read in a lot of different languages, but particularly in French literature. I was familiar with many contemporary authors and playwrights. I read *Le Monde* and the literary monthlies. That fact, together with the facility with which I spoke the language, helped to impress the people we dealt with. Peter and others soon developed confidence in my taste and judgement.

When we were hoping for Marie Bell to appear in London in a season of Racine, of whose plays she was perhaps France's greatest exponent, we found ourselves conducting very difficult negotiations. As she was not part of the subsidised theatre, we were dealing with the French Ministry of Culture in the person of the brilliant historian Philippe d'Erlanger, under whose patronage the financing of overseas tours for the propagation of French culture depended. We reached a serious impasse. There was no time to wait to see him as the Savoy Theatre had issued an ultimatum. From our hotel lobby I discussed matters with him on the telephone for about fifteen minutes whilst Peter stood beside me.

When I had finished, the receptionist said, 'You put your case so well, that you've convinced me!' Peter was pleased – particularly when our demands were met.

The Marie Bell season, at the Savoy in March 1960, was very successful. Her *Phèdre* and *Bérénice* were unforgettable. It was the first time Racine had been seen in London in many years and probably the first time any play of his had sold out in England. Dealing with Bell herself had been a marvellous experience. She was a genuine theatrical *grande dame*, giving audiences in her amazing and vast all-white bathroom overlooking the Champs-Elysées; it was more like a drawing-room, with telephones and chaises-longues. To thank us after the season was over she took us to Maxims and danced the night away to waltzes and tangos.

The first night had a moment of horror. An hour before the curtain was due to rise, the leading man Jacques Decquimine was shown by helpful friends that his name and that of the character he was playing had been left out of the programme. It was a dreadful printing mistake. With some justification he refused to go on.

It was ten minutes to curtain. Madame Bell was poised in her dressing-room. The theatre was packed with the *crème* of Anglo-French society . . .

Peter rushed backstage in answer to my cry for help. Together we went down on our knees to beg him to consider. The show went on.

Most actors are 'difficult' at some time. But I soon learned to deal with the moments. My method – which has always worked very well – is to pretend not to hear what an actor is being difficult about. They rant and rave, but I take as little notice as possible and, the next time I see them, I pretend nothing has happened.

My way has always been to keep them happy, give them what they want – if it is not too expensive. If an actor wants the dressing-room wall painted pink – I paint it pink. Feed their ego. It is easier than arguing. Actually, I like actors. I find that side of them amusing, and I understand it. It is a sign of nervousness, because they are always being judged. That is why critics are so disliked in the theatre. If a critic is really unpleasant about an actor the actor cannot but take it seriously. Personally I am surprised an actor has never shot a critic. (My own most heartfelt complaint about critics is that even when they like something they seem nowadays to go to great lengths to avoid saying so. I read a critic, know he enjoyed what he saw – but he will not say it outright.)

My work with Peter was mostly planning and preparing, doing things he did not want to do – easing the way. But my self-confidence was growing. When I had to make a decision I made it without worrying later whether it had been right or wrong. Occasionally I would cause the most terrible shambles, but not often. That happened far more often later when I started producing on my own.

My growing responsibilities and Peter's acceptance of my taste meant that when I heard Ingmar Bergman was staging Goethe's *Ur-Faust* in Malmo he agreed that I might go and have a look at it. I greatly admired the films of Bergman that were only just beginning to be appreciated in Britain, so much so that I decided I could not possibly remain friends with someone who had professed not to like *Smiles of a Summer Night*.

So, off I went in midwinter to Sweden, where Bergman was director of the Malmo City Company, without buying so much as a fur hat.

It was midwinter. Malmo is a small provincial city in southern Sweden. Visitors in winter are rare. But the company gave me a great welcome and, after the performance, there was a splendid dinner in a turreted castle: huge log fires, furs on great stone floors. All the actors came and the party went on through the night. Since I looked even younger than I was, they were somewhat surprised when I told them that they must be seen in London.

The production of *Faust* was breathtaking. It was very stylised and pure with beautiful lighting in sharp contrasts. There was a spectacular swordfight scene involving Max von Sydow done like a silhouette against the sky. That it was played in Swedish seemed hardly to matter– the play was universally known and the acting seemed outstanding.

Those were my arguments. To my delight – and to that of the Malmo City Company – the Swedish government accepted the deal I had structured.

There was no way then – and it is even less possible now – to bring any show to London for a season only, and expect to cover the costs from the box office. But then, as now, what weighed heavily with the various governments was the fact that London was the theatre capital of the world. Acceptance in London was taken very seriously and carried great prestige, and when I later went on to present the American avant-garde in the 1960s the status of the originators soared enormously in New York because of their success in London. In 1956 Peter had presented the Berliner Ensemble. Brecht had died literally on the eve of their departure, but the visit to London went ahead as it was considered so important.

Faust did respectable business at the Princes Theatre in 1959. It was a critical success but not a great financial one. On the first night, as well as Gilbert Harding, Malcolm Sargent and Tony Richardson were in Peter's box. I did not know Tony then, but was flattered when Peter turned to him and said, 'Isn't this wonderful? Michael found it.'

I could see Tony did not like it. Years later I asked him. 'God, no,' he said. 'Hated it.' But I like things that cause strong opinions and this was one of them.

Bergman himself I found withdrawn and unforthcoming but Peter got on with him famously. Both of us were a rapt audience at a lunch to which David Lean was also invited. The two great directors had a conversation about the technicalities of screen creation that was the most fascinating exposition possible of a craft of which both, in different ways, were masters. What was amusing was that, until two days prior to this lunch, Lean had never seen a Bergman film – he rushed to the Charing Cross Road and saw three in a row.

In the winter of 1959–60 Peter and I went on a trip round Eastern Europe. Peter wanted the Berliner Ensemble to bring over *The Threepenny Opera*, the scintillating, sardonic musical that was Brecht's comic master-piece. We did not manage to arrange it but this was nevertheless an important occasion for me.

It is very hard for any thinking man not to feel that Communism is a wonderful way to run the world – until one actually sees it in practice. Dealing with the East Germans was unpleasant, they seemed inhospitable and paranoid. East Berlin was the bleakest city I had ever seen and, apart from books, there was nothing on sale in any of the shops. Prague was much more interesting, relaxed and prosperous, and its medieval architecture untouched by the war, in sharp contrast to the rubble of Berlin.

With my parrot-like ear I got a slight grip on the Czech language after a few days, and this helped greatly when we went to see the comedian Werek, who was one of the funniest performers I had ever seen. I had never seen an audience behave as that one did. People were literally falling out of their seats with laughter, because his jokes were filled – as he later explained – with double-entendres against the régime.

Werek could easily have performed in London, Paris or New York.

The language barrier would have been swept aside by his overwhelming sense of comedy. After the show we drove with him and a friend to a small country inn. He wanted to be private. We were the only guests. The landlord was discreet. There was a big chicken pot, with a wood fire underneath.

Everything that had happened to Werek in Czechoslovakia, everything he talked about, was tragic. Yet only two hours before we had seen him reduce an audience to helplessness. The woman next to me had clutched me to stop herself falling off her seat. It was profoundly moving: this genius of a comedian, 'free' and a star, but a prisoner no less. He told us of the many times he had been invited abroad. But the government refused to give him an exit visa. They knew he would not have returned.

As I was interested in Franz Kafka, I asked our official guide where he was buried. 'We do not regard Kafka as an exponent of our culture,' was the reply. 'He was a German. A German Jew.'

This was at a time when very few Westeners were invited behind the Iron Curtain. Through his presentations of the Berliner Ensemble and the Moscow Arts, Peter was trusted and respected. But the atmosphere was strange and at times frightening. Sometimes we would meet ordinary people to whom a Westerner was an oddity or an object of envy. One man took my hand when I was in a shop and said in English, 'You are *so fortunate, so lucky* to be British.'

That type of incident made a deep impression on me, but we also had our laughs. When we were invited to lunch at the British Embassy, Peter was so apprehensive about the cooking that he insisted we stop off in an inn for a substantial pre-lunch snack. The Embassy lunch, to our hopeless embarrassment, was excellent and lavish.

*

On one of my trips to Paris I saw a play called *Tchin-Tchin* in a tiny theatre in Montparnasse. I came back and told Peter that it was excellent.

It was a two-character play by François Billetdoux, slightly poetic but not excessively so. The man was an alcoholic Continental, the woman prim and English. Their respective spouses were lovers and they wanted to find out why. They discovered each other – and themselves. It was a play with two tremendous acting parts.

Celia Johnson agreed to play the woman. The man's part was offered to Laurence Olivier, who was then making the film *The Entertainer*. We sent him to Paris to see *Tchin-Tchin*. This turned out to be a mistake; he was put off by the poky theatre, which had only 200 seats and distinctly lacked atmosphere. Today he would perhaps have reacted differently, but then he was in midstream between his great acting career and becoming founder/director of the National Theatre. He decided not to do the play, even though Willis Hall had done a lovely adaptation.

Our next choice was Orson Welles. Welles was a great gourmand, notoriously so, and we had many amusing meetings trying to get him to sign. I remember one lunch that he arranged at his house in Chelsea where for four of us there were four extremely large chickens. But, no matter how well and frequently we lunched, Welles, having accepted the part, hung back from signing a contract. Peter naturally became extremely nervous. We had a good play, Celia, and Sean Kenny, fresh from his triumph in designing *Oliver*, had created a superb set for us, but still no leading man.

Celia was also getting nervous. Much as she was looking forward to teaming up with Orson, whose charm as well as his talent had already endeared him to her, she was in considerable demand herself and wanted matters settled.

Finally a day – 30 May, 1960 – was set for Orson to visit Celia in the country and deliver the signed contract at the same time. He did not arrive for lunch as expected. He then sent word he would arrive at tea-time. Peter, distraught, established that Orson had indeed left home with the contract that morning. No one had seen him since.

When he failed to arrive for tea, Celia called her agent, my old counsellor Aubrey Blackburn, who the next day telephoned Peter to say that his distinguished client was now somewhat fed up. In dread of losing one of his stars without having gained another, Peter was cheered by the appearance at his door of Kenneth Tynan. Tynan, then drama critic of the *Observer*, was a key theatrical figure and also a great friend of Orson's. Peter knew that Tynan quite rightly worshipped Orson. Rather belatedly, he warned Peter that his new star had an innate reluctance to put his name to documents, but nevertheless promised to track him down and give him a lecture. But, even as they were talking, Peter's butler wafted in with a silver salver on which lay not only our copy of the contract, signed, but the actor's as well. Orson had delivered the goods.

Getting his signature, however, did not mean that we got the great actor. Although he had contracted for the part we never saw him again, or at least not until the play had been on for four months – with Anthony Quayle a tremendous success in the part. Perhaps it was our fault for trying to persuade him to do a play against his better judgement.

Meanwhile we all tried to find him. We looked in Paris, in Spain, even in Yugoslavia where he was supposedly making a film. But we never heard from him nor laid eyes on him until at least a year later, when Peter and I were in the Ritz bar in Paris having a cocktail and who should be sitting there in all his grandeur but Orson. 'Ho, ho!' he boomed. 'Fine detectives you would make. It's taken you all this time to find me and I can be clearly seen and in excellent humour.'

We laughed – he was very jolly. Then he said: 'I'm on my way to London tonight but why don't we have dinner, before I get on the train? I know this wonderful little restaurant . . . '

So off we went, driving somewhere past the Bastille, I anticipating one of the great meals of my life. The restaurant was empty. The proprietor fell on Orson as if he were God – which to some people, of course, he is – and we sat down to an extremely ordinary dinner. From the point of view of the cuisine. But not the entertainment. Orson set out to entertain us marvellously. He is a superb story-teller. There was no thought of recrimination. How could we hold such a trifling grudge against the director of *Citizen Kane?*

We took him to the station. He had huge suitcases. There were no porters. Peter only had one arm, and Orson was – well, Citizen Welles. Naturally, the compartment was far away, next to the engine. Orson swaggered down the platform like Louis XIV, I stumbled on behind with the suitcases.

Working on *Chin Chin* (which it was, of course, called in English – foreigners really do think the British say that when they raise their glasses) showed me that I still had a few things to learn. Sean Kenny did the most superb designs. He showed them to a conventionally-minded production manager. 'I've been in the theatre thirty years and they will never work,' said he. 'Nobody's ever done it like that, it will be a disaster.' He suggested another designer to us behind Sean's back. But for me that typified the spirit of the theatre I had already come to hate. I like people who say, 'Okay, I'm warning you I don't think it'll work – but let's try and do what we can.' I liked the adventurous and was wary of technical bluff.

Sean was equal to the challenge, however. He just said, 'I know it will work, I've designed it. I insist it's done this way – otherwise I'll leave.' And, of course, the sets not only worked, they were original and beautiful.

Chin Chin was due to open in Newcastle on a Monday. The Saturday before was the last night of a production of Feydeau's *Look after Lulu*, directed by Tony Richardson and starring Vivien Leigh. So, naturally, Peter and I went up in time to see her performance as well as to prepare for our get in on the Sunday.

In addition to the difficult problems of doing Feydeau in English, Vivien was not relaxed and not at her best. Afterwards, backstage, her dressing-room was crowded. In the midst of the crowd was Cecil

Tennant, the head of MCA in England and the most powerful agent in London. He was staying on for our opening on Monday. Peter swept into the dressing-room. 'Darling-you-were-wonderful,' he exclaimed sincerely.

When we left I asked, 'You don't believe that for one minute, do you?' He replied, 'Listen, she's opening next Wednesday in London. Why upset her, four weeks ago the truth, tonight praise and encouragement.'

So if you cannot be constructive, be enthusiastic. A gentlemanly lesson – yet another that Peter performed with conviction and Vivien, I think, believed.

*

Suddenly, even though I still knew there were so many things to learn, I had come to a decision. I wanted to be a producer myself. I had observed Lucille and then Peter doing it their way and now I wanted to try for myself.

Naturally Peter was very upset when I said I was leaving. He could not understand why; I was now being well paid, and things were at last beginning to go his way. The World Theatre Season he had fought to set up with the RSC at the Aldwych was a reality. Sponsorship from the *Sunday Telegraph* meant that he would no longer be taking such crippling personal risks.

I felt much the same when the assistant I was eventually to take on myself, Robert Fox, left me after seven years to produce on his own. But he did it for the same reason I left Peter, the same reason children leave home: at a certain time you have to stand on your own feet.

The sort of relationship that I had with Peter and that later Robert Fox had with me is generally the best way to become a producer. But it is very hard initially to land the job as assistant, simply because it is a job that has to be created. Robert had the advantage of having worked at the Royal Court and of belonging to a theatrical family. His two brothers, James and Edward, are stars. His mother Angela is extremely knowledgeable about the stage and his father, Robin, was one of the most prominent agents in London, first at MCA and then as Leslie Grade's right-hand man when Leslie was a power in show business. Also Robert's great theatrical gifts have been proven by his subsequent success as a solo producer.

Robin I liked although I had had a few problems with him. In the 1960s I put on a play at the same time that *Spring and Port Wine* opened at the Mermaid. My show was jogging along at the Apollo, not doing well but not going below the break figure, which meant that the theatre-owner, who was Prince Littler, could not give me notice, although he wanted to in order to transfer *Spring and Port Wine*.

I was summoned to a meeting by Prince, a formidable, rather frightening character. Robin Fox was also there.

It was simple. They wanted to bring *Spring and Port Wine* into the West End and did not have a theatre. They knew that I had been offered Wyndham's Theatre. For some reason they themselves did not want to go to Wyndham's. The Apollo was their theatre and that was where they wanted their play. So they suggested that I go to Wyndham's and they would give me five per cent of the profits of *Spring and Port Wine*. Either from stupidity or an excess of honesty, I declined. I said I would move the play, because it was obviously not going to last much longer, if they paid for the transfer. But I did not want any of the profits because I had done nothing to earn them. Their mouths fell open. But I felt it was wrong to take money that should go to the backers and participants who had earned it. It was real money, too, because *Spring and Port Wine* ran for over two years and was made into a successful film and also a television series. It was a waste transferring my play to Wyndham's and having to redo all the publicity, and we only lasted seven weeks.

So Prince and Robin had been cleverer than me. But though there's always more money you only have one name. I feel there are certain principles that are more important than money, and many of these principles I had learned from Peter. In many ways I was silly to leave Peter when I did, but I think, or rather felt, that I would rather be a minor number one than an important number two. Also I wanted to do plays and Peter was much more interested in the World Theatre Season. So on these two counts I left. I had £1,000 capital and a lot of optimism.

CHAPTER THREE

West Meets East

In Peter Daubeny's own autobiography, *My World of Theatre*, he wrote that he decided to let me co-present *The Connection* in order to give me my first chance as a West End manager. In fact I brought the whole disaster on myself. By disaster I do not mean the actual play, but the way we presented it in London.

The Connection was a startling and revolutionary play for 1961. Nothing quite like it had been seen on the stage. It was written by Jack Gelber, a New Yorker, and produced in 1959 by The Living Theatre, an off-Broadway company run by the remarkable Becks, Julian and his wife Judith Malina. *The Connection* had attracted immediate attention, both stylistically and because of its subject matter. Terry Southern called it the first 'Hip' play, and in many ways it was.

Staged and set in a loft, *The Connection* carried realism as far as it could possibly go. The actors play a group of jazz musicians waiting in agonising, poetically emphasised suspense, for a score of heroin. When their deliverer comes, they shoot up dope and drift away transformed, immune to everything, especially the conventional morality as personified in Sister Salvation. It is she who gives safe conduct to 'Cowboy', the angelic-looking pusher. In the production some of the actors were, in fact, real musicians who played jazz to while away the time waiting for a fix. The audience, because of the brilliance of the production, became completely identified with the torment of addicts. As the suspenseful two hours of the performance ticked away the watchers came to feel at one with the watched.

I read *The Connection* and went to New York to see it. I thought it was a marvellous theatrical experience. Meanwhile Ken Tynan, who was beginning to loom significantly in my life, had also seen the Living

Theatre production and urged Peter to take an interest in it and bring it to London. But in New York the loft was the theatre, the theatre the loft. Realism and naturalism intermingled and made everything work for the audience.

Peter went to New York himself and was convinced. In February 1961 *The Connection* opened at the Duke of York's in London with the original American cast and with Peter Daubeny and Michael White sharing the top of the bill as producers: my first credit as an impresario.

Of all the first nights I have suffered through, this, my début, was the worst. It seemed at the time – and for long after – that my career had begun and ended in that very same night of chaos, jeers and despair.

Since the drive to get *The Connection* to London was mainly mine, so were many of the mistakes. The first was not abandoning the production when I learnt that the Becks had already sold the foreign rights to a pair of entrepreneurs. We became partners with them. One is now a famous director and deservedly, but neither knew much about theatre production even though they often behaved as if they knew everything.

The second and more serious error was not insisting on bringing over the original director, Julian Beck himself. It has since become a firm rule of mine never to restage a production without using the original director or one of his disciples if he is not available. For London, the two entrepreneurs had already signed up Alan Schneider, who has since blossomed into one of the leading directors, but was then at the outset of his career. There was little he could do to improve on the original production, particularly since the actors who came over had already been directed by Beck. But in any case the confusion was soon compounded because, before we opened, Schneider left and had to be replaced hastily. Nicholas Garland took over. Then in his early twenties, he was later to reach the top of his profession as a political cartoonist.

Finding the money for *The Connection* had been easy. It was not an expensive production, somewhere between £11,000 and £12,000 to be raised by the four of us. A lot of people – enlightened people – who had seen the play in New York were quite ready to finance it. Peter turned to his usual investors. Richard Wolheim the philosopher was one of them. I raised some of mine from friends like Anthony Blond and Tim Willoughby, son of the Earl of Ancaster and grandson of Nancy Astor, an extremely good-looking young man about town, who had become a close friend and was my first investor.

We were faced with the usual apprehensive wait for a theatre, a far cry from today when people ring up and say, 'Please, Mr White, put on a production, we have an empty theatre.' A Noël Coward play, *Waiting in the Wings*, was no longer doing well. The Duke of York's was offered; the theatre was then run by a tough expatriate from Chicago, Eddie Horan, nicknamed by us 'Deals within Wheels'. He gave the Coward play notice to quit even though the producer did not want to end its run, which caused offence in the West End as it had a very distinguished cast including Sybil Thorndike, Lewis Casson and many other great old actors.

A theatre owner can give a production notice to quit his theatre if the agreed break figure – that is to say weekly running costs – are not met. In other words, if the break figure is 10,000 and the production plays to 10,200, then in theory the play can stay on for ever. But if it is only at eight or nine thousand then the theatre owner can give notice and take in a production he thinks will make more profits for the theatre. More of this later, but producers hate being given notice to quit – thus the animosity already waiting in the wings of the Duke of York's for *The Connection*.

Horan thought he was doing us a big favour. But taking such a traditional chocolate-box theatre, such as the Duke of York's was probably the biggest mistake of all. In New York the cramped setting, the loft, the realism, were vital parts of the experience. The audience, jammed into a forced intimacy with the cast, found the experience intensely believable. They shared the suspense of the addicts, their misery and joys. But a formal Edwardian theatre made everything remote, improbable, indeed unbelievable. The proscenium arch was a barrier we could not surmount.

Also, at the time, no one in London knew or was affected by the drug culture. This was all still to come, and the harshness of the language offended and disturbed the average theatregoer. Finally, the naturalistic style of play was unknown territory. It just seemed aggressive and shocking.

On the first night it soon became brutally clear that most of the audience found *The Connection* disturbing and repellent. The gallery was packed with a collection of oddities who, stimulated by gaudy press stories, were out to defend their own version of public morality.

Sophie, a very large lady from the East End, was the ringleader. She and others interrupted dialogue and even went to the back of the gallery and banged the exit door to prevent the actors being heard. One of the cast, Carl Lee, had to deliver a line, 'I think it's time to go home.' Some of the audience screamed, 'Yes! – Starting with you.' Carl was black.

Richard Buckle, the ballet critic and a close friend of Peter's stood up, turned and yelled: 'Fuck the gallery!' Another first in the theatre, I suppose.

My own parents and their friends fled. They did not like the play, but what they really objected to was the violence and hatred displayed. They happened to be sitting in front of the *Daily Mail* critic who duly recorded that four people in evening dress had walked out in the middle of the play.

Outside the theatre, after the curtain had come down to a storm of boos and hisses, the scene was even more astonishing. The hard core of hecklers led by Sophie and her chums spat abuse at us as we left. Someone even attacked Peter, striking at his face, jostling his wife Molly, and saying, 'How could you put this garbage on stage – you, Peter Daubeny, who have brought us so much.'

There was a first night party at the old Ronnie Scott's jazz club, and I felt sick – sick and unhappy. I woke up the following morning in St George's Hospital, my evening clothes torn, my face battered. Taking the girl I had invited, Charmian Scott, home from the party I had wrecked my lovely XJ120 at Hyde Park Corner. Poor Charmian was badly bruised, but luckily not injured. The next day, I turned on the radio and listened to a report of the first night fracas. Soon I was in the papers along with the rest of it. Producer Crashes; Girl in Car. When I spoke to my father later that day he said, 'Now, now, there's no need to commit suicide just because you've had your first flop.' I was not so good-humoured about it.

Public anger at *The Connection* was staggering. A few nights after the opening, some of the cast and I went to a celebrated restaurant near the theatre. A usually friendly waitress asked, 'Are you anything to do with that play down the road?' Carl Lee said, 'Yes, I'm in it.' She said, 'Well, you can get out of here and take your dirty friends with you.'

It might have been worse. What I did not realise for a blessedly long time was that some of the actors actually were on 'smack' and were shooting up in the dressing-room. The play was doing terrible business, of course. There was a devastating photograph of the auditorium taken by Cecil Beaton for the *Observer* showing about twenty people sitting in the 700-seat theatre. By Easter, the *Evening News* could record:

Tonight that weirdie from the States at the Duke of York, *The Connection*, is thrown out of the nest. The poor little junkies have struggled along for 46 performances – how they managed to survive that long, heaven alone knows . . . Taking the public for a theatrical ride has been going on for quite a time. The abyss had to be reached eventually, and it looks now as if the vast majority of the British public are crying 'enough', for which relief much thanks . . .

Oh well . . . perhaps it was time I tried another novel.

Overnight, I had become somewhat notorious. Still, I had attracted some attention, including that of Oscar Lewenstein, a vigorous and courageous producer whose taste I admired. Oscar had first come to London as general manager of the left-wing Glasgow Unity Theatre in 1955. One of their productions had transferred to the West End. The London manager working out his costs asked Oscar how much he would expect. 'Five pounds, it's all I need,' responded the staunch young idealist. Life has changed for him since then. After a difficult start followed by a period as general manager of the Royal Court, he had spectacular successes with Wolf Mankowitz's *Expresso Bongo*, Keith Waterhouse and Willis Halls' *Billy Liar*, Jane Arden's *The Party* and many other hits of the highest quality.

At this time, Oscar was preparing to go into films. But he was looking for a partner to share the task he had taken on of running the Theatre Royal at Stratford, E.15, which Joan Littlewood had turned into a world-famous centre for adventurous plays. Now that she was going to teach in Ghana and take a one-year sabbatical, Oscar felt he could try out some new work there without incurring heavy West End production costs. (He had already transferred such memorable Stratford East productions as *A Taste of Honey*, *The Hostage* and *Fings Ain't Wot They Used T'Be* to wider West End audiences.)

Joan Littlewood was among the greatest figures of the post-war era, and certainly one of the finest directors in the world. She also had the ability to inspire others to give their best. Her style of directing was special; she was also sympathetic to the working class and understood their fears and hopes and sense of humour. She had teamed up with Gerry Raffles and together they had made Stratford East the most exciting theatre in Europe. To read the script of *Oh! What a Lovely War* or *The Hostage* and then see what magic Joan added to them was an extraordinary experience. The warmth and love that came across the footlights was unique in modern theatre. It now seems a pity that she never made films because it is so difficult to describe her amazing style and her contribution to the British theatre.

I first met Oscar when he bought the British rights to Jean-Paul Sartre's *Altona*, which I had seen in Paris and wanted to produce in London; but for Sartre he didn't need a partner, in any event at that time he was already in management with Wolf Mankowitz. Now, in

September 1961, he had taken Stratford East for a season. But this conflicted with the film of *Tom Jones* with which he was associated and which was to be produced out of the office of Woodfall Films in Curzon Street where I operated after leaving Peter Daubeny and which was run by Tony Richardson and John Osborne.

Oscar suggested that I take a percentage of three plays he had already planned and find another three new plays myself which he would share in financially on the same ratio. I had not put any of my own money into *The Connection* – not that I had much over a couple of thousand saved – but it had anyway closed and September was a long way ahead. So I set out to have a marvellous restoration summer in the South of France, blissfully unaware that the East End was far more dangerous territory than the West.

*

At Stratford East there was a wonderful café near the theatre, with sawdust on the floor, strong tea, sausages and mash and a real mix of theatre and local workers for customers. I was sitting in it one day when the chilling realisation gripped me that the three plays I had set out to produce were the silliest any manager could possibly do in a supposedly working-class theatre. For the second time in a year my career was in grave danger of disappearing down the drain. I was going to be bankrupt, this time for sure, a wipe-out at twenty-six.

One of the troubles of course was that I was not in the same league as Oscar Lewenstein. He had access to money, he was an established figure in the theatre with many West End hits. I only had personal friends as backers who would invest in a show for fun. They were not really interested in doing highbrow plays in the East End, and who could blame them?

Immersed in the therapy of writing and the various distractions to come my way in the South of France I simply had not worked out what was going to happen when I arrived in Stratford East. Only at the end of the summer did it begin to dawn on me that Oscar had chosen his three plays simply because he wanted to do them, and it was a decision he could well afford. Today I can understand that. If there is money coming in from commercial hits one can say, 'I'm going to do this play because it's great and deserves to be seen – this one is for the spirit and the theatre as Art.'

Oscar's choices were considerably more commercial than the plays I had chosen. The financial structure was that we would make ten per cent investment in each other's productions and each of us would then be responsible for finding his own ninety per cent. From Oscar's productions. I got very little, £2,000–£3,000 at most. To do the plays I had chosen I had to raise about £12,000 and it was very hard work.

The first production in my half of the season was *The Jungle of the Cities*, one of Brecht's most complex and difficult works. The rights were owned by Ronald Hayman, now a well-established writer on the theatre but then an inexperienced director for such a difficult play. As soon as rehearsals started, the actors became scared and then rebellious. It was a nightmare. I could not fire Hayman because he owned the rights to the play. But the contract with the theatre to put the play on was in my name. I was locked into a production which I disliked yet which I could not get out of. I did not understand how to resolve the problem and, meantime, the three leading actors left the show.

Oscar Beuselinck, my lawyer, saved the day. He said to Hayman, either leave and we find another director or you take over the financial obligations. Hayman didn't hesitate; he wanted to direct and so he did, with a new cast.

I became so unnerved that, when confronted with a disastrous perform-ance by an actor, I completely forgot the good example Peter Daubeny had shown me with Vivien Leigh. All through the rehearsals of *Jungle* I had been disturbed by the mock-German accent one of the cast had adopted. Instead of discussing it, however, I said nothing until the first preview when the unfortunate man happened to ask me what I thought of his performance. 'Fine,' I said. 'Except for your accent.' His confidence shattered, he went on to give a terrible performance.

Secret of the World, our second production, was a play about a Jewish family, in which the father loses his reason. The author was a Canadian, Ted Allen, and the director was John Berry, one of the Hollywood Ten, who had fled the United States during the McCarthy witchhunt and gone to live in Paris. Miriam Karlin was the star. This was one of Oscar's choices and was a critical and financial success, but not enough of one to transfer to the West End.

My final production was *The Voice of Shem*, a stage adaptation of James Joyce's *Finnegan's Wake* with that great actress Marie Kean. It was brilliant and almost incomprehensible. The first night was made more lively by the presence of an Irish rugby team brought along by my friend Jo Mennell. They came equipped with Irish whiskey which they passed through the stalls. It certainly ranks as one of the greatest oddities ever to be seen on a London stage.

It was the middle of 1962 before I had finished with Stratford East and by then Stratford East had nearly finished me. On the whole, we

43

had what we like in the profession to call mixed reviews. (The *Evening News* critic called *Jungle* 'highbrow German wurst culture'.)

Joan Littlewood was nothing less than a saint to the people who worked there. And, to them, we were a couple of West Enders taking over their working-class theatre to put on a lot of esoteric literary plays. I got out by the skin of my teeth, though my £1,000 vanished forever. I borrowed some money from Peter, among others, to settle up. I was in deep financial trouble. If anyone had predicted that a dozen years later I should have my name on seven West End productions simultaneously I would have laughed in their face.

CHAPTER FOUR

From 'Cambridge Circus' to 'Oblomov'

In 1961 *Beyond the Fringe*, the Establishment Club, and That Was the Week That Was on television, with all of which I had tenuous links, changed the entire concept of public humour.

Without doubt *Beyond the Fringe* was the most important theatrical comedy show since the war and it reflected an entire generation switch. There are productions that alter an entire era. *Hair* was one, *My Fair Lady*, although as big a hit, was not, nor were *Hello, Dolly* or *The Sound of Music*. But *The Rocky Horror Show* and *A Chorus Line* did change attitudes and perceptions beyond the small world of the West End and Broadway.

My favourite haunt at the time was that extraordinary institution, the Colony Club, haunt of painters such as Lucien Freud and Francis Bacon. It was run by the redoubtable Muriel Belcher. The Bacon portrait of her is justly famous. Women – unless like her they smoked cigars, drank a bottle of brandy a day and swore like barrow-boys – were beneath her notice, but it was Muriel's private fantasy that all the world was queer. She referred to every man in the place as 'she'. If one of them came in with a woman she would say, 'Oh, look who she's dragged in tonight. Stop pretending, darling – we all know.' She was what the French call an *animateur* and all successful clubs need such a figurehead.

But Muriel, in spite of her sharp tongue, was kind and understanding of human foibles. Also, she understood painting and literature, her clients were friends, and she gave them much support, although this was often accompanied by a very sharp tongue.

The Colony was a dingy room on the first floor of a run-down building in Soho, but many of the most interesting writers, in addition to painters, frequented it. But one day, as with any relationship that becomes too regular and almost a duty, I decided I had had enough. I simply – for no real reason – never went there again.

Most of my time, of course, was spent in the theatre. It was from my friend Jo Mennell that I first heard of a playwright with whom I am proud to have been involved. This was Athol Fugard and I produced his great play *The Blood Knot* in 1961 at the Arts Theatre Club. Robert Loder, an English friend who had lived in South Africa, helped me finance it. It has been said that, had Fugard written nothing else, his place in the theatre would be secure.

The Blood Knot is the story of two brothers with the same African mother but with different fathers. One of them is black and the other, who passes for white, is actually half and half. The play is about the agonies produced by this difference.

The backing was parcelled out at £50 a unit and I doubt that many have had a more distinguished list of investors. Fugard, a frail, bearded, ascetic twenty-nine-year-old, came to London and stayed with friends in Golders Green. He would walk the five or six miles home after the theatre. He ate but once a day, he was frugal and touchingly modest and remains so despite the international fame he has since acquired.

Superb, fascinating though it was, *The Blood Knot* was a financial failure, even though it was a two-character play with a minimal set and in an inexpensive theatre. Fugard's later plays, *The Island* and *Sizwe Banzi Is Dead*, which won prizes in London and New York, were also financial failures when I co-produced them at the Royal Court and the Ambassadors in 1974. But one knows that quality in the theatre rarely equates with financial rewards. What cannot be denied is that, as much as any other modern playwright, Fugard has fulfilled what he himself defined as one of the theatre's responsibilities in an oppressive society, which is 'to try and break the conspiracy of silence that always surrounds an unjust social system'.

A curious dissident in the generally favourable reception to *Blood Knot* was Ken Tynan. He was then drama critic of the *Observer* and widely followed as the outstanding writer on theatre. The *Observer* was staffed by many who had strong links with the liberal South Africans, and colleagues told Tynan that it was important to the anti-apartheid cause and it must be supported. Perhaps as a declaration of his independence Tynan gave it a bad review. This caused great offence at the time to many of his friends. According to a recent *New Yorker* profile of Fugard by Mel Gussow, the *New York Times* drama critic, it rankles with him to this day. Certainly it caused real damage at the Arts Theatre box office.

The Tynan review caused me for the first time to write to the editor of a newspaper. The letter was not printed. Many theatre people do, of course, write letters of complaint and dislike critics. I never mind as the critics are always on the outside looking in and never part of the enthralling collective feeling that gives so much of the pleasure of working. So basically they are loners which is why I am always heartened when I see a critic accompanied rather than alone.

I had a running joke for years with Harold Hobson, the *Sunday Times* critic, about bringing his wife to important openings. Hobson was a box office critic in that the importance of the *Sunday Times* gave him immense authority, and he often used to drive theatre people crazy with his seemingly eccentric reactions. But he had a virtue which no other London critic displayed. When he loved a play or performance, he would write about it not once but often many Sundays in a row. He realised that, to get people to go to the theatre, it was essential to over-react. Often he saved a production that was fading by his sheer enthusiasm and genuine love of the theatre.

Hobson once told me that he had always wanted to be a theatre critic. He was never afraid of his own opinions – as instanced by the story of comedy called *So What About Love* by Leonard Webb. John Thaw and Sheila Hancock were the stars; it was a pleasant, intimate play with good acting but basically quite lightweight. The daily reviews were mixed but Hobson on Sunday loathed the play and said so - in no uncertain terms.

The author wrote to him, not abusively, a gentle note, suggesting that since his reaction had been so uncommonly strong he might consider having another look. Normally it would have been a sheer waste of writing paper but this time Hobson came to see it again. He then did something unique; he wrote another review reversing his original opinion and giving the play a rave. This he partly justified by blaming the first night audience.

It is true that first night audiences often over-react. There are friends, relatives, lovers, husbands, agents, backers: not exactly impartial viewers. To accommodate newspaper printing deadlines the curtain is normally at seven. So the audience arrives tense, rushed and disorientated. Few are normally in a truly receptive frame of mind. Any reaction, good or bad, is exaggerated – and this applies to the critics too. Often I have felt their hackles rising at insincere laughter or over-eager applause – as a mother or a wife sits beaming, applauding every move.

A genuinely enthusiastic audience can be just as harmful to some critics. At the first night of *The Pirates of Penzance*, my major hit of 1982, the audience rose to its feet applauding at the final curtain. It was not faked. Yet Michael Coveney of the *Financial Times* posed his readers the question: What was the point of this show? The answer was that the show was pure entertainment and enjoyment! How could Coveney have been unaware of the genuineness of those in the theatre? Then on the first night of *Jeeves* (which the critics unanimously hated) one shaper of public opinion turned to my ten-year-old son Joshua, who loved the show, and rebuked him for laughing. The critic was only irritated by this example of audience reaction.

But I have to admit that Hobson's re-thought review – and in his fashion he wrote about the play repeatedly after that – helped business only a little. It never made *So What About Love* a smash hit. No doubt the first review was the more effective. Still, at the end of the run, Sheila and John went off and got happily married.

*

During 1962, while Britain was in danger of being smothered by satire of every kind, and Pop Art, the Twist and Elvis Presley became part of everyday life, I spent some time in New York and Paris. I also caught a glimpse of a new direction: Happenings.

In Paris I had been introduced to Jean-Jacques Lebel, a surrealist-anarchist painter who dreamed up events which involved audiences with unrelated visual mixes and performances. Discussing this turn of events in Cambridge one weekend I was told about the current Footlights Club review called *A Clump of Plinths*, which had been on for two weeks. All the major London managements had looked it over and passed – it didn't for them match *Beyond the Fringe*. I went to the last matinée and felt that I saw pure comic genius at work. It turned out that, embodied in one hilarious sketch at the finale of act one, was the embryo of *The World of Monty Python*.

It was a courtroom scene with John Cleese, then a law student, playing a manic barrister. The accused was a dwarf, Bill Oddie, whose head barely reached the top of the witness box and who had to haul himself up to answer each question. And Tim Brooke-Taylor was the judge. (These two, with Graeme Garden, later became the Goodies.) John gave a performance in this sketch which made me ache with laughter. It is generous of him to say that I discovered him, but this is nonsense, he was born a comedian. All I did was to help him make the theatre rather than law his career. I did this by deciding to bring the show into the West End.

The first decision was to change the title. We called it *Cambridge Circus* which was still confusing since neither of the London theatres into which the revue subsequently went was at that address. And much later, when it went on a very successful tour of New Zealand, people occasionally asked for a refund when they discovered they were not getting lions and elephants.

Cambridge Circus opened at the New Arts Theatre in July 1963, for a limited three-week season. It was very successful though I felt that the audiences were made up just of students and graduates. But Fred Carter, who was then general manager of Stoll, thought differently and offered us a further season at the Lyric, Shaftesbury Avenue. Elated, I gave a party at the Oasis Swimming Pool in Holborn. Since theatrical parties were not usually held in such places, it got marvellous coverage in the press, and I managed to get the mix of people I have always subsequently tried for, ranging from Edith Evans and David Frost – then appearing as a stand-up comic at the Blue Angel – to Miss Daily Mirror and a bevy of beauties in swim-suits.

Cambridge Circus stayed at the Lyric for a hundred performances. It was not enough to make real money but enough to teach me a few more things I had not yet had a chance to learn: for instance, the magnetism of a full theatre. When a show is going well I feel like going to it as often as possible. When a show is a flop it is very hard to hang around the lobby looking cheerful.

If, as in the case of *Cambridge Circus*, a show shows signs of being a success, but has not yet made its money back, the biggest hazard it usually faces is that the actors will try too hard to sell. They oversell. This cast, to the contrary, was most relaxed. Most of them were ready for the show to end so that they could get on with their true careers. But fame was breathing down their necks.

Among the investors in *Cambridge* were John Brabourne and Danny Angel to whom I had been introduced by Richard Goodwin, who, when Pay TV did not happen, produced many successful films with Brabourne. I had bought from Richard the flat and office in Duke Street, St James's where I still work. The three of them were engaged in trying to set up a pay-TV network in Britain to operate in the way that Home Box Office now does in the United States. They took me on as a programme scout for the useful sum of £40 a week. Their vision was correct but the timing was still too early.

Lord Brabourne was also a close friend of the Queen's. She decided to come and see the show. I was pleased since the audiences were beginning to fall off and some royal patronage could only have helped. The tickets had already been bought through the royal brokers when a pregnancy was announced and she cancelled all her engagements. Still, it was fun having had a production on the Avenue.

It had become painfully obvious to me that I still did not know how to structure deals properly. The amiable but amateur manager of the Footlights Theatre knew even less than me. We got into endless trouble about contracts and share-outs. I would fail to work out *all* the costs. That really required a good production manager, and I was not to acquire one of those for some time. Nonetheless, something of crucial significance to my career had occurred. I had not had to go through the humiliating routine of trying to convince the landlord of an empty theatre that I had something that could fill it. A West End management approached *me*.

Nor had I needed to go cap in hand to talent agents begging them to allow their clients to read a script that I was working with. Incredible as it seems I found it very difficult at that stage even to offer an actor a job. In the early 1960s the agency that had all the stars was MCA. Even to get one of their top people on the telephone was a major undertaking. There have been instances of actors saying to me, that part was perfect for me – why wasn't I offered it? You were, I would reply truthfully. But your agent turned it down.

*

Seeing myself as the C.B. Cochrane of undergraduate wit, I then did something really stupid. I saw another review at Edinburgh, this time emanating from Oxford University, and decided to bring it to London. The only theatre available was the Phoenix, a thousand-seater. Talented undergraduates, who had been hilarious in a tiny hall in Edinburgh, were now lost. Nor did it help that the name of the show was ****. That might have looked cute in Oxford, but how could there be any word of mouth promotion when no one could utter the title?

To a large extent I was just spinning my wheels. But the smoke had begun to attract attention. From an agent, as it happened, and an energetic and influential one. One of the theatre's few constant truths is that all writers and actors want to be directors. Everyone else wants to produce. Peter Rawley was the agent who then represented Spike Milligan. He worked with Beryl Virtue who later became part of Robert Stigwood's organisation. He came to see me and said he could get the Lyric, Hammersmith for the two of us to present a stage version of a Russian literary classic starring one of his prize clients.

The story he had in mind was *Oblomov*, the famous realist novel by Goncharov. The central figure has taken to his bed and nothing and no one will induce him to leave it. His estate is disintegrating, he is being robbed, his orchards are neglected, but he has turned his back on the problems of the world. *Oblomov* was of course a metaphor for Russia itself, the sleeping giant unable to rise and deal with everyday problems.

Spike Milligan had agreed to play Oblomov, his first serious role. With such an improbable mixture of play and star my first true success in the theatre was born. We got a splendid cast together for the remaining parts, including Joan Greenwood in the female lead; Peter Eyre, one of my few friends to become an actor, got his first West End job.

Naturally rehearsals were difficult because it was not easy for Spike to be serious. Or indeed for anyone else in the cast to take him as a classical actor. He was not an actor, he was a great comic, then at the height of his Goon Show fame. The director, Frank Dunlop, with whom I was to do many more shows, had been hired to see *Oblomov* produced in the spirit of the book. Spike, on the other hand, saw the part as nothing short of Hamlet. This was a classic confrontation, the thin man struggling out of the fat man.

The previews were nerve-racking. On opening night I hid in a box with Frank as the first act passed in funereal stillness, the audience restless and unexcited.

Act II, Scene I. The audience was still coming back slowly from the bars into the auditorium as Spike walked downstage in his nightgown, with Joan Greenwood on his arm. 'All right' he said, looking at them threateningly. 'Let's start this again.'

That got the first laugh of the evening. Then, a few moments later, his slipper accidentally flew off and landed in the stalls. Instantly Spike's old music hall spirit asserted itself. 'Unless you've got three feet, can you throw me back my slipper,' he yelled down. The house dissolved. From then on Spike just did a brilliant series of expanded improvised jokes.

The response of Joan and the rest of the cast was inspired. No matter how extreme Spike's clowning and verbal contortions became they played it straight, thus heightening the comic effect. By the end of the evening, the audience was ecstatic, the horrors of the first act forgotten. One of my definitions of a star is somebody who gives the best performance on the night that matters – the first night, when the daily paper critics and everybody who will spread the word is there. That is the night you want somebody to reach out and grab the audience.

After the show we all knew that *Oblomov* would have to wait for a serious production, ours was going to be fun. Only the adaptor of the play, an Italian writer Riccardo Arrango, fought to retain the original concept. But soon he, too, was forced to surrender. When he left the restaurant we spent a happy night thinking up more jokes. What had seemed a flop went on to be an eighteen-month triumph, not least for

Arrango who earned enviable sums of money because the book was out of copyright, and consequently he did not have to share his royalties with Goncharov.

We moved to the Comedy Theatre and re-christened the show *Son of Oblomov*. By the end of the run at the Lyric, the show was definitely hot and Spike had invented lots of brilliant comic business. The daily reviews of the Comedy opening were generally good. But, come Sunday, the Observer critic Penelope Gilliat (Ken Tynan was in New York) head-lined, 'The Genius Of Spike Milligan.' That put the full seal of approval on it.

We were all ecstatic. We had a smash hit and so it would have remained except for Spike's acute fits of depression. He had been blown up by a landmine in North Africa in World War II, and he said that the periodic depressions this had caused made it impossible for him at times to appear on stage. But, since audiences came less to see *Son of Oblomov* than to see him, on the nights that he was off a lengthy queue would form for refunds. There was one particularly awkward occasion when, rather than go home, he went across the road to a bar, the bow window of which faced the theatre foyer. There he sat in full view of the disappointed playgoers. Several coachloads from Derby showed up. When they spotted him sitting there, they wanted to tear the theatre apart.

But, when Spike was on good form, he was the greatest of comedians. He would make an audience laugh hysterically just by wiggling his toes. He loved to find a celebrity in the audience and turn them into a target. The Duke of Edinburgh and Prince Charles came and he adapted all his jokes to suit them.

On the last night he rowed with all the staff. They demanded an apology. He refused. I was summoned and for the first though not the last time found myself conciliating between star and staff. I was glad it did not get even more unpleasant; I was only twenty-seven and still inexperienced.

I still have a tremendous affection for him, not only because he provided me with my first real hit. *Oblomov* had made at least £7,000–£8,000 a week profit. Everyone did very well out of it, and I knew I now had a list of backers as well as some status in the eyes of the theatre-owners.

Spike gave us lots of laughs offstage as well. One night I was sitting in a booth at a Chinese restaurant with Spike and Peter Eyre when the waiter announced that a gentleman had sent us a chicken and a bottle of wine. It was Peter Sellers at a nearby table. Spike picked up a knife to tackle the chicken and in best goonish fashion it shot into the air. Sellers had tied a bit of string to it. Spike began dreaming up an equally hilarious revenge.

Anyway, *Son of Oblomov* established me as a serious producer.

CHAPTER FIVE

How to be a Producer

This is the way a producer works. He has a reasonably central office, at least one secretary, probably two, a production manager and a publicity man. Then he must have a sufficient sum of money – or know where to find it from backers. As the cost of the production increases this becomes more and more difficult. Many private investors do not want to invest more than £1,000 in a show. If a play costs £12,000, as *Sleuth* did in 1969, the sum would give the investor one twelfth of the investor's share of the profits. But if a show costs half a million then his £1,000 share will seem a small one.

In London 60 per cent of the profits of a production normally go to the investors, and 40 per cent to the management – in other words, the producer. In America the proportions are more often fifty-fifty. If, however, a backer wished to put up all the financing for a production, he could demand anything up to 80 per cent of the profits.

Once the producer becomes known to the literary agents, then the flow of scripts will commence and eventually an agent or author will come up with something interesting enough for me to want to produce. I might become committed after reading a script, for any of these reasons. I like it. I see that it would attract an audience – whether I personally like it or not – which means I would not produce it, but could honestly recommend it to someone else. Or I decide that it deserves to be presented even if it looks commercially risky because of the high level of its artistic merit. (Robert Wilson, Pina Bausch or Tadeusz Kantor, all of whom I have brought to London and immensely enjoyed, would be examples.)

In this last respect I may be somewhat different from many producers. I have often tried to push out the frontiers by presenting a show which was not really suitable for a large West End audience. When the shows fail to make money, I console myself that they were simply put on in the wrong place or at the wrong time, but artistically they have nearly always been worth doing.

Important actors generally have a secretary, whose role is really to protect and advise the star. Of course, careers can be ensured as much by what an actor turns down as by what he accepts. Warren Beatty is a perfect example of someone who has always chosen the best parts to suit his formidable talents. In some ways, of course, life was simpler for actors in the old days of contracts. The producer in the theatre or the film studio would simply tell the actors what they should do. If they did not want to make a film the studio simply suspended them. But today actors have to make their own decisions. Also films take longer and are more expensive, and therefore the pressure is much greater.

Once a play is selected for production the producer chooses the artistic team. It is usually best to find the director first, because his experience and contacts with actors can be combined with those of the producer's. One of them might be acquainted with an actor ideal for a part, the other may have strong views about who he is ready to work with or, more important, who he is not. The author is also consulted. Preferences apart, the nature of the play often decides the director. I would not waste time sending a straight play to some directors because they specialise in musicals, and vice versa.

In plays – as opposed to films – the author has a considerable amount of influence. Writers, even unknown playwrights, develop favourite directors and stick to them. Angela Huth, whose play *The Understanding* I presented in 1982, wanted Roger Smith. As he is an excellent director I immediately agreed. There was no need for any discussion. However, there are directors I would simply never want to work with, not because of talent but because of previous experiences. Often, it is a question of temperament, sometimes too little, often too much.

The script chosen, the author generally receives an unreturnable advance, say something between £1,000 and £5,000, against his eventual royalties. This sum varies according to the authors renown. The standard West End agreement obliges the author to co-operate with the producer's requirements but obviously it is a question of give and take. Sometimes the author feels the director does not understand his play. A row develops – usually the director wins. This fortunately does not happen very often, although in New York where the business is much tougher – and the money at stake is more awesome – it is not unknown for an author to be locked out of the theatre.

Assuming that the desired director likes the play and is available, the producer negotiates a contract with his agent. Unlike actors, whose price can vary wildly, directors' fees and percentages are fairly well established. The guideline is that a director gets 2 per cent of the box office receipts. Some receive as much as 5 per cent, some as little as 1 per cent. But 2 or 3 per cent is fairly normal, with a fixed fee of £2,000 or £3,000 to cover the pre-production and rehearsal period. Obviously if the play flops no percentage is paid. In 1983 a director might have got perhaps £3,000 for a straightforward play, not much considering all the weeks of preparation and the normal four or five weeks of rehearsal.

But, like the producer and the backers, the director is gambling that the play will be a hit not only in London but in New York and elsewhere; if it is, his income derived from it may go on for years and years. Even when a London production moves to Broadway, with another director using a different cast, the original director often receives a percentage.

With the director, the designer is chosen, a crucial figure in terms both of cost and of helping the play appear at its best. A top designer is like a pastrycook. The actual fillings might not be affected by his work, but he can make the final result look that much more appetising. While a good one can be immensely helpful, the designer can also hinder a play, transforming it into something it is not, emphasising factors that cannot be realised in the performance. Although he can always suggest some of the actors' lines are changed, there is no possibility, when it comes to the set, of a producer saying, let's try it and see. When the designer brings in the model the director must say irrevocably, yes or no, and it is the producer who pays the shop to build it.

Generally, I prefer the director to choose a designer, because it always helps if they have worked together before and get on well. The designer, too, is paid a fee and a small percentage of the weekly box office.

The scenery industry is particularly good in Britain. It was shrinking, but now many of the workshops make sets for television as well. The scenery can account for as much as 20 per cent of the entire production cost. One of my great laments in recent years was over the settings for *Dracula*, a Broadway hit that did not transplant. The scenery, by Edward Gorey, was a work of art, a grey and white dream, stunning scene after scene; it cost £70,000, half the entire production expense. It was tragic having to throw it away at the end of the very brief run. We kept it in store for a while but, like an unlived-in house, an unused set soon decays, and has no other function once the play closes. (That was, incidentally, an instance when I felt the critics were particularly harsh. They did not like the play, but they missed in their dislike an opportunity to praise one of the most beautiful sets I have ever seen.)

The designs will be well advanced before casting is completed, since building the sets will take longer than the rehearsal period; for the catastrophic *I* the scenery took six months to make and then paint. If I am feeling very confident about a production it is easy to exceed the budget; I want perfection everywhere and that always costs more money. My problem in the theatre, as often in life, is over-enthusiasm, I get carried away. I subscribe to the philosophy expressed by Eric von Stroheim. When questioned by the film studio as to why the actors playing Prussian officers needed to be supplied with silk underwear, he replied without hesitation, 'To make them feel like the real thing.' The costumes for *A Chorus Line* were incredibly cheap, just rehearsal clothes, except for the finale, for which the gold tailcoats and hats cost £500 each and there were twenty-two of them; but such a stunning effect at the end of the show was worth every penny.

The producer and director between them pick the costume designer and the sound man whose craft, particularly on a musical, has become extremely complex and vitally important. Until recently, they were available at fixed fees, but now they too, like the set designer, expect a weekly fee for the run of a show and share in all subsequent productions.

Soon producer, author, director and, in the case of a big show, the casting director are making lists of actors, looking through *Spotlight*, the theatrical directory, noting how old everyone is getting. They will not be able to have this one because she is in Los Angeles or that one because he is under contract or filming a lengthy TV series. Despite the legendary horde of unemployed actors, it is always difficult to cast a play. The truth is that there are many more people in the profession than there ought to be. Countless men and women who really earn their living as publicans, waitresses, chauffeurs, models, still keep the Actors' Equity cards for which they once qualified. This overcrowding, combined with the difficulty newcomers have in getting into Equity, makes it surprisingly hard to find fresh faces. It is understandable that a union should seek to protect its members. But, if a member has not worked as an actor for years, he or she ought not to be included in their depressing statistics.

Casting is often a gloomy procedure because there are very few names which can be put above the title of a play and actually sell seats irrespective of the attraction itself – and those that can do not and should not come cheap. My big hit of 1982, *The Pirates Of Penzance*, could have been staged without anyone especially well-known in it. But I decided to launch it with a high-powered – and expensive – cast. Four out of the

57

five original leads, Tim Curry, Pamela Stephenson, George Cole and Annie Ross, were stars. Performers like these command a great deal of money simply because they can pick and choose between so many different roles during the nine months they are tied down in the one show. When people are hot and in demand, obviously they are out to capitalise on their popularity to the maximum, in case this demand does not last. In contrast, the same actors might settle for virtually nothing, if it were a short run in a play that had some kind of special attraction or merit.

Once the ideal cast is decided on, then the call goes out to the actor or his agent, depending on which I know better. Agents, like Alice, can be wonderful or terrible. A good agent will look after clients, be their friend, advise and mother them. A good agent might say, This show may not pay as well as a TV series but as an actor it would be good for you to do it. They are particularly important in the film business. An eminent agent – and there are only a few in the world with whom I have good relationships – makes it far easier to plan a project. Someone like Jeff Berg in Hollywood, whose every client is a household name, has an inordinate amount of power.

I am not a great believer in auditions, although most directors love them. They are always hoping a new Garbo will walk out on the stage. (The exception is provided when there is a foreign director, who would inevitably have to see everyone in an unfamiliar field.) Personally, I prefer to cast on the basis of having seen the actor in a number of shows giving consistently good performances. Which is why I try to see as many productions and films as possible. By now, I have evolved a system for these unavoidable occasions which is as fair as it can be particularly for big musicals with large choruses. A polaroid picture of each actor auditioned, their age, height, experience, type of voice, it all goes into the catalogue. I, the director and, should it be a musical, the choreographer and the musical director, all weigh up the alternatives. It sometimes seems like a jigsaw. The musical director will want another tenor. I tell the choreographer she must give up a dancer. We barter people in order to get the best possible mix overall for the musical, and for the chorus and understudies as well as for the principals.

The understudy who takes over the star role is of course, one of the theatre's most cherished legends. One of my favourite films, *42nd Street*, was based on that precise plot. It does happen – occasionally. My experience is that an understudy, given the big break, will be great on the first night, less so on the second, and by the end of the week may be either a nervous wreck – or a new star. The first time, they have no time to think. They get a call at 5 pm. You're on! Later they have a chance to worry, and unless the director is in London and available they can easily go to pieces with nerves and tension.

In big productions everyone understudies. This gives the promise of a chance to people in the chorus. An actor understudying must, however, be at the theatre all the time. Raymond Westwell understudied both Tony Quayle and Marius Goring in *Sleuth* for three years, and neither of them missed a performance. Then, when we were in our fourth year, I decided he had to be given a chance. He took over and played one of the leading roles extremely well for over two years. However, in the main, understudies understudy. Some actors make careers of it. Many stars have been understudied by the same actor for years, just as they might have the same dresser. It is a very difficult job, and yet absolutely crucial as the curtain always has to go up.

Dressers are a wonderful breed. Some are great characters, like Ralph Richardson's Hal, who looks like a Devon farmer, tanned and fit, charming but not the least bit subservient. Most actors are great friends with their dressers. They know everything, hear everything. It is a job of great mutual dependence and intimacy.

Normally, I will cast a show before setting out to raise the money for it. I then send out letters to about a hundred 'angels', people from all walks of life, some of whom are close friends, some of whom I have never met, who have invested in my previous shows, asking them if they are interested in investing in this one.

At this point I have spent pre-production money, for instance on auditions, and used the resources of my office and production team. I have signed contracts with the author and director and many others. That is how management earns its 40 per cent of the profits. Sometimes the deal with the author seems somewhat unfair. With a hit show an author or authors might be drawing 10 per cent of the box office for six months before the backers and the producer make any profit. For instance, *Annie* took £7.5 million at the box office in London. Of that, over £1.2 million went to the authors although the final profit on the London production was only £415,000. I think writers ought to be content with a much smaller percentage until the cost of a production has been recouped – which in the case of *Annie* was £600,000!

After all, producers contribute quite heavily to the upkeep of many writers. If I commission a film script or a play, I pay an author a non-returnable advance. Out of four projects I commission only one might work – perhaps only one out of ten. But I carry those costs, as well as whatever else might need to be spent in bringing a script to the point where I can ask anyone to invest in it.

Recently, in the theatre, a writer would get 5 per cent on the first £2,000 of the box office and then 7½ per cent on the next £2,000. Then, say, 10 per cent from £5,000 on. Today he wants 5 per cent until recoupment, and then 10 per cent of the box office receipts. These pestilential percentages are a threat to the West End. Since the arrival of the dreaded V.A.T. at 15 per cent it is as though each play has to support one and a half additional authors. For the West End theatre to survive, we must devise a better way of helping the investors to recoup the capital.

On an American hit musical, author, lyricist, composer get, say, 8 per cent; the director might get 2½ per cent, the choreographer 1 per cent, the designer 1 per cent (12½ per cent so far); then the US management and backers 4 or 5 per cent, the theatre between 15 and 20 per cent. That adds up to 36 per cent of takings already paid out. And a couple of stars at 5 per cent each and nearly half the box office has gone before the rest of the cast of, say, forty, orchestra of twenty and all the backstage and front-of-house staff are considered. So it is not surprising that, with a show like *Pirates*, weekly running costs are over £70,000 a week.

While I have been engrossed with the cast, Andrew Treagus, my production manager, has been figuring out just how much financing we need. I have had three production managers in the last fifteen years. The first was Tom McArthur, now head of production at the Royal Opera House, which is the top rung of the profession. Then, during *Oh! Calcutta!* and *The Rocky Horror Show*, I had Edward Burrell who went successfully into advertising. But for the last eight years it has been Andrew, who is extremely efficient and clever and without whom nothing would be possible.

It is the production manager's job to cost everything out and to do the first rough budget. I make the decision about the theatre, but he must understand what the consequences of that choice will be, the rent, the running costs. He takes over the whole technical side. He may ask my opinion about where and by whom we should have the set built or where I think is the best place to have the costumes done. But, generally speaking, I leave it to him to do the best for the show in every respect.

There is usually swift feedback – positive or negative – once the letters reach the investors. If the telephone rings the next day and a lot of people say, Put me down for £1,000, £2,000, £5,000, I know the show has appeal. I do not believe in the hard sell. I never try to persuade anyone. I try to tell the backers as much as I think they need to know on a single sheet of paper. Dear Mr Moneybags, this is a play by . . . We own . . ., i.e. a share of America, a share of rep . . . This is what it will cost to present . . . Our reserve will be . . . Our weekly running figures will be . . . This is how long it will take, if we are a real hit, to get our money back . . .

Nor do I ever describe a play in detail. That can be very misleading. Although with an American show I might say, It won a Tony, it has been eighteen months on Broadway and sold out at every performance. It has always seemed to me that a backer does not want to be overwhelmed with details. The most sensible 'angels' put their faith in a proven management rather than read every play which is offered to them.

Once the acceptances start coming in, we send out an antiquated one-page Investors' Agreement which I have used ever since I started in the theatre. It is somewhat confusing and unclear, but it has served its purpose well and I am superstitious about changing it. It looks ludicrous compared to its American equivalent which might run to fifty or sixty pages. The law in the States is tortuous and diverts a lot of production money into the lawyers' pockets. In Britain, the investor's principal protection, apart from straightforward civil law, is what is called First Class Theatre West End Practice, an unwritten code that specifies, among other imperatives, that the show must go on. It is understood that a producer may not, should he get the idea, give the actors a week off in the middle of a run and close the theatre. A star might have a week off, but the curtain must go up every night, no matter what. If it does not, the investor is entitled to ask why.

Essentially, the code specifies that a producer must do everything that would traditionally be expected in staging a West End production. It is assumed that he will distribute posters, advertise, offer eight perform-ances a week unless it is demonstrably beneficial not to – when, for instance, it might exhaust an actor.

I have never fortunately been sued by an investor, and have only had a couple of memorable rows. One was with a banker who had written to me asking for an opportunity. I was doing that ill-fated musical *Jeeves* with Robert Stigwood at the time. My new investor put a lot of money in – £12,000. It flopped painfully and he wrote me a magnificently rude letter. The Girl Guides could have brought off a better production, he asserted.

The first opportunities are offered to people on my A List. Being on my B List does not mean a prospect is less worthy, only that he or she is less ready to invest. I try the B list if the A list does not do the trick.

What both lists have in common is that they are literate, civilised people who share a love of the theatre.

It is possible to run short of money even when large sums are coming in. A big production can eat up £30,000 to £100,000 (5 to 20 per cent of its budget) before the producer actually gets to the stage of raising the money. If there was a shortfall from the investor lists, I would put my own or my company's money in. I have lost money doing that – it is the famous way of going broke. But I do not believe in unbreakable rules.

If a play is going to cost £70,000 it would be capitalised at £100,000, leaving a contingency fund to cover developments after the opening. For instance severe winter weather might temporarily cut into the box office. In Britain in particular there is always the danger of a strike. It might be necessary to nurse the production through a bad patch. And, expensive as it can be to present a play, it can cost almost as much to get one off. Emptying a theatre – just getting rid of the scenery – can cost thousands and thousands of pounds. On Broadway the unions insist that everything be destroyed.

If the show is successful that extra money might be useful to do a little chest-beating, let the world know through advertising how well it is doing. I do not, though, think additional advertising helps much unless it is on television. And not only is television advertising in England prohibitively expensive but such a wide range of national newspapers has to be covered. In New York television is relatively cheap – and the *New York Times* reaches everyone who matters.

Anyway, once the money is in the bank or pledged, the actors' contracts go out, the theatre lease is signed, and the rehearsal schedule is set up.

Now that London theatres are fairly easy to get, unlike ten years ago, it is possible simply to take a chance and open in the West End proceded only by previews. In fact with a big show there is now no alternative. Even with one of the grand names of the British theatre it is difficult to make money in Brighton or Richmond, because of the cost of travel and accommodation and the relatively low seat prices. The day of the provincial Grand Tour is over, which in some ways is a pity because, even though I never liked them, a six-week out-of-town run could do wonders for a show and the morale of a cast. Although, as I write, this too is changing back as seat prices in the provinces are going up and the theatres are being better managed.

The cheapest way to open today is to go to one of the outer London theatres – Greenwich, Hampstead, the Lyric Hammersmith – for a four-week run. The show will be reviewed by the West End critics and, if they hate it, a lot of money and heartache can be saved by not coming into the West End. If, on the other hand, the critics do like it the play comes in on a greased rail.

With a few rare exceptions among the new breed of out-of-town managements, I dislike provincial openings intensely. One stays in some gloomy hotel feeling insecure, cut off. To the producer the show is a major event, but sometimes to the provincial theatre manager it is just another gig. And provincial reviews can be falsely cheering. They bear no relationship to what might be written in London. I much prefer London previews. I feel much happier in the West End, even if the problems are more immediate and public knowledge.

Two other members of my team will have been working away from the beginning, Audrey Balfour, my permanent right-hand lady, and Peter Thompson, a master publicist, with whom I have worked for years. All of us understand each other very well, have a similar set of values and a sense of humour.

Peter is eccentric and brilliant, with a fine sense of the ridiculous, the ability to prick pomposity. Even mine. When a show is bad he will say, This stinks, but we'll do our best. Now that he works for a lot of different people there is sometimes a slight clash of interests, but to my mind he is the best publicist in the theatre.

Audrey is even more essential to my well-being. We might have several West End productions on the boards at one time and she still makes me feel as secure as anybody could be. Her earlier experience was in films rather than in the theatre and her family are bankers – and gardeners of high purpose. But Audrey has long since learned to *be* Michael White Productions when Michael White is not around. She has a happy gift for always saying the right thing to the right person on the telephone and, above all, she is naturally kind and courteous. I believe one gets more out of people by being kind rather than demanding and she understands that very well. I rely on her to organise my day, my year to a large extent – so that I am never too busy to speak to somebody, see somebody, go to a party – and to put me sharply in my place when needed, which is quite often.

People spend far too much time talking business in my view. Give them a chance and they might spend a week discussing something that could be settled in an hour. I like getting immediately down to a job and doing it. I can never understand people who say, I'm too busy to return your call.

However, occasionally I make the mistake of doing too much, particularly when things are going on in America as well and I have had to zip to and fro across the Atlantic. The effect goes far beyond jet lag. Being met by limousine and parked in a hotel suite, one is engulfed by an entirely false world. Reality is shut out. I like getting out on the street, because otherwise it is impossible to get a true sense of the world as it is. That is why I like seeing films in a local cinema, rather than at previews when the creative people involved are present. It is too inhibiting. Mind you, they probably feel the same about me.

*

It should not be thought that any of this preparation will go smoothly. It is often nerve-racking. However, some of the responsibility for seeing that things do stay on track once the casting, costumes and scenery are in hand is taken by the company manager.

The company manager is the most important member of the crew and earns more than the stage manager. The actual sum matters, of course, particularly to the person receiving it. But it is a better illustration of the costs that must be met to pay the staff to use stall seat prices as a limit. For example just after World War Two the price of three stall seats would pay the weekly wage of a stage manager. In 1984 it takes fifteen seats to cover this cost. I usually have several company managers working for me at the same time. Sometimes I take one off an established show to work on a new production.

Company managers often start as actors, so they know both sides of the footlights. The company manager's abilities are soon evident once a show is on and running. He is, after all, the representative both of the management and the director's artistic standards. It is his responsibility to see that everything is maintained as both would wish, were they themselves in the theatre. He should maintain discipline, yet remain friendly with everyone. He supervises the box office and pays everyone weekly. After the first night he, as my representative, must take responsibility and in my absence make any decisions.

The rehearsals are when the first animosities emerge or – worse – submerge; when it becomes clear that someone is just not going to fit in or the leading lady discovers she does not like the play after all. Rehearsals usually take place in a cold, shabby rehearsal room. I try to stay away in the early days. If a producer goes to rehearsals daily he begins to feel like the director or even the author. I prefer to wait and see a fully assembled performance as it might be shown to early audiences. It is an attitude that has its risks, which, at least on the notorious occasion of *I*, proved fatal.

The way in which the director handles these early days is critical. If he is properly prepared everyone will feel that they are in capable hands and that everything is going to go well. But if he hesitates doubt and anxiety quickly set in; theatre people are very susceptible to both these afflictions.

If the wrong person is hired it is the producer's responsibility to fire them. Naturally there are times when a director makes a mistake. But if they have to go, they go; the result can be poisonous publicity and ruinous additional costs. Firing the director is the most difficult and unpleasant task of all. I have done it only twice. With hindsight, I wish I had done it more often.

There was a play I presented in Oxford in 1968 with Jane Asher and Brian Murphy, *Summer*. I had seen it in Paris and really enjoyed it. In French it had the consistency of a soufflé but in English it changed and became ridiculous and pretentious. Aware of the perils I chose a very good director, Robert Kidd. He was eager and talented, and went on to direct Christopher Hampton's *The Philanthropist* and *Savages*, but he was totally wrong for this particular play.

Romain Weingarten, the author, said to me, This isn't *my* play, my play is poetic. He suggested taking over the direction himself. I had a heart-to-heart in the gardens of Magdalen College with Robert Kidd. Do you think you should pull out of this? I asked. Both the author and I suspect that you don't understand the play. Yes, he said, I've been on the wrong track. But now I think I've got it in hand.

Well, he hadn't. Despite a well-publicised visit to Oxford by Paul McCartney who was going out with Jane at the time, *Summer* flopped quickly once it got to London.

There have been times when I would have liked to fire an author. Deliberately or even subconsciously, an author may try to sabotage the director's work, for instance by going behind his back and talking to an actor, giving him notes that change the emphasis of the part. His advice may be quite contrary to the director's conception. It is usually the director who wins over the author. At about the same time that *Summer* was being produced, Wolf Mankowitz came to me with a play called *Adam's Apple*, a farce written by Terence Feely, an experienced television thriller writer. Peter Finch's ex-wife, Yolanda Turner, got the lead, and we also had Bill Simpson who was starring in *Dr Finlay's Casebook* on television at the time.

One memorable night in Leeds, where we opened at the Queen's Theatre which has beautiful Edwardian boxes down the side of the circle – I was sitting in one with Wolf, Terence was in another with his wife and agent – Feely leaned across and said to Wolf, 'If you change one more line in my play, I'll thump you.' Wolf said, 'That line just got a laugh, you should be pleased. I'm not just any old management, you know. You're getting the benefit of me as a writer as well.'

This was dramatic stuff. The exchanges between the boxes became more and more abusive, to the point where the audience's attention moved from the stage to the circle. There was a better show going on overhead.

Feely had some justification. Wolf had been saying to Yolanda, 'You're not getting a laugh on that line, try *this*.' He did have a great facility for coming up with good jokes. But he was not the director. He and I were the producers.

The curtain came down. Wolf vanished backstage while Terence sat there fuming. But there was only one decent place for supper then in all of Leeds, the dining-room of the Queen's Hotel. We all adjourned there after the show, everybody at their separate tables, Bill Simpson with the actors, Terence with his group, Wolf and I with Yolanda.

The long trek round the provinces began. It was not very happy, to put it mildly, and I also made an ominous discovery. Bill had a following built up through television, a good, sober kind of audience. That same audience came to *Adam's Apple*, thinking they were going to see him as the upstanding clean-living figure they were used to, only to find a buxom blonde ingénue bursting out of her bikini as well as a lot of innuendo served up by Bill. They got very grumpy and word quickly spread: this isn't our 'nice' boy from *Dr Finlay's Casebook*. Also, to be fair, it was not the best farce of all time, so business was slack on tour.

The only West End theatre we were offered was the Saville, which was huge and totally unsuitable, but we had no choice. We had ended up at the Golders Green Hippodrome (now no longer a theatre) for our last week of the tour. By this time I was really worried. I was in for a big loss if the play opened in the West End. I will never know why but for the first time in my career I had taken out insurance on one of the actors, our star Bill Simpson. As the curtain came down on the end of Act One at Golders Green, in this atmosphere of total war between everybody involved, Bill fell to the floor, clutching his heart. At the hospital, the doctor said it was quite a serious heart attack. There was no question of his going on stage again. The insurance people said it was cheaper for us to call it a day than to replace him. They paid 75 per cent of the production costs, we paid off the Saville Theatre and we did not have to open – a great blessing through Bill's bad luck. Fortunately he soon recovered and we all quickly forgot *Adam's Apple*.

When a show opens out of town, the crucial moment at which

the four elements mix for the first time – actors, scenery and costumes, lighting and sound, and the production itself – often taking place somewhere like Brighton, that is when a producer is likely to be most concerned with details. He will be there, talking after the show every night with the director and author, and perhaps also with the star, searching out weaknesses in the writing, the direction or the performances.

I have a perilous tendency towards optimism. Once I find something to be enthusiastic about in a production I am likely to be enthusiastic about everything to do with it. There is always a banana skin waiting for you, however.

You can have an opening night in the provinces, and everything goes extremely well. But in your heart you know you are in terrible trouble, as was the case with *Adam's Apple*. The London theatres have probably been booked already, so you have to see if you can get it right.

I make the same observation to authors all the time. After the play we are having supper and I say, 'I didn't understand such and such.' The writer then explains it. I then say, 'It is no good telling me over dinner. Tell the audience. If you don't tell them in the play, you can't go to supper every night and tell them what you meant. If something is not clear – make it understandable. Now, if that's your intention.'

Sometimes crucial faults can be diagnosed. Sometimes no treatment can be devised.

In 1975 I produced Tony Shaffer's second play called *Murderer*, on which from the outset he and I had very different views. It was directed by Clifford Williams, who had directed *Sleuth*. Tony wanted the first part of the play to be done as Grand Guignol, violent and bloody. I thought that would be repugnant. I was probably wrong. But my view prevailed and when we opened in Brighton the play was not working as a whole. We all knew something was wrong but it was very hard to say what.

Clifford and I had become friends with Ken Tynan. I asked him to see the play and try to see if he could help. Ken, Tony and I had supper at Wheelers with Clifford after the show. But we came no nearer a solution. But we were right to have had doubts. When the play opened in London, reviews were mixed – more good than bad on the whole – but business dropped steadily every week throughout the nine-month run.

Wherever the opening, no matter how many weeks of rehearsal there have been, rest assured that everyone will be a nervous wreck by opening night. Should it be out of London the scenery is very often shipped down to arrive at one or two a.m. on a Sunday morning. There will be a dress rehearsal on the Sunday – if possible – and then the opening on Monday night. Often the crew will have stayed up all Saturday night, worked all Sunday and by eleven p.m. on the eve of opening night everyone will be exhausted.

In addition the producer must concern himself with publicity and advertising. Publicity is never a problem for me since Peter Thompson truly loves the theatre and only seems happy working seven days a week. Films do not appeal to him nearly as much. Once, after I had not done a play or a musical for eighteen months before launching into a series of West End shows, he said, 'Ah, now you'll be back in business!'

I said, 'I *have* been in business – in films.' But that did not count with Peter.

'I'll soon have your name back on the map,' he said.

'I didn't know it had come off,' I said.

But it is true that, except in the case of expensive epic films, a producer's name does not register deeply in the public memory. We are nowhere near as visible as we would have been a generation or two ago. Looking at a 1936 *New Yorker* magazine, one sees the Lunts, Ethel Merman, Bob Hope, Jimmy Durante, Gielgud – staggering names. But even the smallest ad proclaimed: A Max Gordon show or A Shubert Production. That flamboyance has totally gone. People who deal today in the big money which theatre demands feel that drawing attention to themselves works against them with the creative names, who, over the past twenty years, have tended to espouse left-wing views.

But the theatre producer is nevertheless a far more significant figure than ever before. The fundamental difference between the theatre – and the cinema to an even greater degree – as opposed to writing or painting, or even music, is that it can only be powered by money. The most inventive director still needs a stage, actors, costumes, lights. The most brilliant actor, a theatre.

All of which involves a producer in trivial but inescapable matters such as billing. Arguing about billing is one of the things I dislike most of all in the world. Another reason for being an admirer of Brecht is because of his edict that on the posters the names of the cast should simply be listed alphabetically, something not always possible in a world of ambitious West End actors and competitive agents. My solution for solving the billing of a show would be to put all the agents in a locked room with a blackboard and chalk and not let them out until they had sorted out their clients' billing themselves!

When I put on *Arturo Ui* at the Saville Theatre in 1969 I knew I was taking a risk, but I was idealistic. Because it was Brecht I felt an obligation to make the theatre available to the widest audience, and that lack of means should not prevent younger people from attending. I was more interested in filling the Saville than in profits. Ninety per cent of the seats were low priced. So we enjoyed packed houses and did not make a bean.

The production was quite brilliant. Michael Blakemore – well on his way to deserved success – directed. Leonard Rossiter played Hitler and gave a star performance. He has said somewhere that it was the play that made him – at the age of forty-two. Brechtian principles were hard to maintain, though. Driving past the theatre after a preview I saw his agent actually measuring the size of the comparative billings. The next day the agent complained that Leonard's was not in accordance with his contract.

Everyone concerned is tinkering with their end of a show right up to the moment of total commitment, the West End first night. Little details sometimes become obsessional. Certain things nothing can be done about drive you crazy when you see a play a number of times.

Having a good opening is the main goal for the producer whether the play is coming in from Brighton or it has done a series of previews in the West End. That means first of all getting an audience that is neither for nor against the play, and composed of people who can accommodate the critics' deadline demands and are ready to appear dressed up at 7 p.m. And it gets more and more difficult to find them. A big show like *Pirates* might have 70 to 80 investors who will all want to come. They, like the 42 people on stage, will have friends, spouses, lovers, relations, agents.

For maximum media coverage there must be some glamour in the audience as well as on stage. If there are any of my film connections or my personal friends from Hollywood in London, they always come to add a little glitter. As the audience arrives I am most likely to be in the box office, usually with Audrey who has our list of guests. I do not like standing in the foyer saying good evening to everyone and, if I went backstage, I would make everyone there nervous. The box office on opening night is in a frenzy anyway.

Box office thievery, once a considerable hazard, has been largely eliminated by computerised ticket-selling and credit cards. 'Skimming', the most common form, is impossible in any case on a sell-out. It means stealing off the 'top' of the take. Very rarely, an assistant theatre manager or an usher might let people in without tickets if they slip him half the price. 'Icing' is a New York speciality that does not happen much in

London. When a show is in great demand there, a box office manager – sometimes even the producer – simply creates a black market by doubling the price of a sought-after ticket and pocketing the difference. He is robbing the author, director, choreographer, the investors, of that difference.

Ticket agents – libraries as they are called in Britain – are entitled to charge a premium. On every day's seating plan in a theatre a block, roughly half the best seats in the theatre, is pencilled in for Keith Prowse, Lashma and others. The libraries can do what they like with those seats which are marked in red on the plan until a date known as the mark-off, a week before the day of performance, when they must pay for them. But on a hit show they know they will sell the tickets anyway, so they never send any back. And they always hold back a few good seats right up to curtain time for favoured clients who may demand them at the last minute.

On a first night, though, the producer's main requirement of the box office is simply that the staff be pleasant, polite and help get everyone into the theatre on time. It is unnerving to find that with ten minutes to curtain time there are still forty empty seats which belong to investors or their friends. Even more worrying if the critics are already in, waiting impatiently for their wretched seven o'clock. The curtain can only be held so long, perhaps fifteen minutes. I dread the moment when people will start to slow-clap. But latecomers blundering in at the delicate moment can ruin a play at the outset. I give the curtain-up signal on first nights myself. It would be unfair to leave the decision to anybody else.

The audience can make some less serious contributions to disaster; of these coughing or restlessness simply have to be borne. Though the reverse can happen, too. A good laugh early on – where a laugh is supposed to come – can make both actors and audience relax. Trouble can strike from any direction. A lighting cue going wrong at the beginning might send all the actors into a frenzy of tension, convincing them that it will keep going wrong all through the evening. That is why the technical side of the theatre is so important.

That is also why I no longer sit in the stalls nursing my own tension. I either stand at the back of the house or go into the back of a box. Or make a few visits to the bar. Nor do I watch a whole show through. With *The Understanding*, I went next door to the Waldorf Hotel for at least half the show. I was too fraught that night – with good reason. I could feel what was going to happen.

That play had already provided me with my worse experience in the theatre. *The Understanding*, a play by Angela Huth about an urbane elderly couple reflecting on their life-long love affair, it was a play that I knew would attract two big stars, in the event Celia Johnson and Ralph Richardson. I decided to take the play out of town for three weeks, two in Richmond, and one in Brighton, then London.

I had known Celia a very long time. She had been in *Chin-Chin* back in my Daubeny days. She was totally honest and completely natural, the kind of artist to whom everything seemed to be effortless even at the age of seventy.

The tour was a sell-out. On the Sunday before we were due to open in London, Louis Malle, the director of *My Dinner with André*, was staying at my house. I had largely financed the film, which was due to open on the Thursday two days after *The Understanding*. I was cooking dinner – one of my favourite pastimes – for Louis and for David and Barbara Stone who love the cinema and own the Gate Cinemas where *My Dinner with André* was to open its UK engagement. In the kitchen I suddenly felt terribly faint, so unwell in fact that I had to go to bed and leave Lyndall Hobbs as sole host.

I was disappointed because I had been looking forward to talking to Louis, whom I had not seen since the film's success in New York. I was also afraid that for the first time ever I might miss one – perhaps two – of my opening nights. Soon I drifted off to sleep and woke up at midnight feeling slightly better. The next morning I was perfectly all right. I went down to breakfast, and Lyndall told me that the previous night – just when I had been at my worst – John Gale, the producer, had telephoned to break the news that Celia had died. Louis, drawing on his experience of Indian mysticism, had no doubt that was the cause of my illness.

Celia had had a heart attack whilst playing a game of bridge; cards and the *Times* crossword were her passions. I rang up Ralph Richardson, who was understandably shaken. Not only had they acted together countless times, they were very close friends. As to the play, 'Boss,' he said – his usual label for me, 'I'll do whatever you say.'

The boss then made a terrible error of judgement. My first reaction to the awful news had been to open the show on the following night with the understudy. First reactions are often right and in retrospect that is what we should have done – got the curtain up the following night, regardless. We might have had awful reviews, but there would have been a respectable reason for them. Or perhaps I should have understood that God was telling me, You're not going to make it, and called it a day.

Instead I decided to look for another actress. The opening was put off two weeks while we tried to find someone with a name to match Ralph's to take over. Scripts flew back and forth to chic retreats – it was summer – while the costs ticked up inexorably. There had been no insurance this time. Celia had been past the age limit. All told, the tragedy added £40,000 to the cost of production because we had to go on paying the theatre and all the actors and staff and also re-rehearse our new leading lady.

We finally got Joan Greenwood, of whom I had happy memories from *Son of Oblomov*. But the heart had gone out of the production. The notices were bad, although Harold Hobson, now retired from the *Sunday Times*, gave it generous praise in the *Times Literary Supplement*. The play *was* doomed. I should not have prolonged the agony.

That was another example of the danger of keeping something going against the odds. When everything is completely negative – reviews not good enough, no business – a show *must* be got off as quickly as possible, which generally means four weeks. The theatre contract specifies two full weeks and two weeks' notice. Little is saved by not playing the notice out because the actors' contracts would be similar.

The real crunch is that first week in London. There is an old saying that, if your first Monday is better than your first Friday, you have a hit. It is truer than ever today. *The Pirates of Penzance* had the classic signs of a hit from the start. One performance hardly ever sells out in any show in London: the Wednesday matinée. It should be moved to Sunday, then it *would* sell out, but that is still under negotiation with the Unions. The first midweek matinée of *Pirates* took £3,000, two weeks later it was £6,500. By August it was selling out.

You know soon enough when you have an outright flop. It hits you in the solar plexus. You feel as if someone's taken you out into the alley and beaten you over the head. The morning after when you read those bad reviews, you feel terrible, worse than any hangover. You are in a state of shock. Your mind is full of 'if only I had . . .' or, 'How unlucky to get the second string critic instead of the first.' 'If only so-and-so had been as good on the first night as he was in Richmond.'

It is not just losing money – it is the waste of months of work, time and energy. Nobody calls you after a flop – there is nothing to say. The only consoling thought – though it is not much consolation at the time– is that there is nobody good who does not have the odd disaster. Nobody. You cannot have hits without flops. But often it is not a clear-cut case. I have lost a lot of money trying to make a fight for it with a play I believed in against the odds.

High pressure – which means high-cost advertising – works if you are selling a product that is available everywhere in the land. If you are selling something that is only available in the West End of London – to a minority – an awful lot of money goes straight out of the window fast if you take that route.

Television commercials have helped turn some Broadway shows into hits. But television itself treats theatre very badly – steals the worst, leaves the best, rarely supports it except in the most facile way. Plonk down a single camera, shoot a musical number that had taken weeks to produce, and it looks awful. A couple of days with a top director would be needed to do it properly. Whenever British television asks if they can do an extract from one of my shows I refuse. They got quite angry over *The Rocky Horror Show*, which of course would make spectacular television – done properly.

When a producer has a struggling show, a 'nervous' hit, or a 'declining' hit, one which gets very good reviews but only attracts a limited audience, the company may be quite happy. Because I am invariably optimistic to begin with. Everything will be all right, I say. We just need to hang on. A mention in a diary column? Oh, that will help. The star goes on some TV programme. *That* will help. But none of it does help because it takes too long for such publicity to percolate downwards, months and months in fact.

Eric Idle's play *Pass the Butler*, which opened a little before *Pirates* in 1982, was an interesting case in point: good cast, very mixed reviews (because of its attacks on journalists, and its one-line jokes which the English do not like very much). Then came a tube strike, and the Falklands war which hardly helped. But I loved the play and I kept it on far too long. I always had the feeling it would turn the corner. But it was *taking* £11,000 – £12,000 a week and the get out was £15,000. The play that was to follow us could only take £2,500 a week. You think, a lot of people like this play. There must be another 500 of them a week in London. But you never find them. If a show does not sell out in a 1,000-seat theatre, it will not sell out in a 500-seat theatre. I ran it at a loss for over twenty weeks, losing in the end over £50,000, more than its production costs as it had opened at the Cambridge Arts.

There should be a profound sense of relief in giving notice after a long struggle. But there is not. Just depression. It is like a marriage going wrong: people have come close to saving it but only close.

Usually by that time I feel great warmth towards the author, the director, the actors. I want to do well for them as well as for myself and the backers. By contrast it is fun to remember the heights, as when I go

73

to New York or Los Angeles and see people still lining up for *The Rocky Horror Picture Show*, or glow over selling a film that I made ten years ago to U.S. Cable TV.

Hit or miss, however, the investors get their first statement a couple of weeks after opening. They could form a pretty good idea, without even hearing from me about what is happening, simply from the reviews or the ticket queues. The figures are simple: on the left the box office takings and on the right the expenses. Not the production costs (they have been spent), the weekly running costs. The bottom line is either a plus or a minus. Many of them are horrified by the costs: £3,500 a week to rent lighting and sound equipment for *Pirates* – £170,000 a year. Why rent? they ask. It would probably cost £200,000 to buy such sophisticated machinery and more to maintain it.

Thereafter, the investors get a weekly report. Soon the moment comes when the style of bookings, the number of chauffeured cars waiting outside, make it possible to judge the kind of audience a show is drawing, whether it is appealing to the thinnish ranks of big spenders or to a wider range, whether you have something like *Annie*, or *Chorus Line*, that just get stronger and stronger with each week. This is good word of mouth.

Even in that blessed case there must still be changes. Actors come and go, some because they have other things to do, some whether they want to or not. I have tried to insist on contracts of not less than nine months. On the early takings of *Pirates of Penzance* for instance I assumed it would run for at least two years. When an actor's time is up it is prudent to try to lower the salary level on his replacement because the second-year income is liable to be lower than the first. The theatre will not be quite as full. With an established show like *Pirates* there is no need to stir up new publicity with fresh stars, although the replacements must be first class. The idea is to cast the parts slightly differently, find people to bring something fresh to it, not to seek out clones of Pamela Stephenson, Tim Curry or George Cole. It is easier nowadays to replace at a high standard than it was a few years ago, when both actors and audiences rather looked down their noses at the idea. In New York you even sometimes get bigger stars taking over – David Bowie (in *Elephant Man*), Raquel Welch (in *Woman of the Year*) and Dustin Hoffman all did this successfully and without losing any prestige. With *Chorus Line*, when the American dancers left, they said we would never find a cast in England. But we did.

By now I have met most of my investors if only at first nights. Usually they get invited to any big party. One or two of them are close personal friends whom I see all the time. But I do not hear from most of them between shows. Some call to say 'Well done' or 'Tough luck' depending on the results. Some do not. Even when plays fail, investors have written me glowing letters. When I did the musical *Flowers for Algernon* with Michael Crawford I had a shower of mail saying, 'Well I lost my money but I do not regret it – I thought it was wonderful.' And of course it was.

CHAPTER SIX

Happenings

In the mid-1960s, one of the qualifications of being 'with it', according to a glossy magazine of the time, was to be able to tell Michael White from Michael Codron. Codron was the producer in London I admired most. We were to collaborate soon enough on a production so disastrous that Glenda Jackson, who starred in it, has the good sense to keep it out of her official biography. But the difference in 1963 – though not perhaps in 1966 – was that Codron was the one with the money and White the one with the art. Everything I could afford went on paintings. I bought Hockney and Peter Blake drawings for £20, Kitaj prints for £5, a Tamara de Lempica for £300. Jean Cocteau gave me a huge stage design which a mover lost, and an insurance company refused to pay for because I could not prove it had been stolen.

I was not yet a member of the Society of West End Theatre (it is, in any case an organisation I have never been very happy with, even when I was on its Executive, dominated as it is by theatre-owners) but I had presented enough shows to be quite well known.

I was determined to do what I wanted to do. And there were enough enlightened or at least curious people around London to provide modest audiences for the theatrical oddballs, more often than not imported, whom I promoted. 'His persistence is likely to provide enough hits to massage the pain of some of his more way-out experiments,' wrote *Variety*, adding a reference to my 'distinct yen for avant garde'. I hoped they were right.

London knew something of 'Happenings' since word had drifted across from New York, and American Charles Marowitz, who later directed *Loot*, had provided an example centred on Carol Baker on the 'Fringe' of the 1963 Edinburgh Festival. Determined to present an example of this new theatrical marvel, I was delighted when my old friend Jean-Jacques Lebel showed an interest in bringing over his Festival of Free Expression from Paris.

I rented a peeling religious hall in Vauxhall Bridge Road for two nights, telling the owners I was holding a poetry reading, and set up a box office in John Sandoe's Chelsea bookshop. I assured the puzzled but curious press that everyone who bought a ticket (for twelve shillings and sixpence) would become not merely a spectator but an actor in the proceedings. And, since it was a co-operative venture, they would be backers as well. Happenings were supposed to involve the audience, I explained, omitting to add that I was yet to experience one myself. Nonetheless, in this case, I was understating the matter.

Partly because one of Lebel's star performers was the American painter, Carolee Schneeman, who specialised in 'living collage' – herself, naked, covered in paint – there was a wealth of advance publicity. The first performance was a total sell-out. It became a hot ticket. Intellectually fashionable London did not dare miss such an extraordinary evening. Unfortunately it was not to be repeated.

The event started with painted girl happeners parcelling the audience in long rolls of white newsprint. Immersed in this sea of paper, the onlookers were then sprinkled with detergent powder while Carolee went about spraying cheap perfume everywhere. Most of them were clutching a deformed boot or shoe, given to them as they entered, which we had gone to great trouble to collect from the reject dump of a factory. Some of the luckier ones were also given a joint to put them in the right frame of mind.

As Peter Duval-Smith was careful to note in the droll review he wrote for the *Financial Times*, 'Nobody was actually naked, but a lot of pretty girls wore the briefest of briefs as they gambolled about with some bearded young man performing antics that varied from the odd to the very odd.' Curiously, in view of what later happened, Lebel accused me of bourgeois timidity and pandering to respectability because I had decided that the girls must keep their bras on, at least for the first night.

Various tableaux unfolded before the entranced audience. A girl had a picture of the Pope projected on her bottom. More girls were painted, slapped about with wet fish and strings of sausages, parcelled up in polythene bags. Two schoolgirls flogged a policeman. It was sensational, I suppose. But many of the performances were very evocative and effective.

Then on came Norman. Norman Gair was nothing to do with the Festival of Free Expression. But what a performance he gave! He was the caretaker of the hall and had some firm expressions of his own to make. 'I have never seen anything so obscene in my life,' he assured the *Daily Express* later that night.

I had been standing by some swing-doors at the rear having a really good time when he entered. It was wonderful to see an audience totally perplexed, not knowing whether they were watching complete junk or a work of genius. Picasso and the cubists had made people very wary in that regard. I noticed that streams of coloured water were flowing under my feet and guessed we were in for trouble. One of the girls had left a tap running in the dressing-room where they were washing off the paint.

Actually, Norman's wife entered first. She grabbed me by the hair and screamed. She was going to get the police. It was disgraceful. Then her husband, described by the *Express* as a 44-year-old ex-Army regular, entertained us with his views. Since he was also standing alongside me most people took it for part of the show. Peter Brook went up to him and said: 'I think you're the best thing in the entire evening, a most interesting performance.' So the evening ended in a kind of ecstasy, everyone thrilled that the police came and we were thrown out.

I sued the *Express* over their version of events. They conceded that they had been wrong to call the event obscene and paid compensation for our lost performances. The second night's entertainment consisted of Jean-Jacques and a few others chaining themselves to the railings outside the hall, as a protest against bourgeois censorship.

A photograph of that time shows Merce Cunningham, John Cage, Robert Rauschenberg and myself outside Sadler's Wells theatre. Together with Jasper Johns and Roy Lichtenstein, Rauschenberg had created a whole new world of painting in the United States. I deeply loved Cage's music. Even though it is not at all melodic I find it absolutely inspiring. And he himself is a totally engaging person who, unlike a lot of serious people, is great fun to be with. Merce Cunningham had been dancing to Cage's music for years. They are inseparable. I had seen Merce's company in New York and without bothering with a contract we shook hands, agreed on a fee and I said I would bring him to London that September.

By a stroke of good fortune Rauschenberg, who was resident designer of the company, won first prize at that year's Venice Biennale. Nigel Gosling, who under the name Alexander Bland was dance critic on the *Observer*, wrote a full-page piece about Rauschenberg and Cage coming to London, which created a pleasant climate for the visit. So Cunningham danced barefoot out of time to Cage's music and Rauschenberg, in addition to contributing the scenery, did the lighting. He composed a different brilliant effect each night, depending on his mood. It was the best lighting I have ever seen on any stage.

It was the world of art and the theatre which showed most interest in Cunningham and Cage. There was the predictable funny run-in with the Musicians Union. One of Cage's ballet pieces calls for a chair being scraped across the floor of the orchestra pit. The musician assigned to do it took umbrage, saying that it was beneath his professional dignity. There was also a lot of hostility from conventional dancers and composers. Many people simply saw it as ugly, unpleasant, totally unmusical, visually negative. But the Sadler's Wells opening attracted important directors and the cream of London's Art world.

We moved from Sadler's Wells to the Phoenix Theatre to a chorus of acclaim which bewildered the Americans. Neither Cage nor Cunningham had much popular appeal in New York. The four weeks Merce was on stage in London was the longest engagement he had ever played in one place. But the success he achieved in London turned out to have enhanced his appeal when he returned to America.

There were walk-outs, of course, at every performance. But with something experimental if people do not walk out then the impact is not getting to them. Events like the Cunningham season were pre-empting the future. What was done in 1963 – and earlier – audiences now take for granted. All great artists pre-empt the future.

Son of Oblomov was still at the Comedy when, for a couple of nights, we turned the lights on again after the performance so that Graziela Martinez, an Argentine 'abstract dancer', could reel around the stage wrapped in chicken wire to the recorded sound of running water. Clement Crisp wrote in the *Financial Times*: 'I must confess I failed to see it. The whole sorry business seemed to me sadly dated and desperately arch.' With a new world of dance emerging that was the kind of review one had to expect.

My love of dance – and the new lure of Happenings – often produced front-page publicity. One of my imports, Yvonne Rainier, a disciple of Merce's, outdid the Fleet Street photographers at her press conference launch by stealing an armful of cameras, and running down Trafalgar Square with the cameramen in hot pursuit.

She danced for one single night at the Commonwealth Institute. 'An evening for the collector of theatrical oddities,' wrote one critic. 'But otherwise of no interest.' Probably what some people thought of me.

In this age of discovery I had also been exploring a couple of epochal matters. Marriage was one. The other was marijuana. In 1965 I had got married to Sarah Hillsdon. She was very smart, a former model turned designer who with Alice Pollock (who had been Orson Welles's secretary) founded the Quorum design group – as vivid a personalisation of Swinging London as could be found.

Much of our time was spent in the company of another married couple, Clive Goodwin and Pauline Boety, at their house in Notting Hill. He was the presenter of the rock TV programme *Ready, Steady, Go!* and, together with Charles Marowitz, had launched *Encore*, the theatrical magazine. The Goodwins presided over the closest thing to a salon of painters that had emerged in London since World War Two. Pauline, herself a talented artist, was in Ken Russell's film, *Pop Goes the Easel*, with Peter Blake, Derek Boshier and Peter Philips. All the interesting young painters from America and England would converge there.

That, however, was not its only fascination. It was also the first place in London one could smoke grass in civilised circumstances. We used to have heady Sunday tea-times and, from the first, I realised why I had never been at home in the boozy atmosphere of pubs and cocktail parties. Even now when grass is such a commonplace pleasure to so many people it is difficult to recall the romantic thrill of that discovery.

In the early hours of most days I would usually be found at the Ad Lib, probably the best nightclub I have ever been to but about which, at that time, I had somewhat mixed feelings. Alfred Esdaile who owned the Royal Court Theatre had put up a building on the fringe of Soho to house the Prince Charles cinema, office and a nightclub. He offered me the theatre, suggesting that I find a friend to come in on the nightclub.

He over-estimated my financial leverage, which was flattering, although I would actually have loved to take the whole block. It would have been a very good deal because the Prince Charles turned out to be an excellent cinema and the offices were soon leased to the GLC.

However, I did have a friend interested in the nightclub – Tim Willouby. We were going to be partners until Tim started saying we had to have fur on the walls and tanks full of piranha fish from Brazil. If he had blown £50,000 on the venture, he might have been unhappy but it would not have affected his lifestyle. I would have been wiped out.

So I passed and the nightclub – called Wips – opened in a great flourish of publicity, soon to close in an even greater one. The premises then became the Ad Lib, a magical place.

Rauschenberg loved to dance and I would take him there almost every night while he was in town. The Beatles would be at one table, in what became Liverpool Corner, the Stones at another. Everybody was on a permanent high, convinced that the '60s were the golden age of the 20th century – which indeed they were. People under twenty-five were making big money, were totally confident and the future looked great. Anybody with an idea could get backing.

I met Yoko Ono through John Dunbar who was then married to Marianne Faithful. She arrived in London to exhibit her works of art, introducing herself as a friend of John Cage. She spoke English fluently, which is rare for a Japanese, but it was still a highly eccentric version. I had just moved into my office in Duke Street and the place that was going to show her work faced Mason's Yard in which John Dunbar had his gallery.

Yoko asked me if I would present her just for a few days in a one-woman show she had contrived called *Music of the Mind*. It involves as much work putting something on for a week as for a six-month run. There has to be a poster, advertisements, critics invited. But I agreed.

Dealing with Yoko was a daunting task in itself. She was never less than demanding and precise. She would ring up twice a day, turn up at the office and totally take over. It was hard not to respect her perseverance.

Music of the Mind was quite well received by the few who saw it, among them John Lennon who had been taken to the gallery with Roman Polanski.

Later Yoko did a film entitled *Bottoms*. She asked if I would put the money up, but although I thought it was interesting in a weird way, I knew that despite her enthusiasm it would not make a penny. So I managed not to get involved in it. Nor appear in it.

It was hard to be too friendly with Yoko. There was always something she wanted. She was driven by ambition – of which I do not disapprove – but it was tiresome to be the target of it.

But I liked the way she behaved towards children. Sarah and I had two by that time, and were about to have our third, Sasha. Yoko was keen to film the birth and pestered us endlessly. But Sarah would not hear of it. A pity, I thought, because it would have been historically interesting.

After Yoko had moved in with John I went to see them in the basement in Montagu Square where they were under siege by the press. There was his gleaming Rolls Royce Phantom with its black windows parked outside but inside they were forced to live in squalor, not daring even to take the garbage out – empty milk bottles, bread crusts, overflowing ashtrays, newspapers everywhere.

*

The director Frank Dunlop was trying to do me a favour when he rang up and said, in effect, It's all very well doing all this avant garde stuff, but there is not much money in it. By then I could have told him that. He told me he had the rights to an American play which had been a big hit there, a light comedy. What was more, all the finance for the London production was available. He proposed that I should manage the West End run.

I don't like light comedy, I said, somewhat pompously, at first. That apart, the concept of just managing a play was something that had never occurred to me. Rather than starting out to look for money, I would simply do the necessary work, charge an office fee and take a percentage. I should have known it would not be that easy.

The play was *Any Wednesday* by Muriel Resnick in which Sandy Dennis had made her name on Broadway. I read it and had some reservations, but I had to agree that it would be a good vehicle for the right actress. It is not that I really dislike light comedy. I like it if it is done by people who are supremely good at it. Ronald Squire, Cary Grant, A. E. Matthews, William Powell – they all have or had a gift that can transcend the material.

We set out to find another Sandy Dennis – and failed. We had someone I was very fond of in the male lead, Dennis Price, an heroic figure. And we had the lovely Moira Lister. But, after seeing almost every young actress in London for the girl, we chose Amanda Barrie. That we got it wrong was no reflection on her. She just was not an American ingénue. That we let her go on was a reflection on us.

Any Wednesday had an awful first night. One reason was that about sixty backers who had frequently seen the Broadway production flew in from New York with their wives and dinner jackets, looking for supper at Annabel's and toasts to our transplanted smash. And Amanda just did not deliver to the level of expectation Sandy Dennis had raised. We ran successfully for about six months really because of Dennis and Moira. But we were never a real hit.

Michael Codron, I had noticed, did not make such mistakes. He did not put on American plays as a rule, he tended to do new British work and all his productions had class.

I had seen a play at the Open Space theatre, run by Charles Marowitz by whose work I had become very impressed. I was impressed by the play too, *Fanghorn*, written by David Pinner, an actor turned playwright. Glenda Jackson gave a marvellous performance as a razor-wielding lesbian. She rang down the Act One curtain with a spine-chilling line to a tied-up husband upon whose wife she had designs, 'Now I shall cut off the part that offends me most!' At the opening of Act Two the part referred to was revealed to be the husband's moustache.

Codron had an option but I wanted to get involved. Codron like me, had little experience of partnership but he was willing to try.

Among my friends was Sir William Pigott-Brown, the playboy baronet, who was a key 1960s figure. I told him it was quite a sexy play if he was interested in an investment and he decided he wanted to put up all the money. In fact he insisted and Michael agreed to unload his investors. I also got Derek Boshier, a superb painter and my close friend, to do his first poster. It was rather sensational, all black and orange and – weird. We went into the Fortune Theatre and the first night was appalling for several reasons, the first of which was that most of the audience hated the play. A play that sits well at the Open Space can inexplicably fall apart when it travels to the West End. This play was a good example. It got very nasty reviews, apart from one in *The Stage*, but unfortunately *The Stage* never sells tickets.

Another reason was that, thinking it would be good publicity, William asked some prominent friends to the first night. The party showed a grasp of time uncertain beyond my usual fears of keeping the critics waiting. This was the height of flower-power fashion and, about twenty-five minutes into the first act, an entire orchestra of bells tinkled and bracelets jangled, as a couple of Beatles and Brian Jones from the Stones with their ladies came down the aisle to the best seats.

The audience turned away to look at this amazing sight. The onstage action might as well have stopped dead. The first act, which was already going down the chute at the speed of light, plunged even faster.

There was some sort of party afterwards, but the whole evening ended in tears. William went on nightclubbing and got arrested at five a.m. for being drunk in charge of a motor vehicle. He woke up next day in Vine Street police station to find he had lost his driving licence as well as all the money he had put into the play.

Ages later I asked him, 'Why did you insist on putting up all the money? You must have liked the play a lot.'

He said, 'To tell the truth, I'd never even read it. I just thought – Glenda Jackson, White, Codron, Marowitz – must be all right.'

By then I was about to do *Oh! Calcutta!* so I gave him a tiny percentage to make up the loss. Eventually he got back all the money he had lost on *Fanghorn*, and a bit more besides.

Partnerships are, of course, fraught with peril especially if one partner is anything like Willy Donaldson, the celebrated former submariner, literary joker (*The Henry Root Letters*), and entrepreneur (*Beyond the*

Fringe). I first made the inimitable Willy's acquaintance in 1958 through Michael Hastings, the playwright, himself a precocious talent. We went one night to a most beautiful house off Sloane Street with a huge drawing-room. There was this young man just down from Cambridge, who was thinking of going into the theatre – Willy. He was very witty and engaging. He was also lucky because, at the age of twenty-three, Peter Cook, Dudley Moore and the others had let him produce *Beyond the Fringe* in London. It made his fortune, short-lived though it may have been.

When I went to see *Fringe* later on I met Willy in the bar at the interval in his impresario's camel-hair coat. This is such a great show, I said, nearly swooning with admiration.

'Do you think so?' said Willy, casually. 'It's just a nice little bit of light relief.'

He was, I soon discovered, extremely eccentric, the only successful impresario who would lunch at Joe's Café in Rupert Street – eggs on toast and a glass of milk.

For a while I shared an office with Willy. I liked him. He had in tow an incredibly bright young East Ender, Barry Krost, who wanted to be an agent. We thought of setting up in representation. Michael Winner was going to come in with money.

One day Willy said: 'The last seven times I've seen you, you've been with a different girl. I know you know a lot of girls, but you must stop showing off.' He was going out with Sarah Miles at the time so I did not think he was one to talk about showing off. It took me a while to realise that he was pointing out to me a certain emotional rootlessness – it was before I married – of which I was not really aware.

After *Fringe* there came a series of flops in which I shared, sometimes involuntarily. We did a show together at the Prince Charles Theatre, presented Oscar Brown Jnr., the American singer, and just about the time the Beatles were getting hot, but before they had a hit, we planned a show called *Nights of Comedy*. It was going to be a new-style vaudeville evening with different acts every week.

I rang up Brian Epstein who managed the Beatles and suggested that it would be a good showcase for them. If I had turned up to our first meeting at Grosvenor House with a contract, and had Epstein not been so indecisive, we might have signed them up for their big chance along with a clutch of East End comedians, strippers and drag queens.

I went off to Tunisia for a week's holiday, which turned out to be miserable and boring, and while I was away Willy cut me out of the show and brought in Michael Winner. It was a major disillusionment. Willy, however, is not the kind of person who disappears from people's lives without trace. Much later he was about to put on a show called *Dial 1234*. Wherever it played, the idea was, it would be called *Dial* then the telephone number of whatever theatre it was playing in. It was to open at the Royal Court in Liverpool.

Since he was not a member of the right associations he had to deposit enough cash with Equity to cover the actors' salaries for a month. With consummate cheek he asked me to sign the bond – which from me they would accept. He literally begged me to do it. I was in rather better shape than he was by then – it was 1966 – preparing to put on Joe Orton's *Loot* and a play at the Dublin Festival called *Hogan's Goat* by William Alfred. For old times' sake I signed.

David Conyers, who was then an important agent, woke me up at eight-thirty one Saturday morning to tell me that *Dial* had not opened in Liverpool the previous Monday as scheduled because the company had not been able to get the scenery to work. Too bad, I said sympathetically, but what did that have to do with me?

'Well, actually,' said David. 'Willy's disappeared and Equity has been on the phone asking when Mr White, the bond-signer, is going to come and pay the cast.' He had several clients in *Dial*.

David's idea was that I should go to Liverpool, see the show and, if I liked it, take it over under my management. I did not want to go to Liverpool. I certainly did not want to pay the money – although I would have to. But to Liverpool I went, out of a sense of duty.

At the stage door of the Court, a vast old-fashioned theatre, I was greeted by the sight of two women and a man from the cast standing just inside wailing. Really wailing. One of the actors, David Kernan, said, 'At least let us do a run-through. It's got lots of good things in it. We could open in Leeds next Monday.' Amanda Barrie was in it, too.

So I sat through the show, which was pretty bad. It had already struck me that, if the actors had not been paid, many others would not have been paid either, let alone the scenery and costumes. I could have been hit for £30,000 instead of about £2,000. So at the end I had the unpleasant task of explaining that I could not help.

So there were a lot more tears and a terribly gloomy trip back to London. It was sad that Willy had not been able to say to me, Look, I'm in terrible trouble, you're going to get caught. But as soon as I have some money . . .

Once Equity had sent the money represented by my signature up to Liverpool Amanda Barrie and David Kernan very decently gave it to the dressers and backstage staff who have no such insurance. A few weeks

85

later someone rang up and told me where Willy was skulking. I went to see him. He defused my anger instantly. He was still funny and likeable. And eventually he paid me back.

*

My first business encounter with David Merrick came about because of a new partnership venture with Oscar Lewenstein. Oscar had seen a Walter-Mittyesque play by Brian Friel at the Dublin Festival called *Philadelphia, Here I Come!*, about a young Irishman who dreams of Philadelphia, land of hope and promise, pavements paved with gold. It had two wonderful parts played beautifully by Donal Donnelly and Patrick Bedford. We took it on a fifty-fifty basis.

David Merrick, not only the leading American producer of our time but, as I had amply heard, the most difficult man to deal with, came over and bought the play for America without demur. We decided that, as it was set in America, it should open there before London, which meant a very nice situation for Oscar and myself. We put up a relatively small amount of money to support the Festival production and we then had a free ride because Merrick was financing the US production.

It opened – in Philadelphia naturally – for a two-week run-in and the first night went splendidly. The audience loved it, as did the local critics. The next morning I had a meeting at which Merrick was seemingly out to justify his reputation for awkwardness. 'I think,' he said, 'we need to do something to liven this play up. I think we should get a new director.'

The director was a most distinguished Anglo-Irishman, Hilton Edwards, who had worked with Michael Macliammóir for many years and ran the Gate Theatre. My jaw fell open.

'Why on earth do you want to do that?' I asked. 'Look at the reviews, look at the advance.'

'Well,' said Merrick. 'We need to make it lively, get some action going.'

Over my dead body, I said, and Merrick did not persist. The play went to New York and was very successful. It was on Broadway for over a year and won a Critics' Circle award. We brought it to London, afterwards, but there is an unfortunate prejudice against Irish plays here and it did badly. It was a lovely play though and I remember it with affection.

It also provided me with important personal milestones. On the night it opened in Philadelphia my second child, a daughter, was born and promptly called Liberty – for the statue not the store. And on the day that the West End production began eighteen months or so later Sasha, my second son, arrived.

*

Philadelphia was only the second Broadway production with which I had been concerned. But, by the end of 1966, I was quite accustomed to living like an impresario. Our house had more paintings in it than furniture and I had bought my first racehorse.

From experiences like *Any Wednesday* I had learned that I should not produce shows that I could not really love. And the time and money eaten up by the farther-out productions had taught me not to do something simply because I liked it.

At the beginning of 1967 I gave an interview to the *Daily Telegraph* in which I impudently said, 'I have made all my mistakes.' Little did I know. But it showed the optimism of the times.

CHAPTER SEVEN

I Am Desired by the Lord Chamberlain ...

In the 1960s – and for decades before – British theatrical life was dominated not by great acting stars, mercurial playwrights or adventurous producers but by the far less well-known figure of the Lord Chamberlain.

The Lord Chamberlain is not just a fancy title given to a faceless civil servant; he is – and always will be – a true-blue British peer by birth. But why a member of the British aristocracy was ever given unlimited power to censor beyond recognition or ban a play completely is beyond my comprehension. He also decided the appropriate dress for state and ceremonial occasions and advised the monarch on who should be permitted in the Royal Enclosure at Ascot, but that did not affect the informed enjoyment of millions of theatre-goers.

This preposterous misuse of power began in 1900, when Queen Victoria became concerned that some of her many relatives abroad were becoming the subject of disrespectful references in the theatre. The Lord Chamberlain's office was promptly given the duty of licensing every theatrical performance in Britain. Until 1967, this bizarre institution had to be consulted from the first moment a play seemed likely to be produced.

No other form of expression was subject to censorship. But the Lord Chamberlain's rules were that no stage presentation might represent recent members of the royal family, heads of state, religious dignitaries – or *any living person*.

That was before he got around to thinking about public decency. Modest semi-nudity was permitted provided that the nudes stayed as still as statues. But words? Words were the real worry. The task of establishing and enforcing strictures provided full-time work for a panel of advisers and staff and, in the process, they seemed to become a trifle obsessed with bodily functions. Look at the changes that were insisted upon for Frank Dunlop's production of Alan Sillitoe's *Saturday Night and Sunday Morning* at the Prince of Wales Theatre in 1966.

Dear Sir,

"Saturday Night & Sunday Morning"

I am desired by the Lord Chamberlain to inform you that the above named play in 2 Acts, has been passed for public performance on the understanding that the following alterations are made to the script:

Act I 2–9:	Omit 'beggar'
Act I 2–10:	Omit 'beggered' (twice)
Act I 4–17:	Omit 'begger'
Act I 5–23:	Omit the stage direction 'Brenda looks behind screen.' and substitute 'Emily pushes Brenda a screen and there Brenda undresses where she is not seen by any of the audience. While she is undressing and while she is in the bath, no part of her body is seen by the audience, and when she comes out from behind the screen, she is swathed in blankets.
Act I 5–23:	Omit 'Christ'
Act I 5–23:	Omit 'beggered'
Act I 5–24:	Omit 'Jesus'
Act I 5–27:	Omit 'begger'
Act II 1–1:	Omit 'begger'
Act II 2–8:	Omit 'Christ's'
Act II 2–9:	Omit 'bogger' substitute 'bastard'
Act II 3–11:	Omit 'bogger' substitute 'bastard'
Act II 3–13:	Omit 'beggar'
Act II 3–15:	Omit 'Christ'
Act II 4–18:	Omit 'beggary'
Act II 6–31:	Omit 'bogger' substitute 'bastard'

From the additions to Saturday Night & Sunday Morning, submitted on January 25th: omit the following:

Page 1:	From '. . . a fellow come into the bar last night . . . to and inclusive of 'It's not a dance, it's a raffle'
Page 2:	'. . . did everything come out all right.'

The Licence will be forwarded to you in due course.

I am to add that any proposed alteration or addition to the above play, or change of title, may not be acted or presented until allowed by the Lord Chamberlain.

Yours faithfully,

Assistant Comptroller.

In 1967 I submitted the script of *Fortune and Men's Eyes*, a play about prison homosexuality. It was ripped to shreds. A year later, with the Lord Chamberlain's office abolished, I was able to present it at the Comedy Theatre without interference, marking the first time male actors had appeared in the West End naked and fully lit. What had been a threat to public morals had, in only a year, become mere entertainment. (A week earlier, *Hair*, which for me was the best musical of the decade, had marked the Lord Chamberlain's departure by a début in which the cast showed all. But, so intimidated was everyone by years of heavy-handed repression, that it was done with the lights dimmed.)

Often, a producer and author, desperate to save a play from being wrecked, would go in person to the Lord Chamberlain's office to plead its cause. It had been asserted that a scene in *The Connection* might encourage sodomy because of the way an actor stood while making a remark like, 'Bugger that!' The author Jack Gelber and I acted the whole thing out in the Lord Chamberlain's office in St James's Palace to try and show him that it would *not* corrupt an innocent member of the public.

Because the Lord Chamberlain controlled the licensing of theatres as well as the plays housed in them, he could enforce his ruling by threatening an owner who would, of course, lean on the producer. One reason the Establishment Club was so welcome was that, since it was a club, performers could ad lib outrageously and to their hearts' content, a pastime utterly forbidden in a West End theatre.

This hypocritical, and therefore typically British, device could be used to evade censorship. A club performance was presumed to be private rather than public. In practice, however, it usually meant being confined to small, and therefore unprofitable, premises. The English Stage Company, which owned the licence for the Royal Court Theatre, was a club. The Arts Theatre operated in the same way. Members were not legally supposed to be signed up less than twenty-four hours before a performance, but of course they were.

The person most responsible for the final abolition of the Lord Chamberlain was George Strauss, then Member of Parliament for Vauxhall, an old-fashioned liberal in the true sense of the word. He was a man of great charm and intelligence. He was also a serious theatre-goer who invested in many plays. He, more than anyone else, pushed for the change of law. There was plenty of opposition, naturally, from the press. 'Can you imagine what will happen if censorship is lifted? The theatre will be one big porn show.'

This was blatant rubbish. For a start theatre-owners, like most people with money, are pretty conservative. There was no prospect whatever of the country being invited to wallow in salaciousness. And, even if there had been, I stick by a comment I made at the time, '*I* do not believe in any form of censorship.' People who take exception to a spectacle are not likely to go to see it, and no one under eighteen should be granted admission. When I put on *The Beard*, notices outside warned that it was an adult play. To my knowledge there was never an instance of an innocent passer-by wandering in off the street and being offended.

In 1966 and 1967, a time of fierce polarisation over the Vietnam War, politics preoccupied the Lord Chamberlain's office far more than sex. This meant that a brilliant anti-Lyndon Johnson play, *Macbird*, was banned outright, while the Lord Chamberlain's actions over the anti-war *America Hurrah* turned a sure-fire hit into a loser.

At this time Nicholas de Jongh described me in a *Guardian* interview as a 'capitalist revolutionary', which was slightly exaggerated. But I *was* imbued with more than the fashionable amount of indignation over Vietnam and other world situations and was quite prepared to do or say something about my feelings in public. If you feel strongly about an issue you cannot divorce it from the rest of life. Politics is a part of it.

But I was not, by any stretch of the imagination, anti-American. I loved New York and went there three or four times a year and it was, in fact, what I saw and heard from Americans that largely formed my opinions. In London I was a frequent guest at the United States Embassy. Both the Ambassador David Bruce and his wife Evangeline were sympathetic to the arts. I was even at a party of theirs at the height of the Vietnam war which turned into public unpleasantness when some of the guest 'doves' pinned anti-war slogans on the backs of people who seemed to them to be 'hawks'.

I was, however, sufficiently indignant about much that appeared to be happening in American life to rent a theatre in London where Mark Lane could air his theories of conspiracy in the Kennedy Assassination. I also supported papers like the *Black Dwarf*, founded by Clive Goodwin and Jim Haynes, a marvellous spirit who started the Travers Theatre in Edinburgh and who was at the centre of every avant garde cause.

But back to *Macbird* and *America Hurrah*, those two explosively controversial properties which landed me in so much strife with the Lord Chamberlain. The first, *Macbird*, was a brilliant lampoon based on Macbeth, written in rhyming couplets by Barbara Garson, a twenty-five-year-old Californian. It had trouble enough finding a stage in America but eventually was put on at the Village Gate in New York in January 1967. After that, productions sprang up all over America.

It had only just got under way in America when the Joint Select Committee appointed by Parliament in Britain began the hearings that were to lead to the Lord Chamberlain being relieved of his duties in regard to the theatre. The two star witnesses were Peter Hall, already director of the Royal Shakespeare Company, and Ken Tynan. The principal inquisitors were Norman St John-Stevas and Michael Foot.

Peter Hall pointed out that the theatre should have the same right to comment about public figures as the Press. Ken brought up *Macbird*, calling it 'an extremely funny and wildly scurrilous play', but adding, 'I doubt that American society is being seriously undermined.'

Michael Foot seemed to be the more interested of the two inquisitors in political freedom. Norman St John-Stevas seemed principally concerned about the Royal Family and blasphemy. He wondered if the common law rules on blasphemy would be acceptable in the theatre, should censorship be abolished.

Certainly, Ken told him. 'After the first case the gale of public laughter would be such that this House would have to modify the law.' Reported *The Times*, 'Mr St John-Stevas lapsed into brooding silence.'

My first approach to the Lord Chamberlain about *Macbird* received this reply:

Dear Sir,
The Lord Chamberlain regrets that he cannot licence this play, for the time being anyway.
If, at a later stage, evidence could be produced of a considerable run in the United States without undue unfavourable comment, and you then wished to re-submit the script, the Lord Chamberlain would be prepared to reconsider the matter.

The second show which incurred the Lord Chamberlain's displeasure, and the one that was the more painful financially, *America Hurrah*, was written by Jean-Claude Van Itallie, an American playwright. In fact it was three unrelated one-act plays which, when I had seen them in New York directed by Joe Chaiken, had bowled me over by their economy and brilliance. I felt they would be a success in London.

As the *Daily Telegraph* critic, Sean Day-Lewis pointed out, the plays owed something in their form to Artaud's 'theatre of cruelty'. One of the three plays, *Motel* – among the finest ten-minute plays ever written – was presented by actors in grotesque papier-mâché masks who systematically destroy a motel room. In another, the set was smeared with four-letter words, but that did not seem to matter to me nearly as much as what had been said – actually said publicly, by both President Johnson and Vice-President Hubert Humphrey– about the war.

I decided to present *America Hurrah* first as an English Stage Company club production at the Royal Court, financing it entirely myself. I was certain it would prove a draw and it did. Both critics and public were impressed. For four weeks fashionable London lined up to pay the two shilling membership that entitled them to buy a ticket. But there were fewer than 500 seats in the Court and there was little chance of recouping after the thirty members of the Open Theatre Company who had brought the show from New York had been paid. We had to move to a suitable-sized West End theatre.

I had hoped that the show's reception at the Court would persuade the Lord Chamberlain to give it a licence. I was wrong. He was not worried, curiously, about the four-letter words. He wanted all the political material removed, which, apart from emasculating the plays, would have left the audience with an evening of entertainment a mere fifty minutes long.

There was a satisfying public outcry at such blatant censorship. It reflected the impact the plays had had on thoughtful audiences. One of the few public voices raised in support of the Lord Chamberlain was that of Lord Longford. I believe indeed that the experience of *America Hurrah* had the historic effect of inspiring the anti-porn crusade he has fought so tirelessly ever since.

If I was to rescue the substantial investment for which I was responsible, there was only one thing to do – turn a West End theatre into a club for the run of the show. I made a deal for the Vaudeville in the Strand with gracious old Mr Gatti, whose family had owned it and the Adelphi for years. It was a very British compromise, but tortuous and hypocritical and involving an enormous amount of extra work. However the end seemed to justify it all as we really were coming into the West End.

The American cast was ecstatic. They signed leases on flats, put their children into schools. The season at the Royal Court had been a sell-out, so when the box office opened at the Vaudeville business was great.

But we blew our trumpets all too loudly. The blare of publicity and attention which *America Hurrah* attracted was too much for the Lord Chamberlain. His office officially warned Mr Gatti that he was putting the licence of the Vaudeville at risk. When we arrived at the theatre on the Friday before we were due to open, it was locked and bolted.

On the Saturday we held a press confernce. On the Sunday we were on the front pages all over the country. There was more public outrage. West End theatres had been turned into clubs before. But the protests did not help me, left with somewhere between £5,000 and £10,000 at stake and nowhere to put on the show.

Then something perfectly wonderful happened – which showed the tremendous spirit of the acting profession. The cast of the production due to follow us into the Court, *Fill the Stage with Happy Hours* (Hylda Baker and Harry Corbett among others), decided that they would transfer to the Vaudeville instead. They would play there for the same salaries they would have received at the Court rather than at their normal West End rates, which were five or six times higher. *America Hurrah* would be able to move back to the protected haven of a club in which it had earned its deserved success.

And so it did, but with no chance of covering the costs from the box office receipts. This side-swipe of bureaucratic vindictiveness in the Lord Chamberlain's dying hours ensured that my timely hit lost money, instead of making a profit.

Although the sexual vigilance of the Lord Chamberlain was no more by 1968, the Attorney-General could still prosecute for obscenity. And plenty of people were eager to see if he would when, with Tony Richardson, I put on another American play at the Royal Court.

This was *The Beard* by the San Francisco poet Michael McClure. Two characters, Jean Harlow and Billy the Kid, are in heaven wrangling over various cosmic issues including who had been the greater celebrity. At the end of the play, Billy turns himself on Harlow and pretends to perform oral sex.

Even in America it had had lots of problems. In Los Angeles, the principals had been arrested dozens of times. It almost became a part of the performance, the sheriff taking them away to be booked, the producer delivering a homily to the audience on freedom of speech. Then eventually someone burned the theatre down.

In London the parts were brilliantly played by Billy Dixon and Richard Brighton and the play was directed by Rip Torn. We put it on late for London, at 10.30 p.m., when a revival of *Look Back in Anger* finished. This was to emphasise that it was for 'adults only', as the warning notices plastered outside the theatre clearly stated.

'A crescendo of sexual desire, in its four-lettered expansiveness and in its sexual frankness,' said one review. Ken Tynan called it 'a milestone in the history of heterosexual art'. But you can always tell when something has grown beyond the inner theatre circle and through to the bigger world. Articles appeared even in the *Daily Mirror*. The half-page one *The Beard* provoked was headlined, 'Do We Need This Filth?' The *Observer*, on the other hand, under the heading 'The best in London', said: 'Billy the Kid and Jean Harlow locked up together in a blue velvet eternity. Funny with two stunning performances. Not for the prurient.'

Even without that kind of attention the play was already very hard on both actors; its intensity was like a nightly and public bout of psycho-therapy. They both became a little crazed. It is hard for any actor to play in a two-hander about crazies and not become affected. One night Brighton was angry with Dixon – she was a difficult lady – and in the crucial scene he bit her.

Dixon screamed and slapped his face so hard that the production nearly disintegrated there and then in front of the audience.

She swore she would never speak to him again let alone appear on stage with him. She was going to take it up with Equity. But tempers cooled the next day and the show went on its bumpy way, although the longer it ran the more fevered and crazed the relationship between the actors became.

The Beard is still talked about. There is no doubt it was a very important poetic play. Sandy Lieberson wanted to produce it as a film with Mick Jagger playing Billy, but it came to nothing. Michael McClure, the author, was a lovely man. He often had Jim Morrison in tow while he was in London; Jim was very good-looking, civilised and modest but, onstage, a tornado of violence and sex appeal the likes of which had never been seen before in the music business. Once, when we went to a night club, every woman around devoured him with her eyes.

*

Despite these mischievous activities I had begun to cut a more serious figure around the West End. I had joined the council of the Institute of Contemporary Arts when it moved to the Mall, which was fascinating but time-consuming, and eventually I helped get the theatre off the ground by paying for the lighting equipment. It was my seven years of meetings there that taught me to be suspicious of committees. My way would be to choose the right people, give them a budget and let them get on with what they're supposed to be doing.

I have to accept that the future of the theatre may rest with a body like the Arts Council. But, instead of putting a huge annual grant behind certain productions, the Council, in my view, should buy two or three theatres, in which new productions could find their feet, and donate them at a peppercorn rent. In that way, fresh, interesting work could be done commercially without it costing so much and with such attendant high risks.

Simply being in a theatre eats up far too much of the box office, up to 20 per cent of the gross box office receipt. To use Drury Lane at £11,000–£12,000 a week rent as an example, a flop can mean losing an additional £100,000 in rent alone.

CHAPTER EIGHT

'Loot'

Among the dozen or so productions of 1967, my tenth year in the theatre, was the novelist Brigid Brophy's first and only play *The Burglar*. I presented it with Michael Medwin and Albert Finney of Memorial Productions.

It had a sound cast, Siân Phillips, Gerald Flood, Jim Dale, James Villiers, and a good plot, and it was splendidly directed by Frank Dunlop. Originally Peter O'Toole wanted to be in it but would not have been free for nine months to a year. We decided not to wait for him – which led to his turning up at the first night in Brighton, and pacing up and down backstage, reducing everyone to gibbering wrecks with advice and exhortations.

Despite that, *The Burglar* was well received in Brighton and had good advance publicity into the West End, including a curious pre-opening rave from Tariq Ali in *Town Magazine*, which caused trouble with the other daily critics, who did not take kindly to being pre-empted.

How could it fail? Fail it did, however, closing afer ten days at the Vaudeville, sending thousands down the drain and reviving all my confusion about critics and their abilities.

I have never known a play in which so much attention was focused on the author, and the play and production so ignored. The critics kept comparing Brigid with George Bernard Shaw and decided that she was not his equal. The play had certain Shavian similarities, in the sense that it was a witty comedy of manners and ideas, rather than action. But it had been written by a woman novelist. A lot of critics seemed not to like the idea of women novelists turning into playwrights. I remember thinking at the time that we should have waited for O'Toole, and what a pity Tariq had written his advance rave.

But, above all, 1967 was the year of doomed, inimitable John Kingsley (Joe) Orton.

I first saw *Loot*, Joe Orton's second major play, at the Golders Green Hippodrome in February 1965, the night before Joshua my eldest son was born. It was produced by Michael Codron and Donald Albery and had opened at the Arts, Cambridge in February 1965. It was directed by Peter Wood and Kenneth Williams, a close friend of Orton's, starred. I will never forget the set: a complete white fantasy, brilliant but out of sync with the abrasive realism of the play which was the root of much of its humour. It toured but fell apart on the road, coming to rest in Golders Green where I saw it.

I thought Orton was an amazing writer – *Entertaining Mr Sloane* had already established him – but it never occurred to me then that I would resuscitate *Loot* eighteen months later. Even in the shape in which I saw it, though, the play was a masterpiece. It is a farce, the action centring around the hiding of a mother's corpse, removed from its coffin and hidden in a cupboard so that the loot of the title can be concealed. Its deep black comedy conveys some of the most marvellously pungent observations made on life in modern Britain. The character of Inspector Truscott seems a good deal less fantastic now when we know rather more than we used to about the ways of the British Police.

Oscar Lewenstein inspired the resurrection. He was going to Ireland to produce the film of *The Girl with Green Eyes*. He wanted to give a second chance to *Loot*, but not on his own. He proposed that I come in with him on a try-out at the Jeannetta Cochrane Theatre. We would each put up £1,000 to underwrite the production and I, being in London, would take the responsibility for the day-to-day management.

I did not rush to accept. Very few plays have been known to return from the dead. Orton's agent was Peggy Ramsay now the most influential theatrical literary agent in London. I was wary of her as we had fallen out over a play by her client Eric Kahane *La Philosophie du Boudoir*, based on the Marquis de Sade, which in a moment of folly a year earlier I had said I would do. It was very dirty but it seemed like a challenge. I sent it to Harold Hobson for an opinion. He said, If you do this, you'll go to gaol. So I did not do it, and Peggy had taken offence. It made me uneasy. She was a very formidable lady. Funnily enough, she too had once worked for Peter Daubeny, as his secretary. Orton worshipped her. She was the central figure in his life, much more than an agent, she was his friend and confidante.

While I was considering Oscar's offer, Peggy did something that annoyed me – but it worked. She telephoned and said, You're the only

Licensee and Managing Director : DONALD ALBERY

Proprietors : THE WYNDAM THEATRES LTD.

Criterion Theatre

PICCADILLY CIRCUS, W.1.
Telephone: WHItehall 3216

By arrangement with Donald Albery
OSCAR LEWENSTEIN and **MICHAEL WHITE** present
The LONDON TRAVERSE Theatre Company's production of:

LOOT

£104,000 BANK ROBBERY

Michael Bates

alias Truscott gives 'a gem of a performance' SUN

'a superb comic creation' EVE. STANDARD

'which establishes him as one of the most brilliant farce actors on the British stage' TIMES

Sensational West End crime drama !

Held responsible for this daring coup is author **Joe Orton** 'the Oscar Wilde of the Welfare State'- (Observer), and actors
**Michael Bates
Sheila Ballantine
Kenneth Cranham
Gerry Duggan
and Simon Ward**
are also involved. Have you seen them? Dial WHI3216

"
The most genuinely **QUICKWITTED PUNGENT & SPRIGHTLY** entertainment by a new young British playwright for a decade
ALAN BRIEN — SUNDAY TELEGRAPH.

'OUTRAGEOUSLY FUNNY'

PHILIP HOPE-WALLACE — THE GUARDIAN.

directed by **CHARLES MAROWITZ**
★★ designed by
TONY CARRUTHERS

FULL STORY INSIDE !

Designed by MICHAEL CARNEY

Printed by LAKEMAN & CO. LTD. 2 HERBRAND ST. WC1 ·

Michael White, Lyndall and children in 1974

On the roof of Duke Street in 1968 (*left to right*): Michael White, Sarah White, Pauline Fordham, Gala Mitchell and David Hockney

At Sadlers Wells in 1963 (*left to right*): John Cage, Merce Cunningham, Robert Rauschenberg and Michael White

With Frank Dunlop during rehearsals for *Any Wednesday* at the Apollo Theatre in 1964

© *Marc Boxer*

"I dare say Kipling did write a splendid story about Calcutta but somehow I don't think this is it."

© *Sir Osbert Lancaster; from a* Daily Express *Pocket Cartoon by Osbert Lancaster*

Two faces of the reaction to *Oh! Calcutta!* when it first appeared in 1969

A restaurant in Rome in the late Sixties: Peter Daubeny (*left*), with whom Michael White spent 'five happy years of apprenticeship', and Federico Fellini

Kenneth Tynan, critic, friend and deviser of *Oh! Calcutta!*

10 Downing Street
Whitehall

February 20, 1969

Dear Mr White,

    I am writing on the Prime Minister's behalf
to thank you for your letter of February 17. The
Prime Minister manages only infrequent visits to
the theatre and in the event of his being able to
increase the number of visits would have on his
list a considerable number of other plays to which
he would wish to give priority.

Yours sincerely,

D. Andrews

Michael White, Esq.

An invitation to Harold Wilson to attend a performance of *Soldiers* received a dusty answer

FROM THE
EDITOR

THE DAILY EXPRE
FLEET STREET, LONDC
FLEET STREET 8000

July 21st, 1964.

Dear Mr. White,

    On June 9th the Daily Express reported various critical
comments made of the performance of "The Happenings" by member
of the Paris Workshop of Free Expression at Dennison Hall, London
and produced by you.

    It has been pointed out to me that this report gave a
misleading impression of some aspects of the performance. In
particular none of the cast was naked on the stage as bikinis or trunk
were worn and there was nothing obscene about the performance.

    In these circumstances I would like to record that the
show has not been banned as obscene in Paris or Rome and to apologise to you and your cast for any wrong impression created.

Yours sincerely,

Robert Edwards

Michael White, Esq.,
c/o Oscar A. Beuselinck,
18 Bloomsbury Square,
London, W.C.1.

But the *Daily Express* had to apologise for misrepresenting another of Michael
White's shows

Hewison's *Loot!* cartoon

A card from Willie Rushton

WHITE BARN THEATRE
WESTPORT, CONN.

LUCILLE LORTEL, Founder

PROGRAM

Band: George Adie — guitar   Bill Stronach — vibes   Iwan Williams

ROBIN GROVE-WHITE

DOUG FISHER

JANE BRANSHAW

in association with Bernard Jefferson

Michael White

Vanessa Redgrave   Joe Melia
Ronald Radd   Annie Ross   Barbara Windsor
And Hermione Baddeley

in

THE THREEPENNY OPERA

by Bertholt Brecht music Kurt Weill
English adaptation Hugh MacDiarmid

with Lon Satton
Victor Maddern Dan Meaden Arthur Mullard
Derry Power   Henry Woolf

directed by Tony Richardson

associate director Keith Hack
sets by Patrick Robertson costumes by Rosemary Vercoe
lighting by Richard Pilbrow Musical director Marcus Dods
Choreography Eleanor Fazan

PRINCE OF WALES THEATRE
Coventry Street W.1   930 8681

ST. MARTIN'S THEATRE
WEST STREET, CAMBRIDGE CIRCUS, SHAFTESBURY AVENUE, W.C.2 01-836 1443
SOLE PROPRIETORS: S.M. THEATRE LTD.   LESSEES: PETER SAUNDERS LTD.
LICENSED BY THE G.L.C TO RICHARD PHILLIPS GRISTOR METER

MICHAEL WHITE
PRESENTS

ANTHONY QUAYLE
KEITH BAXTER
in
SLEUTH
A NEW THRILLER BY ANTHONY SHAFFER
DIRECTED BY CLIFFORD WILLIAMS
LIGHTING BY FRANCIS REID. DESIGNED BY CARL TOMS

WINNER! 3 TONY AWARD NOMINATIONS
Including BEST PLAYS
AND BEST ACTORS JOHN KANI & WINSTON NTSHONA
AND BEST DIRECTOR ATHOL FUGARD

"THE STRONGEST AND MOST IMPORTANT
THEATRE ON BROADWAY RIGHT NOW!"
— Jack Kroll, Newsweek

"A THEATRICAL MASTERSTROKE!"
— Clive Barnes, New York Times

"A POWERHOUSE!"
— Martin Gottfried, Cue Magazine

"A MEMORABLE EXPERIENCE!"
— Martin Gottfried, New York Post

ATHOL FUGARD'S

SIZWE BANZI IS DEAD
and
THE ISLAND

"JOHN KANI & WINSTON NTSHONA OFFER
THE GREATEST FEATS OF ACTING ON B'WAY!"
— Brendan Gill, The New Yorker

"THE ONLY 2 NEW PLAYS THIS SEASON OF SUBSTANCE
IN ACTING & WRITING." — Harold Clurman, The Nation

"VIRTUOSO PERFORMANCES!" — Douglas Watt, Daily News

"ATHOL FUGARD'S DIRECTING IS BRILLIANT!"
— Clive Barnes, ABC TV

"BRAVO!" — William Raidy, Newhouse Papers

Edison Theatre 47th Street, West of B'way / 757-7164

THE

C
O
N
N
E
C
T
I
O

THE ROCKY HORROR SHOW

ALIVE ON STAGE

Music Book & Lyrics by RICHARD O'BRIEN
Director JIM SHARMAN
Designer BRIAN THOMSON Costumes SUE BLANE
Lighting GERRY JENKINSON Musical Arrangements RICHARD HARTLEY
The Theatre Upstairs Production presented by MICHAEL WHITE

ALL SEATS BOOKABLE

KINGS ROAD THEATRE
(ex Essoldo Cinema)
279, KINGS ROAD, SW3 BOX OFFICE: 352 7488

Kington — bas

Barry
HUMPHRIES

MICHAEL WHITE
extremely proudly presents

HOUSEWIFE-
SUPERSTAR!!!

FOR 8 WEEKS ONLY
EVENINGS 8.0pm
Saturdays 5.30 & 8.30pm

GLOBE THEATRE
Shaftesbury Avenue, W.1   01-437 1592

ael White

cis Perry

MICHAEL WHITE &
THE TRAVERSE THEATRE
present

yoko ono

All persons with bicycles
phone WHI 1424 or HOL 4818

PHOTO by IAIN MACMILLAN

"MUSIC WITH NO AUDIBLE SOUND" — Daily Telegraph   "A HIGHL

AY with JAZZ
Jack Gelber

UKE of YORK'S
THEATRE

THE
COMIC
STRIP

Opening 7th Octobe

HAVE A NICE DAY

London's
newest anarchic cabaret
Boulevard Theatre Walker's Court Brewer St
Tel. 437-2661 Tues. to Sun.

DUCHESS THEATRE

CATHERINE STREET WC2   01·836 8243

LICENSEES·THEATRE CONSOLIDATED LTD   CHAIRMAN·D.A.ABRAHAMS   MAN.DIR·JOHN HALLETT

ROBERT STIGWOOD
in association with
BOB SWASH and **MICHAEL WHITE**
presents

THE DIRTIEST SHOW IN TOWN

WRITTEN AND DIRECTED BY **TOM EYEN**

1970 – *The Dirtiest Show in Town*

1973 – during filming for *The Rocky Horror Picture Show*

1976 – *A Chorus Line* directed by Michael Bennett at the Theatre Royal, Drury Lane

The Young Vic production of *Cato Street* with Vanessa Redgrave

Spike Milligan and Marjie Lawrence in the 1963 production of *Son of Oblomov*

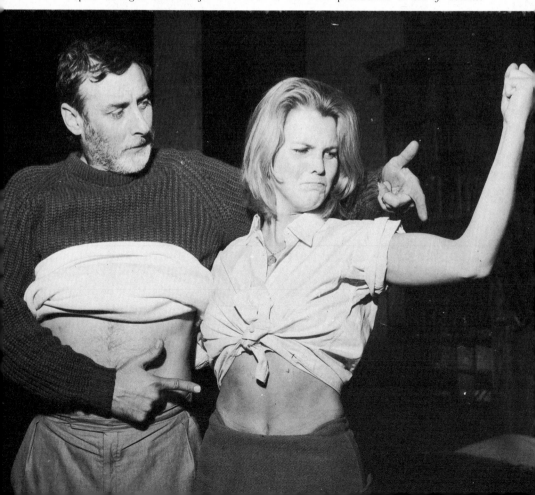

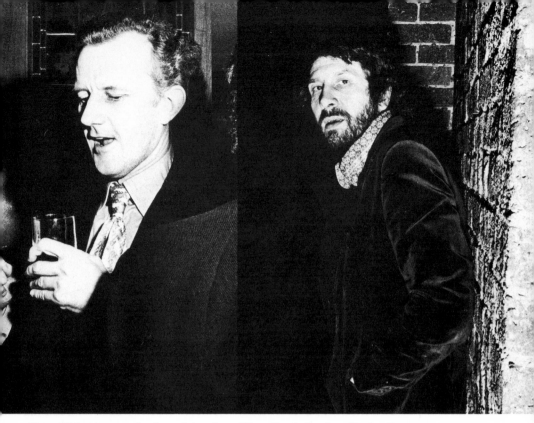

Tony Richardson at the first night of
The Threepenny Opera

Clive Goodwin, key Sixties literary
agent

American glamour in Earls Court: Diana Vreeland and Jack Nicholson with Michael
White at a Bob Dylan concert

The Comic Strip, Rik Mayall, Nigel Planer, Jennifer Saunders, Adrian Edmondson,

intelligent manager in London, the only one who understands this play. (She did the same thing again years later when, happily, she talked me into putting up the money for *My Dinner with André*.)

This time the director was Charles Marowitz, and now at rehearsals the play worked. Orton had rewritten it incessantly, even obsessively, throughout an interim production in Manchester directed by Braham Murray. Soon there was additional dialogue by the Lord Chamberlain.

We had a very good cast, but not very well known, Michael Bates, Simon Ward, Kenneth Cranham. Almost immediately, Marowitz insisted on replacing the young actress cast as the nurse – a key part – with Sheila Ballantine. That was fine by me. I agreed that the first girl had not been right. I did not even ring Oscar in Ireland about it.

When Oscar came back he blew his top. I don't know Sheila Ballantine, I don't want anyone strange. He wanted to withdraw. I was short of ready cash or I might have bought him out. So Oscar did not insist. Sheila stayed in too – and was tremendous.

The first night was a triumph. The audience laughed throughout, a tribute to Marowitz's decision to keep the farce in hand so far as the acting went, and leave the jokes to the writing, as it were.

We had always agreed on this. The Inspector, for instance, was certainly exaggerated but he ought to look and talk like a real copper. The house must look like a real house in Kilburn. It was a masterpiece of comedy, and the critics recognised it. Orton was compared to Oscar Wilde, Ben Jonson, Lewis Carroll, GBS. Orton fully agreed. He was acutely conscious of his success. 'I have a lot of vices,' he said in an interview with the *Evening Standard*. 'But false modesty is not one of them. The best thing about *Loot* is the quality of the writing.'

Orton was a constant caller at my office in Duke Street and a tireless critic of the shortcomings of the actors or the director or myself. He was business-like, precise, opinionated. His dislikes were almost pathological.

He had kept an unblinking eye on the Manchester repertory production prior to ours, writing me frequent letters of advice.

Fay. The way it's being played at Manchester – as a real woman, a real nurse, is right. If you can think of a starrier version of that OK. Otherwise I'd be delighted to have a Manchester girl. A name I'd be happy with is Vivien Merchant. Otherwise there hasn't been a really good suggestion on the part so far. It is the third part in the play. I don't want any of these 'monsters'. I want a real woman. Not a man in drag. And this is about the most difficult thing to achieve in the West End Theatre. So please Merchant or the girl in Manchester. Or someone who really can suggest a real nurse, a real woman. The boys in Manchester are poor. My first choice for Hal would be Derek Fowlds. John Hurt. Ian McShane. For Dennis I've only got Hywel Bennett or Barry Evans. That type anyway.

Not Bolam. He's good but oh, dear, he's as clean as a whistle sexually. This is what is wrong with the Manchester boys. One can't imagine them having each other or Fay or anyone.

Unless you or Oscar have any violent objections to the actors suggested you could go ahead (once the director problem is settled) on this list. But any other suggestions I must know.

The director. This is up to you. I'm not good on directors. Get somebody straightforward if possible. Somebody who'll know his onions. I'm dead against anyone too arty. I think it's a good 75 per cent casting anyway. Depending on what you think after you've seen Manchester I wouldn't violently object to Braham Murray. But then, on directors, I'm a blank.

The style of the set in Manchester is right. It could do with being better for London. But the tone is right.

When Joe came to see me he was only rarely accompanied by the mysterious figure of Kenneth Halliwell, the man whom he lived with and who was soon to kill them both. On these occasions Halliwell was as retiring and unobtrusive as an Indian wife. But in their hair-raising private life – both were hyperactive homosexuals – he was embittered by Orton's unashamed enjoyment of the spotlight. He considered himself equally responsible for his partner's triumph. 'A genius like us,' he once, unforgettably, described them. Well, Halliwell did think of the title for *Loot*.

Orton was desperate for the play to be a success. We transferred to the Criterion Theatre but, despite the glowing reviews, the box office was less than stunning. Halliwell by his side, he would go in person most days to check the takings. But many people – like my own mother – were put off by the uncompromising rawness of the play.

Naturally he was thrilled when the play won the *Evening Standard* Drama Award for best new play of the year, the most important award in London theatre. There were no more quarrelsome demands for recasting. True to his reputation as a gaudy dresser, he went to collect his honour wearing a tie like a neon sign. 'I look better in cheap clothes,' he had once told me. 'Because I'm from the gutter and don't anyone ever forget it. Because I won't.'

Soon Orton was masterminding the next step, Broadway and a film.

100

Arthur Lewis and Bernard Delfont bought the film rights for £100,000 – of which Oscar and I got a satisfying percentage – and in my view made it into a very bad film. Various people including David Merrick dickered with the American theatre rights. Eventually the play was bought by a lawyer, Harold Orenstein, who although very pleasant, successful and highly-thought of in the music business had never produced a play on Broadway.

New York is full of people who say: I've got the money, I like this play, I want to be a producer and become one – once. I suppose that anybody with a bit of money could set themselves up, and if they had the foresight to get hold of a good general manager you might think – why not? But it does not work that way.

I had the strongest doubts about Harold's ability to get together the kind of production *Loot* deserved in New York. But in the end it was the only firm Broadway deal we were offered. *Entertaining Mr Sloane* had, after all, only lasted one night.

Oscar had left the arrangement to me and I signed. Joe, as usual, was determined to advise. Soon he was sending me long lists of likely actors and letters detailing his views.

LOOT — America

Possibles

TRUSCOTT	McLEAVY	MAY
Alec Guinness	1. Arthur Lowe	Maggie Smith
Anthony Quayle	2. George Rose	Joan Plowright
Leo McKern	3. Liam Redmond	Julie Andrews
Peter Sellers	4. Leo McKern	Dorothy Tutin
Michael Redgrave	Ed Begley	Sarah Miles
Peter Finch	Boris Karloff	Susannah York
John Clements	(I've just realised	Geraldine McEwan
Nigel Patrick	who Ed Begley is –	Fenella Fielding
Donald Pleasance	he played the father	
Nicol Williamson	in Sweet Bird of	
Richard Attenborough	Youth. He's wrong	
James Mason	for McLeavy.)	
Christopher Plummer		
Anthony Newley		
Trevor Howard		
Jack Hawkins		

(I don't know anything
about   Christopher
Plummer

'A few words on the Broadway production,' began one of his four-page letters. 'It seems to me that the American producers, with the best intentions, have got hold of the wrong end of the stick. *Loot* is a serious play. A director who imagines that the only object is to get a laugh is not for me.'

Actors were all-important to him.

Only actors who can play the characters I've written should be in the play. Comics who see everything in terms of funny lines are out.

The boys. We should take Kenneth Cranham. And another English boy. I don't think American actors can understand the parts. And I don't want there to be anything queer or camp or odd about the relationship of Hal and Dennis. Americans see homosexuality in terms of fag and drag. This isn't my vision of the universal brotherhood. They must be perfectly ordinary boys who happen to be fucking each other. And the girl as well. Nothing could be more natural. I won't have the Great American Queen brought into it. I hope I make myself plain on that point. It is an important one.

Fay. V. difficult. She must be kept in her place (always a difficult thing for Americans to do with their women). Of course she must be more exuberant than Sheila is. And it would be nice if she had a decent pair of tits. And blonde hair. It would be much funnier. But she isn't a play about Fay. If only there were someone like Marilyn Monroe. But there I'm echoing, I'm sure, every Hollywood producer. Your idea of Rosemary Harris is v. good. She should ideally be under thirty. I want the erotic idea behind a girl in her late twenties and boys in their 'teens. She isn't a mother-substitute. None of your Tennessee Williams drag-queens. Having said all this I am probably going to undo it by saying that I wouldn't object to Fenella Fielding. I don't like her – she's a camp lady – but if she could be controlled I wouldn't say no. And I'm sure she'd be v. popular in New York (for so many reasons).

Another letter ended:

I also think that it might be wise to reconsider Marowitz as a director. God knows I'm not a fan of his. I think a lot of the direction in *Loot* is atrocious. But on the principle of Better the Devil you know than the Devil you don't, I'd think about it. With a stronger cast his direction wouldn't stick out so much. And it is a success in London!! Remember that.

Loot did go to Broadway. George Rose was excellent in it. It got atrocious reviews – like all Orton's plays there – and did not last at all. It really should have gone off-Broadway. Obviously Joe was bitter. His disappointment centred on me. In a series of letters that surfaced after his death I was blamed for *Loot*'s failure. Me alone. Oscar and Peggy Ramsay were never mentioned. Which was, at least, unrealistic because all arrangements had to be referred back to them.

Oscar and I also fell out rather badly over Orton's disenchantment. When he was about to do *What the Butler Saw*, the third major Orton play, with Ralph Richardson, at the Queen's (it failed but at the time it seemed like a red-hot play), he told me Orton had expressly said that I was not to be involved.

I never really understood why he said this. All Oscar needed to say was, It's my play, I'm Orton's manager, and I want to do it with somebody else. It would be a very ugly story if it was true, and even if true, it should not be repeated. And I found it particularly odd that Bernard Delfont came in as a partner on that as well as on the *Loot* film. Delfont was something of a prude, very nervous about doing anything anti-Establishment, and *Butler* ended with an obscene gesture, a statue of Churchill with an erection.

The night before Orton was murdered, Halliwell came to the theatre. There was an old doorkeeper there, of about eighty-five, the traditional old-time doorman. Halliwell spent a lot of time talking to him, sitting on the stage-door steps. And then, evidently demented by the idea that fame and fortune were luring his lover away from him, he went back and killed Orton and then himself.

All funerals are miserable, but Orton's was particularly depressing. He was so young and he would have written great plays. He had written so mockingly about death. It was a very weird occasion, Beatles tapes in the Golders Green crematorium, an odd mix of mourners. Predictably, Orton's murder sent the Criterion box office shooting up. But we had already been given notice to quit by Donald Albery. There were only two weeks left of the run.

Loot, nonetheless, remains among my favourite plays. And to show that wounds heal faster in the theatre than in the real world I did it again – with Oscar – at the Royal Court a dozen years later. In fact we presented all three Ortons and transferred *What the Butler Saw* and *Entertaining Mr Sloane* to the Whitehall.

But at the time I felt that I had met my match in Joe Orton. The knife-edge resuscitation of *Loot*, the endless nerve-jangling confrontation with author and agent, the sight of a fine play going to waste on a Broadway which wasn't ready for it, then the grisly climax, had cost me more energy than any one man could afford and it temporarily cost me my nerve. As Cochrane said, 'You've got to have some chips on the table, even if it is only one;' Something that anyone who fancies himself as a gambler should not need to be told. But when *Loot* closed abruptly in New York I had nothing and thus I missed a great opportunity: to become the English producer of *Hair*.

Derek Goldby, who had directed *Loot* in New York, Sarah and I fled to the Bahamas as soon as the show closed. Not only did we have a miserable week of sunstroke and nervous crisis but I missed the first night of the epic show which replaced it at the Baltimore Theatre.

Hair was directed by Tom O'Horgan. I had put on his first production *Tom Paine*, about the American revolutionary in London, which was wonderfully directed – epic avant-garde theatre. Tom and I got on very well, and he had been telephoning me to urge me to take an interest in *Hair* for London.

It had been produced by Joe Papp and Arnold Weissberger, the lawyer who represented the production and whom I already knew. They had also telephoned me several times to say they had offers, but they would really like me to have it for London. They wanted a $25,000 advance, which was a lot of money then, and I was too immersed in Orton and *Loot* to apply myself properly to raising it.

By the time I got back to New York to see the show Robert Stigwood had snapped it up for London. I did not know him then although I was soon to know him very well indeed. Stigwood did a very nervy and stylish thing. Knowing that the Lord Chamberlain was soon to go, he kept that show waiting for six weeks after it was ready and paid everyone. It was a terrific risk, because the Attorney-General could have prosecuted anyway. In fact the only thing that stopped that was the glowing reviews.

I deeply regret missing out on *Hair*. I loved it, saw it a dozen times. Every ten years or so a musical comes along which changes the face of the medium: *Oklahoma, Hair, The Rocky Horror Show, Chorus Line, Cats*. It is curious how unusual it is for a successful film version to be made of these great theatrical events. Most memorable film musicals – like *42nd Street* – were original scripts. The film of *Hair* would have been an assured success if it had followed the stage show within a reasonable time, say two years. But it came so much later that it just seemed . . . historical. Like *The Boyfriend*.

CHAPTER NINE

'Soldiers'

I was to do some important productions in partnership with Robert Stigwood once *Hair* had put him on the West End map. *Joseph and the Amazing Technicolor Dreamcoat*, for instance, and *Jeeves*, an infinitely less successful Andrew Lloyd-Webber creation. But the historic opportunity I offered him was a share in *Oh! Calcutta!* in which I was already united with a far more profound influence on my life, Kenneth Tynan.

To an astonishing degree the London theatre of the Sixties and Seventies revolved around this exceptional figure, languid and over-assertive by turn, an expert on the stage and everyone who trod it, dandy, epicure, wit, master of gamesmanship. I was already in awe of Tynan when I first encountered him as a critic; even more so later when he became Literary Manager of the National Theatre under the rule of Laurence Olivier. Scott Fitzgerald once wrote that, when he admired someone, he wished to imitate them. There was something of that in our relationship, too. Tynan also had that interesting mixture of the intellectual and the social. I remember seeing him once in a limousine, over-dressed to the nines, with Laurence Olivier and Vivien Leigh. They flashed past me as I stood outside the Park Lane Hotel. He had his showbiz side as well as a fine intelligence; and, as someone once said about him, 'wrote like an angel'. He also loved good food and wine and the ladies. He had none of the puritanism of the English intellectual, and something of the vulgarity and razzmatazz of Broadway and Vegas. It made for an extremely entertaining companion and a master of gamesmanship.

Tynan and I first became partners in the vintage political year of 1968. French students were digging up paving stones in the streets (and my 'happening' partner Jean-Jacques Lebel was encamped on the steps of the Odéon). Lyndon Johnson was deciding he would not run for President again, and the B-52s were bombing North Vietnam. The left-wing intelligentsia of London gathered at Clive Goodwin's flat in the Cromwell Road to hear 'Red Danny' Cohn-Bendit, fresh from Paris, who was smuggled on to deliver a private lecture and predict the overthrow of every government in sight.

Tynan was even more active in these circles than I was. He brought me a play that the National Board had turned down, a four-hour-long polemic by an earnest German playwright Rolf Hochhuth, called *Soldiers*, and said he had a backer. Beguiled by the friendship that developed between us as much as by the emotional commitment the times seemed to demand, I said that I would manage it with him. It is about the only thing in my entire career that I wish I had never done.

It was not an easy alliance. Tynan always interfered in every aspect of a production, no matter what task he was supposed to be engaged in. He took himself very seriously, and never doubted he was in the right – even when he was wrong. He could become completely hysterical with rage but half an hour later be laughing and joking. A great intriguer and bluffer, he really could have been in politics.

Once, much later, at an *Oh! Calcutta!* rehearsal at the Roundhouse he shouted at me in front of the entire company, 'If you do that' – whatever it was – 'I'm walking out. I'm going straight down to Fleet Street for a press conference, *and* I'm taking my name off the production.'

Fine, I said. Just fine. But if that had happened during *Soldiers*, a year earlier, I would have run after him and begged him not to go. Now I knew better. Off he went. About ten minutes later he reappeared at the top of the circle steps. 'By the way, Michael,' he said, 'there aren't any cabs around. Are you going back into town? Can you give me a lift.'

But, at the early stage of my intellectual infatuation with Ken, what he wanted, I wanted. I was quite aware that he was a spoiled darling of transatlantic liberal society, an archetypal left-wing trendy. But I believed – and still do – that he was totally sincere in his desire for a more just society even though most of our talk about revolution took place in high-priced restaurants.

This was a particular weakness we had in common. I treasure the memory of a meal with him and his wife Kathleen in Paris, which ranks as one of the great dinners of all time. Between us we tackled three bottles of serious Burgundy. It was one of those occasions where no one thought of the price or indeed of anything except having the best.

Tynan was greatly adept at friendship; he had a positively creative talent for sharing his experiences. Long after we had survived our

107

vicissitudes, whenever he and his wife Kathleen struck out on one of their frequent gastronomic expeditions he made sure that I was made to feel as though I had been there too, via the punctilious, mouth-watering reports he sent back.

I had already heard of the discussion about *Soldiers* that had gone on at the National, and I had seen Hochhuth's other play *The Deputy*, which I thought very moving and truthful. *Soldiers* seemed to me to pose a searching question. Even if the enemy had abandoned all moral considerations, was the bombing of civilians justified? (Apart from any morality, Albert Speer wrote in his memoirs, the allied bombing of Germany achieved the reverse of what was hoped. No Germans rose up and tried to get rid of the Nazis. Nobody did anything except work even harder in defiance. German production was 40 per cent higher at the end of the war in 1944 than in 1939.)

Just before the Lord Chamberlain's rule was abolished I told an interviewer, 'I don't think that the main difficulties in the future will be over sex. They will still be over politics.' I was right. *Soldiers* caused a national outcry even before it reached London. The main reason was the emphasis given to an episode which implied that, in order to placate Britain's Soviet allies, Churchill may have been aware that an air crash had been arranged to 'eliminate' the Free Polish leader Sikorsky.

In fact the real message of the play was contained in a stage argument between Bishop Bell of Chichester and Churchill. The Bishop goes to Downing Street to make a personal protest over the bombing of German cities and civilians – all of which, had strong overtones regarding the current bombing of Cambodia.

Both propositions were interpreted – usually by people who had not seen or read the play – as an attack on the reputation of the recently deceased great man. Hochhuth was, in fact, a great admirer of Churchill, indeed revered him. He wanted to illustrate how war can make even a great and good man into something different – the destroyer of Dresden, in this case, or the proxy executioner of another good man in the interests of a strategically vital alliance.

The play had been performed in Canada without any difficulties. Now Norman Granz, the American jazz promoter, was prepared to put up the money for London. I never did know why he was willing to do this except that he was fairly liberal politically. He was a great supporter of jazz and black musicians, and presented Ella Fitzgerald.

Theoretically, *Soldiers* should have been an inexpensive production but things went wrong from the start. The Canadian actor George

Colicos had been a great success as Churchill in Canada. We decided we had to have him, at £400 a week against 7½ per cent of the take. This was expensive for someone unknown in Britain. The best stalls in 1968 were £1.30.

We decided to open in Dublin. We needed to run the play in for two weeks – it had been cut from four hours to two and we wanted to be some distance from London. The start of production unleashed feverish press coverage, most of it hostile and sensational. London theatre-owners rushed to declare that they would not have it in their house even before they had been asked. Bernard Delfont, the brothers Littler and Lew Grade all said it again when they were actually asked, thus taking the role of censor unto themselves.

It was interesting to see which side was taken by whom. Victor Lownes, whom I did not even know at the time, telephoned and said, I don't know whether this play is right or wrong, but I'm against censorship. He offered us £1,000. Sidney Bernstein did the same. So did Peter O'Toole.

Finally, Donald Albery agreed to take it in. But, instead of the normal two weeks' deposit, he required £5,000, which added to our financial problems. You could almost have done a complete play for that in those days. We were in no position to argue. But, in a way, it would have been far better if we had not got the theatre at all. It meant that we had to find a lot more money. Soon there was a rift between Granz and Tynan. Granz, I had realised by then, had some kind of intellectual crush on Ken. He wanted recognition. Ken thought he was making some kind of benevolent gesture in allowing Norman to participate in such a great event.

The production costs had already risen well above that and the burden of meeting them fell on my shoulders. I had been told I was just the manager – no question of fund-raising. But the contracts were in my name and, when we had to get more money, I was the one sent out to bat.

It was hard going. Even my family disapproved of this play – the only time they have ever criticised my activities. I was disturbed enough myself by then. I was beginning to get serious hate mail, postcards of Coventry after the Blitz, scrawls calling me a Nazi sympathiser. And yet many of the backers I eventually found were Jewish liberals; they saw that it was ridiculous to label the play as pro-Nazi.

Feeling the need of moral support, Ken and I went to see Laurence Olivier at the National. We did not get much. We knew that *Soldiers* had been rejected there in deference to Oliver Lyttelton, later Lord Chandos, who was chairman of the National and after whom the Lyttelton Theatre is named. He had been a member of Churchill's War Cabinet.

One of our less welcome allies was also an investor, David Irving, the right-wing historian, who seems unable to stay out of any debate about the Nazis. He more or less adopted the play's more dubious contentions and kept appearing on television to argue his views, which was distinctly unhelpful.

Not unnaturally, I suppose, Winston Churchill Jnr took strongly against the play and set out to do whatever he could to hinder it.

In this contentious atmosphere, off we went to Dublin where there was a key meeting which I, unfortunately, missed. It was unfortunate, since that was the only time before the play opened that the question arose whether the name of Edward Prchal should be removed from the script.

Prchal, a Czech, had been the pilot of the RAF plane which, the play postulated, had been deliberately crashed off Gibraltar in order to kill its principal passenger, General Sikorsky. Only Prchal, of the dozen or so on board, had survived.

Clifford Williams, the director, and Ken decided in their consultation that, since the play had already been done in Germany, Canada and America, they need not worry about any slight to the pilot's reputation. But the Theatres Act of 1968, which displaced the Lord Chamberlain, had specifically made the publication of defamatory words in the theatre actionable as libel. And, although Ken was an experienced journalist, he did not take into consideration how much sterner the libel law is in Britain than in most other countries. Prchal, reference to whom could easily have been excised, was alive in California. He was soon to appear in London to assert his innocence and make our lives a misery – the Lord Chamberlain's revenge, in a way.

But there were still endless difficulties to be confronted before the play even went on in London. My distaste for billing wrangles may be better understood if this letter from my old friend and benefactor Aubrey Blackburn illustrates the trivial wrangles that can materialise.

You asked me yesterday what I understood had been meant by the reference to 'unspecified feature billing' during the Basil Langton negotiations. My reply was that whereas Langton had requested that his name should come in second place in the list of artistes supporting the star JOHN COLICOS, he later agreed to leave it to you to decide the actual position. This was after I informed him that I understood that the cast would probably include ROLAND CULVER and ALEC

CLUNES and that you did not know at that time what other artistes would be included in the list. It was always clear to me, and to Basil Langton, that in any event his name would appear in the same group as the others and that none, other than JOHN COLICOS, would be in a larger size. Since you are honest, you will agree that this is what we both meant and understood and that this formed an important condition of the verbal contract.

Consequently, I have to say that your present proposal, that a group of Artistes including ALEC CLUNES, GEORGE COULOURIS, JOANNA DUNHAM and RAYMOND HUNTLEY should appear with JOHN COLICOS above the title and that Basil Langton's name should be relegated to a position under the title (with 'and' preceding his name) underneath the names of two minor artistes, is quite unacceptable. You have said that Mr Colicos objects to Mr Langton being above the title but I imagine that you will confirm that he has no contractual right to dictate to you in this way, and I ask for your assurance that you will see to it that Mr Langton receives billing in the form agreed between the three of us.

If I am right in thinking that this would mean that the names of five artistes would appear under the name of JOHN COLICOS all above the title and that you have already promised ALEC CLUNES billing on the first line by himself, and RAYMOND HUNTLEY (with the word 'and' preceding his name) on the last line by himself, you would seemingly fulfil your obligations to all concerned if the five names are billed together in the same size as follows:-

ALEC CLUNES
BASIL LANGTON
or
JOANNA DUNHAM
or
GEORGE COULOURIS

BASIL LANGTON	BASIL LANGTON
or	or
JOANNA DUNHAM	JOANNA DUNHAM
or	
GEORGE COULOURIS	

Clifford Williams had already directed the play in Toronto and the amazing sets and staging by Ralph Koltai were to have been kept. But in Dublin the actors had mutinied over the harsh revisions caused by cutting the play from four hours to two and the addition of a prologue.

They sent me a telegram:

UNSHAKEABLY CONVINCED PROLOGUE MUST GO STOP ACT ONE PROVING DANGEROUSLY INEFFECTIVE AND WILL REMAIN SO EVEN WITHOUT PROLOGUE STOP REPORTED TUESDAY PREVIEW ALARMS US PROFITABLE USE OF REMAINING REHEARSAL TIME VITAL TO SUCCESS = COLICOS HUNTLEY CLUNES.

They were right. We cut the prologue. The play got good reviews in Dublin and on the opening night eight curtain calls. The Irish audiences had been spared the farrago of prejudicial publicity we had suffered in England and were able to judge it on its merits.

When we did open in London on 12 December 1968 it was in a virtual state of siege. Threats had flooded in by mail and telephone. The security arrangements drawn up for the New Theatre included:

Before house opens attendants to search all lavatories, bars, etc., and under every seat. Also all exit corridors should be inspected.

A list of Michael White representatives who are permitted to circulate during the performance to be given to Mr Hunter, who will issue them with special passes.

All electrical switchrooms, dimmer banks and switchboard to be kept locked during the performance.

Cloakrooms to inspect any parcels, suitcases, briefcases, etc., left by patrons, and draw attention of a manager to them at earliest possible moment.

If objects taken into auditorium, attendants to make a note of where patron is sitting, and draw attention of a manager.

The controversy at least guaranteed us a top-drawer audience for the first night. Lord Harewood, Lord Harlech and Hugh Carlton Greene, Director General of the BBC, represented the Establishment. But many people were there simply in the interests of free speech.

After the shouts of 'Bravo' from the packed theatre, Ken, weeping with joy, told a reporter, 'This proves the essential sanity of audiences in England.' Winston junior was still telling the press, 'This is an infamous libel,' while John Colicos observed that the play's reception answered those who said it attacked the old man's memory. 'On the other hand,' he said, astutely. 'I feel that it increases his stature as a tragic hero.'

There was some well-justified criticism of the play, artistically. So much had been taken out of it. Some of the critics thought Churchill was played in a hollow and lightweight manner. Not that there was anything lightweight about Colicos's preparations. It took him an hour to convert himself into a facsimile of Churchill, filling out his cheeks with wax. I disagreed myself with the idea of an *impersonation*. I do not think real people should ever be played like Madame Tussaud figures.

Largely because the first-nighters decided that the play was less a scandal than a slightly turgid historical drama, we did not do well at the box office after the first week. Then, a month after we opened, Prchal unleashed his lawsuits.

He took out one writ against Hochhuth and the translator, David McDonald; another against myself, Granz and Tynan, Donald Albery and Ian Albery, Wyndham's Theatre and Clifford Williams. A third went to André Deutsch who had published the play.

We excised the relevant lines immediately. But the hostile controversy came to the boil again. Tynan was bitter. 'Such a weight of editorial disapproval and Establishment frowning has built up,' he told the papers, 'that I think a lot of people who would enjoy it feel that there is something shameful about going to see it.'

The Prime Minister of the day, Harold Wilson, took it upon himself to announce that *Soldiers* was 'scurrilous'. When I invited him to come and judge for himself he had me sent a marvellously condescending letter.

I am writing on the Prime Minister's behalf to thank you for your letter of 17. The Prime Minister manages only infrequent visits to the theatre and in the event of his being able to increase the number of visits would have on his list a considerable number of other plays to which he would wish to give priority.

The damage was fatal. *Soldiers* closed at the end of March. But the battle with Prchal was only beginning. In those days there were six QCs in England who specialised in libel. At one meeting I attended there were five of them in the room. I was mightily impressed, particularly since we did not have a leg to stand on. An English jury was bound to find against us.

I could see we were going to lose. The only question was how much we were going to have to pay. The Tynans – Kathleen had identified herself with the cause as firmly as Ken – thought that an out-of-court settlement would be a tremendous loss of face. Ken found it difficult to admit being at fault, even though it had been he who slipped up in the first place by not deleting the references to Prchal. He also made a considerable fool of himself by claiming in public that he had consulted eminent military authorities who believed that in the matter of Sikorsky there was 'an open case' against Churchill. Challenged, he could not say who the authorities were.

Rolf Hochhuth was no more help. He had always insisted that he had evidence of the conspiracy to do in Sikorsky locked in a bank vault in Zurich, but that to produce it would be a betrayal of his source. My view was wholly pragmatic. We were in the wrong. The case was certainly going to cost us £50,000. Why risk having to pay perhaps £150,000?

We spent weeks with lawyers. There was a preliminary hearing, and after a lot of huffing and puffing between the Tynans and me in the corridors I insisted that we capitulate. Ken agreed with very bad grace but it was certainly the most mature decision I had made in the theatre up until then. Prchal went on with his case against Hochhuth and three years later was awarded £50,000 damages.

Sharing this ordeal brought Ken and me on to a much more even footing; closer in a way, since I no longer felt that I must idolise him. As someone I once met who had known Scott Fitzgerald said to me, 'Sure he was a hero. But like everyone he was less of a hero when you actually met him.'

CHAPTER TEN

'Oh! Calcutta!'

By the time Prchal settled with Hochhuth *Oh! Calcutta!* had been on in London for nearly two years. It was to run there for ten and in a score of other places for financially very satisfying periods.

Ken's job as Literary Manager of the National Theatre was a strange springboard from which to plunge into the scandalous venture of *Oh! Calcutta!* But his prestige was an important factor in getting the concept of the show accepted. Subtitled 'An Evening of Elegant Erotica' it was, as anyone old enough will recall, an episodic, largely naked romp in which a wide array of behaviour hitherto thought of as strictly private was lampooned publicly. As I described it at the time, 'A nice healthy dirty show.' Nothing in the theatre the world over was the same after *Oh! Calcutta!*

It was generally thought that Ken created *Oh! Calcutta!* out of his own fantasies and his not inconsiderable daring. It was billed as 'devised by Ken Tynan'. Now, long after his death from emphysema aggravated by his refusal to stop smoking, it has to be admitted that a number of other people had been thinking along similar lines.

I believe the inspiration came originally from the New York producer David Merrick, to whom I now belatedly offer acknowledgement. Sometime before 1969, Merrick remarked to me that the people who went to see musicals were actually going to look at pretty bodies as much as anything. There was a terrific amount of sex in the theatre, he said, even when it was disguised – as in ballet.

I mentioned this to Willy Donaldson while we were sharing an office. It was becoming clear then that censorship would soon go. I got the idea that I might try to do a show about sex and nothing else, and not hide behind any artifice of Art. When Willy and I fell out he went behind my

115

back and wrote to Ken suggesting the idea. He was so entranced by the possibilities that – even while the writ of the Lord Chamberlain still ran – he wrote in detail to Willy about how such a show might be done and, incidentally, what it might be called.

120 Mount Street
W.1.
June 28

Dear W.D.

Just returned from Paris and Sweden, where I thought a lot about our talk. Here are some tentative conclusions:

1. The idea is to use artistic means to achieve erotic stimulation. Nothing that is *merely* funny or *merely* beautiful should be admitted, it must also be sexy. A certain intimacy is therefore necessary – i.e. a theatre seating not more than about 900, such as the St. Martin's or the Criterion. It should preferably have (or obtain) a variety licence, so that wordless items would not have to be submitted to the Lord Chamberlain. The show would be devised (or produced) by me, directed by some like-minded person (Jonathan Miller?), and choreographed by a non-queer.

2. Title. I made a long list of possibilities, including such outside chances as THE CONSENTING ADULTS SHOW, LET ME COUNT THE WAYS, HOW COME, etc, etc; but I've since found a beauty. I showed you a painting by the ancient French surrealist Clovis Trouille of a reclining girl displaying her bottom, with the caption: 'Oh Calcutta!' While in Paris I discovered that this is a pun – 'Quel cul t'as!', meaning 'What an arse you have!' I therefore suggest calling the show 'Oh Calcutta!', subtitled 'An Erotic Revue' and using the Trouille painting as a poster. Those who get the joke will get it, and those who don't will be intrigued. Anyway it's unforgettable.

3. Component parts. The cast should consist of 8-10 girls, all vivacious dancers and about half of them reasonable singers; plus around 4 men, all expert comics. None of the company need be English: foreigners speaking broken English, whether male or female, can get away with far more outrageous things than home-bred performers (*vide* 'La Plume de Ma Tante'). Also English comics tend to be coy and domesticated in matters of sex, unlike their French and American-burlesque equivalents.

4. Possible items—

   (a) As an opener, I would suggest a pseudo-drag stripper – i.e. a male-looking girl singer dressed up to look like a female impersonator. She would need a baritone voice. At the climax of her strip, she would

116

reveal her breasts – thereby baffling the smart-alecs in the audience who had decided that she was a man. To drive the point home, one might make this a double act, of which the other member was a *real* female impersonator – who would disclose his masculinity at the same moment that his partner disclosed her femininity.

(b) Later, there should be a pseudo-lesbian singer in a dark serge suit, wearing no make-up and singing (in a Dietrich-like voice) a ballad about love betrayed. As the song ends, the singer should strip to the waist and reveal that, despite what we guessed, he is male.

(c) A serial film. This should be specially commissioned and used to cover scene-changes – a sort of sexy *Batman*, preferably in colour. About six episodes should be used in the course of the show, each of which leaves the audience cliff-hanging. The film should be silent, with a dubbed commentary: I can't think offhand of a British director who could make it, but there are many continentals who would be interested, from Jean-Luc Godard to Roger Vadim and the sensational Swede, Vigo Sjoman (director of 'My Sister, My Love.)'

(d) Vaudeville routines. These, at their best, are always very sexy – I'm speaking, of course, of American burlesque and Parisian music-hall. One could, if money allowed, import a trio of American burlesque comics – the kind of people who work in the Ann Corio show, 'This Was Burlesque.' Alternatively, Robert Dhery could be engaged to devise three or four routines for French comics such as Jacques Legras and Christian Duvallix.

(e) Dance numbers. These might include:

(1) A ballet based on the paintings (and the world) of Clovis Trouille. He is the Douanier Rousseau of surrealism - in fact, a French poet once described him as Rousseau with balls. His fantastic visions of begartered nuns, girls with bats on their cunts and *fleur-de-lys* on their behinds, novices doing the splits, circus performers who are half-girl and half-horse, would make the ideal erotic ballet. We'd have to get his permission, because he hates being exploited by people who aren't seriously erotic.

(2) A Beardsley ballet, based on Aubrey's erotic drawings.

(3) A French 18th-century ballet, based on the erotic paintings of Boucher and Fragonard.

(4) A Homage to the Crazy Horse Saloon. Alain Bernardin, who runs this Paris strip-club, is without doubt the greatest and most imaginative innovator in the history of striptease. With his permission, I would borrow several of his best numbers –

e.g. 'Hurray for Mr. Touchdown', in which the girls are dressed as American football players; 'Tracy Tiffany', the life-story of a stripper, in which op-art slides are projected on to the dancer's nearly-nude body while she recounts her history in recorded broken English ('My name is Tracy Tiffany. I'm an Aries.'); the classic bath number in which a stripper is first seen in silhouette, projected on a downstage screen, and later perched on a black marble bath, meditatively soaping herself; and of course Bernardin's famous 'La Veuve', in which a widow, sitting in a pew at her husband's funeral, devoutly strips as the organ plays. For all of these numbers we would have to get Bernardin's OK, and although it would be hard for him to prove violation of copyright, I think it would be wise to offer him some kind of payment. Also he might be useful in recruiting girls – the Crazy Horse employs the glowingest, prettiest, most animated strippers on earth.

(f) Semi-documentary items. These might include:
  (1) Tableaux representing national erotic obsessions – such as a nun being raped by her confessor (Italy), a middle-aged bank manager bound hand and foot by a Superwoman (USA), and a St. Trinian's sixth-former being birched by John Gordon (Great Britain).
  (2) The history of knickers. Unknown until the late 19th century, knickers began to be manufactured by crafty textile tycoons. When they first appeared, the church reviled them, since they were constructed like trousers and the Bible forbade women to wear men's attire. Knickers were condemned in every pulpit, and girls who wore them were considered dangerously fast. Later, sensualists like Frank Harris led a crusade for open as opposed to closed knickers – for Free Trade (as he put it) as opposed to Protective Tariffs.

(g) Straightforward solo strip numbers. Such as:
  (1) Gypsy del Rio, the uninhibited acrobat now appearing at the Sunset Strip in Soho.
  (2) Dailly Holliday, a fantastic stripper from Guadalupe whom I saw last week in Paris. She is a buxom Negress, built for wrestling, who performs the first and only Black Muslim strip I have ever seen. Instead of attempting (like most coloured strippers) to be more sophisticated and elegant than the whites, she doesn't even try to be charming. She comes on pure black and brutally militant, snarling at the audience and shoving her

118

arse and tits straight into the onlookers' faces. She is Black Supremacy incarnate, and we might have to built a shallow runway down the centre aisle in order for her to operate.

(h) Erotic sketches by well known writers. The authors' names would be announced, but not attached to the sketches they had written – which would allow the critics to indulge in a fascinating guessing-game. I would approach people like Harold Pinter, Terry Southern, J.P. Donleavy, Henry Livings, Jean Genet, James Jones, John Mortimer, and of course John Osborne. (In fact, I would even use an excerpt from Osborne's 'Under Plain Cover' if he didn't feel like writing something new.) And there should also be an extract from de Sade's 'Philosophy in the Boudoir.' The writers should be told that if they wished to remain anonymous, their names would not even be mentioned.

All these items would be shuffled and interspersed, so that a strip would be followed by a sketch, a sketch by a ballet, a ballet by a film excerpt, etc, etc.

Re-reading what I've written. I see that I've omitted – under section (e), dance numbers – a pop art ballet designed by Pauline Boty, based on paintings that focus on the principal erogenous zones.

When you've pondered the foregoing, let's meet again and make plans.

Willy dropped out of theatrical production, but the notion stayed afloat.

After long discussions with Ken I decided to produce *Calcutta* – even though the name was then as uncertain as most things about it. In great secrecy – astoundingly successful secrecy in retrospect – Ken began generating the material and I began putting together all the other elements. We were not sure where or when it would all end but we were determined to give the world a thrill it hadn't seen before.

Ken wrote to every major writer he knew and many whom he hoped knew of him. No one was spared in the unrelenting search. He was convinced, correctly, that every one of them must have at least one erotic idea. The question was – would they share it with us?

Our first choice of director was Harold Pinter, who surprisingly agreed to direct. But, when the publicity machine began to warm up and his name was mentioned, he changed his mind. It is interesting to speculate on what kind of a show he would have created.

This letter to Gore Vidal is an example of Ken's approach:

Harold and I are co-devising and directing (under Michael White's management) an erotic evening for presentation next October. Tentative title: 'Oh Calcutta'. Small cast (8–9 girls, 2–3–4 men), small chamber orchestra, using mime, sketches, dance, film, songs. The aim of the show: to be elegantly but intensely sexy. No crap about art. We are approaching about a dozen writers for sketches. The details go like this:

(a) Sketches can be any length from a few seconds up to as much as 10–12 minutes. Preferably with not more than four–five speaking parts (plus non-speaking girl extras)

(b) Sketches can be of two kinds – (1) you can create a situation that you would find highly erotic: i.e. stage your own ideal erotic fantasy; or (2) you can make an ironic or satirical comment on eroticism. In other words, you can be either subjective or objective. And you don't have to be funny: the sexual fantasy could be slow, ritualistic, serious if you wish.

(c) We're excluding straight homosexuality – but all heterosexual fetishes and obsessions are OK, and so are sexual ambiguities.

(d) In order to let your imagination run freely riot, we're proposing to list all the contributors in alphabetical order at the top of the programme, leaving it to the audience and critics to decide who wrote what. (Though this isn't obligatory.)

(e) For Lord Chamberlain reasons, moving nudes are out.

(f) Deadline in March. Casting won't be completed until we have the bulk of the material, but Eleanor Bron is hoped for.

(g) Dead secrecy, please.

Well before the March deadline the Lord Chamberlain had become one of our lesser worries. We had at first weighed the idea of a London club production. But the essence of the whole concept was that it be *public* entertainment. New York with its more liberal climate struck us as the only possible launching pad – and even there trouble could not unnaturally be anticipated.

The responses quickly came from the writers. Roman Polanski said he would create three short films on voyeurism. Samuel Beckett offered an unperformed piece of mime. Edna O'Brien would be delighted to write an erotic sketch. Norman Mailer would not be. Penelope Mortimer tried to write one but gave up. As did John Mortimer to whom she was then married. Joe Orton insisted on being included and wrote a brilliant send-up of a drawing-room comedy.

The net was cast ever wider on both sides of the Atlantic – John Arden, Willis Hall and Keith Waterhouse, Bernard Kops, Henry Livings, Charles Wood, Robin Chapman, Roy Boulting, John

120

Osborne, Peter Cook, Terry Southern, Elaine May. Some would be happy to provide. Some could not. Some would not.

But one thing there was no doubt about. *Oh! Calcutta!* was an idea whose time had come.

Jacques Levy, the off-Broadway director we finally chose (he had done one of the *America Hurrah* pieces), understood this completely. Soon after we approached him he wrote:

The climate for a piece like Calcutta is perfect now – *on* Broadway at that! I am almost certain that, if we don't open here in the Fall, someone else will do an 'out-rageous' piece on Broadway and steal our thunder. With regard to both the content (eroticism) and the form (an omnibus of writers) there have been a couple of productions that have just begun to catch on and I'm sure that there are more planned – I know that there are such plans for at least three films. Many minds are moving in the same direction.

Jacques also understood exactly what we were trying to do. It is interesting to look back on what we discarded from the writers we approached. Of some fifty to sixty items the majority were impossible to stage, could have been done only on film, or were hopelessly uneconomical. We soon found that what was fine between consenting adults in private was not necessarily appealing performed in public. There was a fascinating distinction between sexy in theory and sexy in practice.

Through thinking about sex almost incessantly, Ken became extremely dogmatic about what was or was not erotic. This led to some very funny debates. Naturally, he always had very strong convictions about the value of his own work, some of which touched the borders of the extreme. (Three of the many pieces he wrote for *Calcutta* were in the staged version.)

Ken loved lists. Here is an example which might surprise some of the people on it.

Possible men:

Ed Bishop
John Bird

Possible girls:

Joanna Dunham
Charlotte Rampling
Susan Hampshire
Nyree Dawn Porter
Yvonne Antrobus
Eileen Atkins

	Elaine Taylor
	Wendy Craig
	Eleanor Bron
Possible composers:	Paul McCartney
	Marc Wilkinson
	John Dankworth
	Rolling Stones
Possible designers:	Carl Toms
	Sally Jacobs
	David Hockney
	Michael Annals
	Julia Oman
Possible choreographers:	Claude Chagrin
	Norman Mayne
	Geoffrey Moore

We chose Margot Sappington, a former dancer, as choreographer, a fortunate decision as her contributions were always singled out for critical praise. The Pas de Deux which opened Act Two was beautiful – strongly erotic yet not overtly lascivious.

All this organisation was using up a great deal of money, although we were not paying the writers a fortune – £20 against a proportionate share in a royalty 'pool' of 6 per cent of the gross receipts. I got Michael Medwin and Albert Finney involved for a while but it all took so long, over a year, and the publicity gradually became so unnerving that they decided against being co-presenters. Eventually they were to be repaid and they withdrew. But, without their good-natured support, it all might have come to nothing. They provided much of the £10,000 of pre-production expenses, at that time a considerable amount of money.

Having made the decision to start the show in New York the question arose of which Broadway producer we would link up with. We talked to several including Merrick, who was my candidate. But he alarmed Ken who feared that, once involved, Merrick would take fright and try to censor the show– which indeed any Broadway partner we acquired would have the power to do.

In the end we took the plunge. I made a deal with Hillard Elkins, a boy from Brooklyn who had made the traditional leap from agent to hit producer with Sammy Davis Jnr in *Golden Boy*. As deals go it was sweet-and-sour, it had its good moments and its bad. I went into it far too casually.

Unless everything concerned in such an agreement is specified and agreed before the start there will inevitably be many problems later on. Even in the four-page agreement that linked Hilly and me there were plenty of grey areas. In short it was a real mess.

Hilly was married to Claire Bloom at this time. He was a man of great charm and energy, with a telling weakness for personal publicity. But he was also an accomplished negotiator. There is no doubt that in the early stages anyone else might have been frightened off by the obstacles confronting such a show. But Hilly reacted to challenge as though he had been given a vitamin injection. His talents stood us in good stead not only with the City of New York and the various theatrical unions which had to be faced but also with the writers. And, above all, with the actors.

The auditions were a positive minefield of sensitivities and principles, often hilarious, sometimes unnerving. Would these respectable and ambitious actors take all their clothes off on stage? Some would without a qualm. Some would do anything but. Some, particularly women, would agree. Then after a chat with their mothers – or lovers – change their minds.

I was not involved in the early New York confrontations but later in London we got into some hysterical problems over whether somebody's private parts looked offensive or not. Men were the lesser difficulty, strangely. It was much harder to find girls who could do the quite tricky moves required and also look great.

Hilly had obtained the Eden Theater, a hippy stronghold down on the Lower East Side of Manhattan, renovated it, and surrounded himself with extremely proficient people, including Emmanuel Azenberg who was later to become a most distinguished producer in his own right, and Norman Kean, his general manager. Previews began in the summer of 1969. It was very hot in every sense when I arrived. The whole town was buzzing about *Oh! Calcutta!* Would it be stopped by the police? Would it even open? It was – with the help of Hilly's publicity drive – the show everyone from the taxi-driver to the doorman was talking about. One thing seemed certain: if it did open, it would be a smash hit.

I had a quick shower and headed down to the theatre. The Clovis Trouille picture which had become the show's logo was plastered all over Manhattan but I was surprised to see that Hilly's name on the posters was three times the size of mine. My resentment was not a question of ego. To those in the theatre world it made it look as if I had just come in with some money, instead of having initiated the project. It was the first sign of the spirit in which Hilly regarded contractual obligations.

At last, though, I was seeing *Calcutta* on stage, nearly three years after the idea had first germinated. I came away in a confusion of delight and depression. Both Ken and I had seen many things we did not care for.

Hilly, Ken, Jacques Levy and I had to go on the Barry Gray show immediately afterwards. Hilly had forgotten to warn us that, unlike any British radio show, this one lasted most of the night. Both Hilly and Ken, born debaters, were in their element. Ken, argumentative by nature, could play verbal games and use the English language better than most. By the time we got to the Brasserie, an all-night restaurant, for supper it was 4 a.m. I was too exhausted to offer any coherent suggestions. I could not have been in much better shape a couple of days later when I met Hilly and his lawyer in Sardi's to be told that not enough money had yet been raised to ensure that the show would actually open.

We had already signed our deal so far as I was concerned and I had handed him all the ingredients for the show. With regard to the film rights, we had made the 20/20 split that is normal in the case of a British show. On a film sale the producer receives 40 per cent of the price and this is divided between the Broadway production and the British production. In the case of a completely original American work the whole 40 per cent would belong to the Broadway producer and his backers.

Hilly explained that his backers indeed wanted the whole 40 per cent. If the show were to go on I would have to give up my share of the film rights. I agreed, but on certain conditions. The conditions were forgotten and it ended with my giving away what turned out to be a valuable percentage. On the other hand, if I had not done so and Hilly had not raised all the money needed, the show might never have opened.

So, despite the healthy glow of publicity Hilly generated, Ken and I were fairly unhappy over the way things were going. But Hilly was fascinating. On the day of the opening he said to me, 'Let's do some shopping!' He tore through the Fifth Avenue stores, spending thousands of dollars on his American Express card. Suddenly, one shop queried whether he had reached his limit on the card. They could not have known what a master of the telephone they were dealing with. Hilly got very excited with American Express at the other end of the line, and then it was on with the spree.

He was a total telephone freak, never happy without one in his hand. There is a story that one day he was going to New Haven to see a new

124

show. The limousine broke down and he and the driver called for help on an emergency phone and started to walk. As they passed the next emergency phone along the freeway it was ringing. The chauffeur, aware of his weakness, said, 'It'll probably be for you, Mr Elkins.' Hilly picked up the phone and, sure enough, it was his secretary in New York. She had talked the highway patrol into putting her through to where she guessed he would be.

Headquarters for Hilly was a wonderful house-cum-office on East 62nd Street. There were always limousines outside, mountains of food being sent in, and, of course, telephones buzzing. One buzzed while we were having supper there one night. Hilly pushed a button and a sort of wobbly mechanical arm with a phone on it extended towards him. He then proceeded to speak for thirty minutes, while everyone sat around pretending nothing was happening.

The opening night of *Oh! Calcutta!* was an extraordinary event. Everyone who thought they were anyone in New York wanted to be there, because there was a strong feeling the show might run one night. I cannot think of any other show which attracted so much electricity and anticipation.

Many people struck an attitude of, Well, we haven't really come to see the sex, we're here because we have a duty to see it. The theatre was full of media as opposed to merely show business stars, network TV heads, magazine editors and other opinion-makers. I was standing at the back of the stalls, just before curtain up, and Hilly whispered the bad news in my ear. He had just heard that Clive Barnes of the *New York Times*, who had seen the show the previous night, had given us something like the worst review ever written; *Oh! Calcutta!* gave pornography a bad name, he was saying.

I had known Clive Barnes in Britain when he was the dance critic of the *Spectator* and the *Daily Express*. In the world of ballet a critic can say what he likes, but rarely affects the box office. However, Barnes was now by virtue of being the critic for the most important paper in the country also the most powerful man in the American theatre. It was said that a bad review in the *New York Times* closed you by Saturday. But, convinced by Hilly whose mighty promotional efforts had got us sold out for two weeks, we knew we were not a goner. Yet.

The show went much better than any of us could have anticipated; although the audience were not warm in their response they were obviously impressed. We trooped uptown for the traditional first night party at Sardi's. At 11 pm the first TV reviews came up on two big screens placed on either side of the first-floor restaurant. By this time

125

one knew they would be bad, and indeed they were. Then at midnight the head waiter walked in with the *Times* under his arm, and the cast fell on him. I had been at enough New York first nights to know that when a bad review in the *Times* appears within ten to fifteen minutes the room empties. But such was everyone's confidence – probably for the first time ever – the party went on until dawn.

When I met Ken in the Plaza Hotel the next morning for an early cocktail he had convinced himself differently. Barnes has never written such a bad review, he said. Our reputation was in shreds. The other critics had done hatchet jobs, too. Kathleen was always tremendously supportive, and she and I tried to cheer him up; after all, there was a queue around the Eden Theater.

Quickly it became evident that we did indeed have an enormous hit. Not just in New York but all over the USA, as the shocked but enticing word spread. Unfortunately a lot of people were making much more money out of the show than either Ken or I. Icing. The tickets were $25 at face value, already by far the highest ever charged for a theatre seat in New York. But they were going to out-of-towners for $100. A number of people became millionaires.

I was also irritated that, although Hilly was wonderful at promotion, he was a trifle slow in dealing with the accounts, a side of the business which is less fun but no less interesting if you are waiting for a cheque. When you have a money-making proposition as good as this, I would often say to him, you must protect it. What I meant was, protect Ken and me.

Not all the complaints were about money. One of Ken's sketches was titled 'Who? Whom?' In it a girl playing a nun kept her bare bottom pointed at the audience throughout. Ken went to Italy to recover from the strain of the opening and I went back to London. Soon he was writing to me.

I'm embroiled in a great row with Hilly, who has cut 'Who: Whom' out of the show because it turns off some members of the audience. This after our agreement the night before Barnes saw the show that the sketch should stay in. I'm objecting strenuously to this absurd censorship (in a show like ours, of all things) and to the breach of agreement. I've suggested that he should merely tell Nancy T. to expose herself less – this, and not the content, is what some people object to. At a party here in Rome the other day, 'Who: Whom' was the only thing people wanted to discuss.

One or two other things:

(1) Is Hilly paying your percentage promptly? He isn't paying mine *at all* – at least, not since the week after opening.

(2) He is talking blithely about European productions. I've looked at my author's contract and he doesn't own any non-English-speaking rights. Shouldn't we be doing something about this – getting the rights so that we can think about a Swedish or French or German production?'

(3) Reports reach me about the new Arts Council recommendations on obscenity. Could you find out anything concrete on this from someone like Michael Foot? If there's any chance of their becoming law, we are in business.

Hilly in fact did not own the rights to Ken's sketches. But he did have the rights to the show as a whole; as well as conceding all the film rights, I had committed one of the stupidest commercial errors I have ever been responsible for – handed over all the foreign rights to Hilly, who then proceeded to do deals, in other countries. *Calcutta* was a huge hit in all of them but very little if any income ever came back to London. In France he had licensed it to Roger Vadim. While I was busily preparing the London version of *Calcutta*, Ken wrote to me to put his case in the financial wrangles which were developing:

This show is the one chance I have of making a little capital, whereas you are always putting on productions any of which might be a hit. I earn a decent living in journalism and public-service work at the National, but 'Calcutta!' offers a slim possibility of safeguarding a few years of the family's future - hence what may have seemed to you like my greediness over the British production. Hilly is not (to my amazement) paying my full percentage on U.S. productions outside New York, and by becoming authors' agent on foreign deals he is able to screw me down to an even smaller amount on European productions. In June we agreed that I would get 4% of gross plus 5% of profits. I'm prepared to come down to 4% of gross plus 4% of profits. Is this OK with you – and if so, could you drop me a line confirming it.

This I did of course.

I still think Hilly was very brave to put *Oh! Calcutta!* on – as were we in London the following year. Trouble threatened in New York, but never actually came. Hilly had accurately gauged the mood of the city authorities, indeed of the nation. The show made the cover of *Time* magazine.

The secret in all successful events lies in their timing. Five years earlier or later, the whole venture might not have come together, but this was the perfect psychological moment. Now it can be seen as a healthy landmark, and an honest attempt to come out into the open about sex – nearly half the audiences were women.

*

When *Oh! Calcutta!* was proposed for London, every traditional theatre-owner in the West End, true to form, said, We Won't Have It In The House. Even Donald Albery, who had taken *Soldiers*, said that he believed it deserved to be staged in the interests of free expression; but not in one of his theatres.

All of them were well aware that it could be as successful as it was in New York, but they thought we – and they – would be prosecuted, which could have meant going to prison. We managed to get the Roundhouse, a vast dingy former locomotive shed in North London, for a short season and began rehearsals.

John Mortimer was called upon in his professional capacity for a legal opinion. After he had seen what we were up to, what he told us was none too heartening.

> I have no doubt that we are seeing a period of retrogression and backlash against permissiveness in the Arts, and that a production of 'Oh Calcutta' would be at serious risk of prosecution. My own opinion is that there is nothing to deprave and corrupt in 'Oh Calcutta', but I would not like to say that an Old Bailey judge and an average jury would not form the view that the repeated references to oral sex and sadomasochism are not depraving and corrupting. I therefore think that if a prosecution were to be launched, the chances of a conviction would be about 50/50, given the present mood of the Courts.

There was an atmosphere of intense excitement. And more than a little paranoia. Nobody was allowed into the Roundhouse without a badge which, as the place was run by a bunch of amiable freaks, was a fairly ludicrous state of affairs. The same kind of unpleasant mail threats and phone calls I had had with *Soldiers* rolled in, but this time I was a porn merchant and sex fiend. Some of them were quite frightening. When you probe the public subconscious a lot of funny stuff pops out.

My solicitor and friend, Oscar Beuselinck, suggested that I needed a partner and proposed Robert Stigwood. I did not need anyone financially but I was beginning to feel a little nervous about standing alone against such hostility. I still did not know Stigwood personally, but I had warmed to him because of his show of nerve over *Hair*. He seemed like someone who would not easily be frightened off. And when I met him I thought that, if I was going to prison, he would be good company. The Lord Chamberlain was no more. The decision to prosecute was, technically speaking, up to Peter Rawlinson, the Attorney-General. While he was making up his mind – and while the public argument raged – a police officer named Cluff from the Vice Squad was detached to keep an eye on me.

He and a colleague turned up at the run-through, hung about disapprovingly, and then came to the office solemnly to inform Robert, Ken and myself of the peril we were in. Stigwood and I were sufficiently alert to it to have formed a company separate from our own Somerford Productions, which owned nothing except the rights to *Calcutta*. If we were going to be prosecuted, we would not be dragging our other interests into the pot – although we each could be prosecuted personally.

But the good news came, however reluctantly, from Cluff, after weeks of seeing him every night. He returned to my office with a long face and said, 'I am here to inform you officially that the Attorney-General has decided not to prosecute you.' Then he added, 'But it would be dishonest of me to say that I agree with him. It is entirely contrary to the advice I presented to him.' Once again we were lucky with timing. A new Conservative Government had taken office in the summer of 1970. Later on, I was told that the Prime Minister Edward Heath after only being at Downing Street for a month did not relish the prospect of a fight over censorship with every liberal in the land.

Cluff sat there looking unhappy. I laughed and said, 'Let me send you a few bottles of champagne to help you recover.'

'Out of the question,' he said. 'I could not accept a gift.' A few years later I met him in the street outside my office. 'I'm doing real police work now,' he said, seriously. 'Murder Squad.'

The publicity was overwhelming, helped unintentionally by the fuss caused by Mrs Mary Whitehouse and her curious collection of supporters: the Dowager Lady Birdwood for instance, Lord Longford, and Councillor Smith of Bromley, a Tory party agent, who when he heard we were away free said, 'Sir Peter Rawlinson has set back the cause of civilisation and a decent way of life in Britain. This decision is a disaster.'

It all sold tickets, of course. Every paper had a *Calcutta*-based cartoon. I had often groaned about the popular press, but it serves a very useful function when it does whatever you want it to do. It was the Whitehouse factor, however, that really made *Calcutta*.

The night before the first public preview the actors suddenly came to me in a group. We can't go on, they said. Can't do it. Not ready for it. It was abject group fear. They had suddenly realised that they were going out in front of an audience that might include their agents, their friends, their parents, their lovers past or present, to jump around with no clothes on and be stared at. They wanted the first preview postponed to give them more time to adjust to the idea of public nudity. It was a bad case of unusual stage fright.

I could understand their apprehension. But there was a lot at stake quite apart from money – the irreplaceable bonanza of the publicity building. And my reputation. I was aware that plenty of people wanted us to fail and I knew, if we postponed for even one night, we might never open at all.

I called for Stigwood to come to the theatre – what is a partner for? 'Tell me what you want me to do,' he said. 'Just repeat what I've already told them as strongly as you can,' I said.

By this time there were only a few hours to curtain. He came out to the Roundhouse and delivered a rousing speech. Between us we won the company over.

That first preview was sheer exhilaration. The cast were thrilled at the reception, their misgivings disappeared. However at the real first night – just as in New York – the reviews were not good. Some of the pieces in the popular press might have been written by Inspector Cluff. But it was Milton Shulman of the *Evening Standard* and Harold Hobson who mattered. If they together had said that *Calcutta* was a filthy show and should have been stopped, then I believe a way would have been found.

But Shulman, wrote, '*Oh! Calcutta!* will certainly shock some people – it will corrupt and deprave nobody.' Hobson even tried to be kind. He wrote, 'Ken Tynan and Michael White who are responsible for *Oh! Calcutta!* are intelligent and witty men who naturally incur the jealousy of hosts of people who are neither. But since this is what they are, it is incredible to me that they should have passed the sketches which make up the verbal part of the review.' And his conclusion was that despite the deplorable taste of the show it was not harmful.

Robert Stigwood, who was a renowned host, insisted that, rather than having the first night party at the Roundhouse, it should be at his extraordinary manor house at Stanmore, even though it was half an hour's drive from town. The party of course was also a joint venture, so we were equally responsible, but Robert set out to orchestrate the whole thing. All of London wanted to be there, of course. The telephones had been ringing ever since we heard from the Attorney-General.

In fact when I got to Stanmore it seemed that everyone I had ever met was squeezed into the vast rooms. Except Robert. Marvellous food in abundance had been laid out in a room next to where the drinks were being served. Everyone was hungry by then and, as the champagne and cocktails went around, they eyed the spread in happy anticipation.

Once everyone had their drinks, I looked about for Robert and, not finding him, suggested to the chef that it was time to eat. 'Sorry, sir,' he said, the waiters drawing up alongside him in support, 'Mr Stigwood ordered nothing was to be served until he gave the word.'

Still there was no sign of Robert. The guests were muttering mutinously into their second and third drinks. I said, 'Well, I'm the joint host, take my word for it.' But the chef would not budge.

By now it was midnight. Starving myself, I grabbed one of Robert's young men assistants and set out to find him. We banged through the forty-room house, to which both of us were strangers, until by elimination we finally reached the master bedroom. It had a massive oak door on which we hammered until he stuck his head out.

'Just tell them to start,' he said, when I explained rather crossly.

It was not as easy as that, I made him understand. Only their master's voice would get the faithful servants going and the guests fed. So, with slightly bad grace, Robert came down and gave the order, then went back to getting away from it all.

In the end people simply would not stay away from *Oh! Calcutta!* no matter how hostile the press. Partly because of its success, I think, it became extremely fashionable *not* to like *Calcutta* in London's more fashionable circles. Some people were very dismissive in public even though they went more than once. Laurence Harvey, of whom I was very fond, said, 'If you laugh at knickers you'll enjoy it. It's the sort of thing I used to giggle about as a six-year-old.'

Different people had different ways of coming to terms with it. Bernard Delfont, who had refused to have it at his theatre, rang me personally for first-night seats for an 'important investor'. Others stick to their moral guns. Peter Saunders was honest enough to say: 'Although I usually invest with you, I'm not going to on this. If I was not ready to have it in the Vaudeville Theatre then I should not be ready to make money out of it in any way.'

Many of the cast never lost their inhibitions entirely. I inadvertently walked into an actress's dressing-room one night without knocking. She

131

had nothing on, just as she had been naked on stage all evening. I did not even notice, but she instinctively reached for a towel.

Those who refrained from investing for whatever reason made a noticeable sacrifice. *Calcutta* earned its investors 600 per cent. But, even when we opened, we still did not have a West End theatre to transfer to. The only person interested was Paul Raymond, the Soho sex revue baron, who offered us the Royalty, the ugliest theatre built in London since World War Two, the worst in every way. The beautiful old Stoll theatre, which had stood on the site, had been torn down by Charles Clore, and an office block built with this travesty in the basement.

Ugliness apart, it is hideously situated. Its entrance in a narrow street off the London School of Economics makes it a trial to reach. And, naturally, we were charged the highest possible rent, £3,000 a week. But there was no choice. We moved in. And of course we were an even greater hit, played to packed houses for two years, making a great deal of money for the investors – for ourselves and, of course for Paul Raymond.

Then Raymond, who was a very amenable landlord to deal with, decided he wanted us out. It is quite normal after a certain amount of time for either a theatre-owner or the producing management to give each other adequate notice to quit without any specific reason. But we got notice while we were still doing extraordinary business, so that Raymond could produce a Folies Bergère-type show – showgirls, feathers and so on – which was quite a major flop. It must be one of the few occasions when he has made the wrong decision.

We were then offered by John Hallett the much smaller Duchess Theatre and there we stayed quite happily for another seven years. The original cast stayed for nine months. It included people like Bill Macy, who then became a major TV star in America; Anthony Booth, of *Till Death Us Do Part*; Dominic Blyth, who went on to become a very good and serious Shakespearean actress; the beautiful Brenda Arnau; and Linda Marlow, who has also proven to be an outstanding actress, and Arlene Phillips, dancer turned very successful choreographer.

The American production was revived in Miami in 1979 and then it reappeared on Broadway, managed by Norman Kean, Hilly's former aide. I find it quite distressing to walk down Broadway, see the sign and watch the theatre fill up. The Tynan estate eventually got something tiny from the American company. But four years after the show had been back on Broadway I had not received a single dollar.

In retrospect I think *Calcutta* was an enjoyable show, particularly with the original company. It had a healthy effect on public consciousness. It forced people who would never have discussed their own sexuality to think about it responsibly. Not everyone, of course. I was interested in steeple-chasing at the time, a pleasure one could still afford. A trainer asked me to go and look at a horse which a member of a well-known tobacco family was selling. I liked the horse and agreed the price.

Two days later the trainer telephoned.

'I don't know how to tell you this,' he said. 'The owner asked if you were Michael White, the theatre producer. I said yes. "The man who put on *Oh! Calcutta!?*" "Yes." "Well, I don't want any horse of mine to be owned by anyone concerned with such a spectacle."'

CHAPTER ELEVEN

Partners

Robert Stigwood and I had co-operated successfully enough on one Lloyd-Webber show, *Joseph and His Amazing Technicolor Dream Coat*, which has the most listenable score of all his musicals. It was originally staged at the Edinburgh Festival by Frank Dunlop, though it was written with school performances in mind. Stigwood said he would bring it into the Roundhouse for a try-out. Then I had a call from Denis Foreman at Granada, who were interested, since they were the publishers of the music. So I did some marriage-broking.

It clicked just well enough at the Roundhouse for us to move it to the New Theatre where we proceeded to lose quite a lot of money. It never quite took off in the West End. But it was soon to become the most performed musical in British rep and, although it took seven years, we did get our money back.

We also went into *Grease* together. I saw it in New York off Broadway before it moved uptown. Although I admired the energy and the choreography, I thought the book was crude and decided not to buy the rights for London.

Much later, when it had been an outstanding hit on Broadway, the British rights were bought, and I was asked if I would like to invest. Richard Gere had been signed for the leady and they had assembled a very good cast. I agreed to put £10,000 into the production. A few days later I told Robert about it, and he asked if he could share the investment.

The Broadway success was certainly not duplicated in London, where *Grease* had a very short and unprofitable run. But it set Robert off on the path of the movie, which is probably one of the most successful films ever made.

A very enjoyable musical we did together was the Joe Papp production of *Two Gentlemen of Verona*. This had music by the composer of *Hair* and had started life, like so many of Papp's shows, in the Free Theatre in Central Park. It moved to Broadway, where I saw it, and we agreed to take it to London. We had a magnificent company, including Diane Langton, Bennie Lee, Michael Staniforth (who was later to appear in *Chorus Line*) and Derek Griffiths. John Guare, one of New York's most amusing authors, wrote the book. But, although we got terrific reviews, we never actually sold out. I think the general public always felt it was true Shakespeare rather than a rock-and-roll musical. Moral: If you are going to adapt any classic to a musical find a totally new title.

We also co-produced a show in 1971 that Stigwood first described to me as the nudest, prettiest and dirtiest show ever staged: *The Dirtiest Show in Town* in fact. It was a real piece of New York ultra-realism, a satire on pullution written by Tom Eyens who later did the book for the wonderful Michael Bennett musical, *Dream Girls*. Its setting was a Greenwich Village bar, it had a very heavy gay-macho, aggressive style – and some really filthy language. There were some excellent people in it. And of course the title was perhaps one of the most commercial ever contrived.

In New York one of the critics said *The Dirtiest Show in Town* made *Oh! Calcutta!* look like *Little Women* and, when we got to London, the *Daily Mirror* – which had been at pains to defend *Calcutta* – sailed right into us with a front-page attack.

Garbage on the stage. Garbage was the 7-letter word used yesterday in the *Mirror* to describe *The Dirtiest Show in Town*. Garbage stinks and so does this latest stage import from America. It's repulsive without wit, crude without a salt of genuine social criticism. What a gift to those who would like to see censorship return to the British stage.

It contained something far worse, had anyone known, an incident unparalleled in the legitimate theatre. There was a scene in the show in which sexual intercourse was simulated. But one night the actor, presumably fed up with faking it, decided upon the real thing. The audience did not realise it, of course. The actress involved behaved like a trouper but, once offstage, she went berserk. She threatened to accuse him of rape, even though they were friends and had been working in the company together for months. There was nearly a huge scandal but fortunately the actress decided that she would not gain anything by it and that the enemies of free expression would be delighted. I gave the actor a stern frightening lecture and that was the end of it.

Then in 1973 came *Jeeves*, Alan Ayckbourn's first musical and one of the great fiascos of all time. When I read the script, I thought it had tremendous potential. Alan had a record of hits. The world is full of P. G. Wodehouse fans, including myself. David Hemmings would head the first-class cast. And there was a marvellous melodic score by Andrew Lloyd-Webber.

But, at a rough guess, it was over four hours long.

The arrangement we had was that, even when we were fifty-fifty on the money for a show, either Robert or myself would always be present as the day-to-day producer. *Jeeves* was left entirely to Stigwood. We agreed that he and his capable associate Bob Swash would supervise, among other things, the cutting of the play down to a reasonable length before we opened in Bristol.

I was involved in another project in America, and I only attended one or two rehearsals before going out there. But there was something wrong and unfortunately it was the director, Eric Thompson. My first objection to him was that he addressed the actors through a loudspeaker system while sitting midway down the stalls. He had had a huge success with *My Fat Friend*, but this was his first musical, and musicals are not light comedies.

Had I known that Robert was deeply involved in various other projects, I might have put off my trip. But, when I returned and went down to Bristol for the dress rehearsal, I immediately saw that the show was in serious trouble; there was an atmosphere I didn't like and don't want to experience again, but of course with every flop one does.

The cuts which should have been made had not been made; the show was still running at the dangerous length of four hours, and morale was low. David Hemmings, who really held the company together, was extremely pessimistic. Sure enough on the first night, while the end of the show was only just approaching, seats started to click. The audience had already been there three and a half hours. They had to catch the last buses.

Unfortunately there was panic after that and the cuts made were drastic, involving the virtual elimination of one of our more distinguished actresses, and some of the better parts of the show. It was a situation the producer most fears, big musical thundering toward the West End like a train that cannot be stopped for long enough for drastic repairs.

I have always thought it would make more sense with such a show to rehearse for five to six weeks, play a week out of town, then stop for a week in order to make the cuts and changes that are always necessary. Doing eight shows a week while trying to work in rewrites is the wrong way to prepare for the West End opening.

As with many musicals that go wrong in this way, by the time we got to London the company had had so many changes and had worked so hard that the actors were in a state of complete exhaustion – in particular David. I watched the faces of people coming out after one of the charity previews at Her Majesty's. They were in a state of disbelief. The first night was a disaster.

The next day I went on *Nationwide*, the TV show, with Michael Billington of the *Guardian* who suggested that, as a penance for having been involved with *Jeeves* (although why he picked on me I don't quite know), I should be chained to the railings of the theatre. What is generally called a lively discussion ensued.

That was the last show Robert and I were to do together. One reason of course was that he went off to America, where he proceeded to conquer Hollywood. His yachts got larger and larger and larger – to the point where, I understand, he now cannot find one big enough to satisfy him. Robert Stigwood is unquestionably the most brilliant entrepreneur of this time. I still have great affection for him but I doubt very much whether I will ever do another show with him, any more than I would do one with Hilly Elkins. The score always seemed to read: Stigwood 3, The Rest O. But he is still very good company for an evening out or, presumably, an ocean voyage.

Soon after the *Jeeves* catastrophe *Calcutta* passed into the realms of the respectable. I gave the first anniversary party – on my own – at the Hard Rock Café, which got enormous publicity. Princess Alexandra came, and we even got into the old respectable *Tatler*.

Up until the mid-1960s I had simply run Michael White Ltd and Michael White Productions with financial sleight-of-hand – bank loans, the income from whatever shows I had on. The ones that worked, that is. I had lunch with Hal Prince sometime at the end of the 1960s after I had just had a ludicrous run of bad luck. He said, 'If you were in New York you'd be out of business by now. It's insane to be sitting here discussing new productions after you've had six flops in a row.'

Later, despite the early difficulties in getting the money to start flowing from the wells of *Oh! Calcutta!*, flow it eventually did. And, when it was joined by the takings from *Sleuth*, a much more modest – but eventually much more rewarding – venture which I had undertaken at the same time, I might have become rich had I been a more dedicated businessman.

Hal Prince had been right, of course. But I had never even thought of doing anything else, never thought that I might not permanently be in producing. I always knew the sun would shine, if not today then next week. I was not one to worry unduly, which is marvellous for avoiding ulcers, but dangerous when the bank rings up and announces that you are dramatically overdrawn. I have never sat down and worried about my position in the theatre – or in life. I had never questioned that I would go on. However, after getting married and having three children under four years of age, there were some fairly difficult moments financially and personally. Even so, I never even considered an alternative career.

By 1960 I had acquired a partner in the most curious way. Sarah was very friendly with an English writer, Merlin Pearson Rogers. He had become celebrated by being gored in Pamplona during the bull-running festival in full view of 20,000 people as he stopped to take a photograph. Everybody in the arena except him could see what was coming. His stomach was covered in scars and he was lucky to be alive.

Sarah had gone to see the running of the bulls yet again and they persuaded me to join them. Whatever else it is, Pamplona, despite its association with Hemingway, is not glamorous. It is six days of continuous carousing, noise and fatigue.

In the famous café, the Hemingway café, John Crosby, the ex-critic-cum-journalist, whom I knew from London, introduced me to another American, Clement Brown Jnr, who lived in Paris and Biarritz. The upshot was that Clem became a partner in Michael White Ltd. He had run a major American company in Europe for many years. He knew everyone from Art Buchwald to the porters at the Gare de Lyon. He was immediately helpful in finding new investors, bringing in American money.

The other shareholders were more or less obliged to go along with my decisions. *Arturo Ui*, a great critical success, and *The Au Pair Man*, a failure, were both in the offing in this part of 1960. *Sleuth*, which was to be a phenomenal hit, was being polished but, just as the need to finance it became acute, Clem ran into personal difficulties and I had to go looking for another partner.

I found the amazing Leo Feldsberg. He found me, actually, because he wanted to do *Arturo Ui* on Broadway and asked if I would help. He was not deterred when I said that it would probably cost him a quarter of a million dollars which he must realise he might lose.

Leo could have been a writer's invention. He was born in Vienna and

138

came to London in the late 1930s where he opened a wine shop which attracted a lot of theatre and opera clients. He was a man of considerable culture but rather unprepossessing to look at. When the war broke out he was supposed to be interned on the Isle of Man like every other Austrian or German alien. But, when his convoy got to Liverpool, he was put by mistake on a boat to Australia. He arrived there with no luggage and no money but, after a series of extraordinary adventures, he managed eventually to find his way to Colombia in South America, where he set up a huge fruit-canning business and built it into a major corporation.

Leo never did find the right set-up for *Arturo Ui* but he loved the theatre and asked to be taken aboard. So, just before *Sleuth* opened, he put £20,000 into the company, which led to his making a fortune from the theatre and from his involvement with Michael White Ltd.

By the time I met him he had bought an apartment in New York where he spent half the year seeing every show in town and every opera. He was still busy running his business so he came to London quite rarely at first. But, one day, he sold up in Colombia and then he was in London a great deal of the time. In my office. He wanted us to make a film with Pontecorvo, who had directed *The Battle of Algiers*, about the life of Jesus Christ as seen in a political as opposed to a religious way; I am sorry we never did it.

Much as I liked Leo I soon discovered the difference between a sleeping partner and one who was always sitting opposite me. There was always a problem of entertaining, of finding a girl to be Leo's date.

That was one reason I set out to reorganise Michael White Ltd. The other – much more important – was that I suddenly realised that, although I was making a lot of money, since I was an employee of the company it was all going in tax. A friend, John Bishop, who was in business and had invested in the theatre with me, told me that the only way to get together some real money was to sell out and make a capital gain.

So, after a lot of discussion with Clem and Leo and an array of accountants, in 1972 I sold Michael White Ltd to the Erskine House Investment Trust, a small public company which John Bishop had taken over, and of which Graham Dowson became chairman.

It was a terrible mistake. Not that they got in my way or anything like that, but I was totally unsuited temperamentally to be a company director; to go to meetings, sit on a board, face shareholders' questions. Erskine House had started as a mining company with conservative Scottish connections, and there were still some original shareholders. One, a

Scottish engineer, told me that his father would turn in his grave if he knew the money was coming from *Oh! Calcutta!*.

My great error was to take shares instead of cash. Leo and Clem both took cash for their Michael White holdings and got out. But, as I was going on with Erskine House, I opted for shares. My father, who probably had some first-hand experience of such folly, warned me not to take shares unless their price was guaranteed at the time of issue.

Came the hurricane of 1973 and our minor speculative public company nearly went down the chute. The shares dropped, like everything else, and the net result was that instead of finding myself well off I wiped out 70 per cent of my Michael White Ltd worth. This included much of my earnings from *Sleuth*, a project I had taken up while the London opening of *Calcuta* was still a year away. No play apart from *The Mousetrap* has ever made such profits, although because I had shouldered all the risk on so many other shows (this one cost a mere £12,000) I had laid a lot of it off. Certainly no play has made the investor so much profit on such low costs. After all, it only had a cast of two.

One morning at breakfast in Brunswick Gardens, where we lived in a large, creaky Edwardian house, Peter Shaffer telephoned to ask if I would be interested in a thriller his brother had written. The twin brothers Shaffer are a phenomenon of modern English literature, although it would be hard to think of two writers more different. Peter won immediate recognition when his first play *Five Finger Exercise* was staged in 1958. He had the rare ability to please both critics and public. *Equus*, his masterwork, still lay in the future. But *The Royal Hunt of the Sun* and many other plays had confirmed him as a major talent.

As children the twins had been fascinated by the thriller form and, although Tony now worked successfully in advertising, he continued to write plays. While I lingered over breakfast the manuscript was delivered by hand. Then – something I have rarely done – I stayed put and read it through in one go.

The play revolves around a traditional, upper-class English gentleman who invites his wife's lover down to the country for a discussion, which ends in murder. The lover, Milo, is everything the husband would dislike. Smart, foreign, deep tan, gold chains, smooth. Not only did the play have a very brilliant idea at its heart but it was also – extremely unusual for a thriller – written with consummate literary skill.

By midday I was on the telephone to Tony's agent, Terence Baker of Richard Hatton, to buy the rights.

Although I thought I had a winner, my view was not shared by the actors and directors whom I then approached. In fact it took twelve months to find a cast for *Sleuth*, which came as a great surprise to all of us. Why couldn't everyone see that this was a natural? Word got round to me that the play had been turned down by other senior managements and producers. That did not bother me. I thought *Sleuth* was a thoroughly commercial play. The reason it *had* been rejected by other managements was the singularity of its plot.

I - rightly in this case – thought that it did not matter if the audience tumbled to the fact that one actor played two parts. If they did, the play would still be exciting, and if they did not – as it turned out – it would be even more exciting.

After much negotiation I luckily got Anthony Quayle and Keith Baxter to star. Clifford Williams reluctantly agreed to direct after I broke a rule of my life which is never to persuade people to do things against their better judgement. We got Carl Toms to design the set and costumes, a most fortunate contribution. He came up with one of the best designs imaginable, tremendously enhancing, bringing the play to life.

Clifford, who had directed *Soldiers* and *Oh! Calcutta!* in London, is Welsh, a former dancer and a delightful person to work with. Although we have had our squabbles, they were always minor. Life in the theatre is like an endless series of affairs – you work closely and well with someone, have lunch with them every day for six weeks, then not see them for years. My relationship with Clifford followed this pattern.

We soon saw how fortunate we had been to get Tony Quayle. Not only was he a distinguished actor but, having been director of the RSC for a number of years, he had often been through the process of getting a new play right. Therefore he queried every clue and line in the play, which was wonderful in helping make everything in *Sleuth* foolproof.

Why does the character do this now? Would he really say that? And through this process of questioning, although it caused many temporary difficulties, when we finally opened in Brighton the play was razor-sharp and flawless, a classic of the thriller form.

I thought *Sleuth* was perfect when the curtain went up for the first time except for one tiny thing. In the highly realistic country house set a fish tank, which was a crucial clue, sat on the floor. Carl had not been able to find anywhere natural for it in his design. Everything else was absolutely perfect for a Wiltshire drawing-room – except for this bloody fish tank. We opened in Brighton, then toured Eastbourne and Stratford. Often I expected some critic to seize on it, demand to know why there was a fish tank lying on the floor in this implausible fashion. But no one ever did.

The crucial deception in the play was carried through the programme.

It had three actors listed, though there were only two in reality. Walking on the beach at Eastbourne, we had fun inventing a background for the actor playing the third part, who was, of course, Keith Baxter in disguise, putting a couple of clues in the biography – which nobody got.

On the first night in Brighton, I knew we had a hit. The Theatre Royal was full of electricity. We had a very high-powered theatrical audience. A lot of people had come from London, even from New York. Word had got round that it was a potential blockbuster.

One major stumbling block lay before us, however. We still did not have a theatre in London. It was not that West End owners did not want us. There was simply no room. We did our week at Brighton, then went to Cheshire for a week, then Stratford-on-Avon. And on to Eastbourne, carrying the costs of touring and not knowing when there was to be a West End opening.

This made my life difficult. With a West End house waiting I could print posters and start getting the word round, taking bookings. Michael English, the designer who had already done a couple of posters for me in the past, notably *Arturo Ui* and *The Beard*, had done a brilliant poster for *Sleuth*, and I wanted to see it plastered round the West End.

Then someone else's ill fortune became our good. A play opening at the St Martin's Theatre got such bad reviews that there was no question of it running. Even though the St Martin's had rather a small stage for our set, when Peter Saunders telephoned me I jumped at the offer.

The first night of *Sleuth* in the West End in February 1970 is a night everyone will remember as perfect. The acting was impeccable, all the tricks worked, the audience were completely riveted. Nobody seemed to guess that Keith Baxter was playing the two parts. When he took his mask off after the opening of Act II, there was a gasp of amazement from the audience, and I knew then we had a strong hit.

We had come in very quietly, little time to spread the word, unable to get much publicity or action because another Shaffer play, Peter's *The Battle of Shrivings*, had just opened, with John Gielgud starring. After it was clear that we were in for a long and happy run, I met the critic from *The Times*, Irving Wardle, in the street. He explained why their notice had been so small – although favourable ('a most dazzling performance whose higher qualities of character and dialogue gain enormously from being held firmly within a modest form . . .'). 'I thought it was just another thriller.' That, *Sleuth* most definitely was not.

For once there was no anxiety about a Broadway production. Tony's American agent, Robert Lantz, had sent a copy of the play to Morton

Gottlieb, who had served a long apprenticeship under Gilbert Miller, the most fashionable and successful Broadway producer of the 1930s and 1940s. Gottlieb had now set up in management with Helen Bonfils, of Denver mining fame, so he had access to plenty of money. He had for a time been Robert Morley's manager. He was very experienced and able.

Gottlieb had been more than slightly put out to discover that *Sleuth* had been sold to me a couple of days before he was ready to buy it. So, after a certain amount of natural haggling (the London production wanting more and Gottlieb wanting to pay less), we made a deal.

While the London company settled down to a complete sell-out Gottlieb went ahead with arrangements for the New York production, for which he wanted to wait a year so that Tony Quayle and Keith Baxter could duplicate their London success. He handled *Sleuth* perfectly. It opened in Washington then went straight to Broadway. He got the right sort of publicity, the right advance, the right theatre – the Music Box, a beautiful house owned by Irving Berlin. Of course a lot of people said *Sleuth* could never work in America, that it was too English – would they know what a Lagonda is over there? But, if the article is a genuine one, people anywhere will appreciate it. *Sleuth* even broke records in Kansas City. In fact it did marvellously the world over, everywhere but France. There, the major actor was Pierre Fresnais, a great name but an ageing one. *Sleuth* required a lot of physical energy and perhaps he was too old for it.

The first night in New York almost exceeded our London opening night. I was really nervous, because I felt that we had such a good chance of being a hit. During the interval I wandered over to Sardi's and drank brandy, something I've never done before or since. There's nobody in Sardi's during theatre-time. Just before opening night something had happened which really set back my relationship with both Tony Shaffer and Robert Lantz. I had said to Tony that, in my opinion, he should not sell the film rights. You are making plenty of money for the moment, I counselled. Let's keep them for ourselves. I thought *Sleuth* could be made as a wonderful low-budget British film in which we could all be involved, retaining profits which would normally have gone to a film company.

But, the day before the play opened in New York, Lantz rang up and said they had been offered $250,000 with escalations for film rights by Palomar Productions and that Tony wanted to accept. I said I thought that the timing of such a deal was absurd. We had already held out for fifteen months, gambling on success. *Sleuth* was doing well everywhere.

143

[handwritten marginal note: no, Bonfils was the publisher of the Rocky Mountain News, a highly successful Denver daily.]

If it was a big hit on Broadway, we could expect even higher offers. Or, better still, we could do it ourselves.

However, Lantz is a very brilliant and persuasive agent and his opinion prevailed. By the next morning – the morning of our opening on Broadway – the deal had been agreed. I was genuinely upset, because I felt that for once here was an opportunity for the author/producer/director to retain a valuable property, and for once there was a real opportunity of filming ourselves and going to a major film company simply for distribution. Such opportunities occur very rarely.

I suppose that it was a lot of money, although it always sounds more than it is. But by the time 10 per cent has gone to the author's agent, 20 per cent each to the English and US managements, the author is left with less than 50 per cent.

The film was directed by Joe Mankiewitz, who although a fine director was then towards the end of a great career. And, although he had two great actors, Laurence Olivier and Michael Caine, I personally did not think the film was anything like as good as the play. It was overblown and did not have the same tautness. It could have been one of the great film thrillers of all time. The amount of money it grossed was nothing like what (I still think) we could have made if we had done it ourselves.

I was also distressed to discover that the producer of the film was to be none other than Morton Gottlieb, the producer of the play. It is a less-than-endearing custom of American producers to buy a play, make the film deal in their capacity as producer, and then move in and produce the film – double-dipping. I think that is wrong. My feeling is that, if you are in partnership with someone, such as an English producer, you are partner all the way up and all the way down.

In the meantime *Sleuth* had changed casts. Paul Rogers and Donal Donnelly had taken over and, although the performances were quite different, they were just as memorable. *Sleuth* won a Tony Award in New York as best play of the year and sailed serenely on.

Meanwhile, in London in its seventy-fifth week, it was making a profit of £1,900 on takings of £5,330. It is instructive to look at where the rest went. Royalties £645, rent £550, backstage salaries and expenses £433, front-of-house £346, printing/advertising £310, props £95, light/heat £86, management £80, accountancy £16, sundries £20. Those were the days.

At the end of the year it was time for another change of cast. Apart from salary and billing the biggest argument between actors and management are over length of run. Managers always want someone for

144

a year. An actor will want to do only three months. I signed up Marius Goring for *Sleuth*, overlooking the clause in the contract that said I needed the theatre-owner's permission. Peter Saunders did not think Goring was suitable so he gave us notice to quit. It seems to me, in retrospect, that he must have thought there must be something better around, since the houses were no longer totally full. And from his point of view there was – *The Mousetrap*, transferring from the Ambassadors. From a purely business point of view Saunders might have been justified. I could not be too cross, because he had taken the play when it had no home. I did not take the decision badly, I just thought it was ridiculous.

Then John Hallett, a charming man who ran the Abrahams theatres – the Garrick, the Duchess, the Fortune, the Aldwych – rang up and offered the Garrick. *Sleuth* stayed there until it closed after 2,386 performances, which put it in the top twelve longest West End runs. I had long since parted company with Erskine House by then, in quite a friendly way. But a look at the accounts for 1973–74–75 will show what a major contribution Michael White Ltd made.

Finally, in 1978, I parted company with Erskine House, with the assistance of Clem Brown and a friendly Dutch banker, Paul Verburgt. I was more relaxed not being part of the *Financial Times* listings.

CHAPTER TWELVE

A Star is Someone to Whom No One Tells the Truth

Immediately after *Calcutta*, I presented a season of *Hamlet*, directed by Jonathan Miller, at the Fortune Theatre – perhaps the smallest theatre in which *Hamlet* has ever been performed. It was fascinating to see it played in such intimacy. Hugh Thomas was Hamlet. He turned director soon after and directed a couple of other plays I presented; *City Sugar* by Stephen Poliakoff was one of them.

I put the profits of *Sleuth* and *Calcutta* to work, financing smaller shows. I revived *The Blood Knot* at the Royal Court. There was a play by a Trinidadian writer, Mustapha Matura, which I liked so much that I did it twice, *As Time Goes By*, about a hippy girl and a West Indian bus conductor. It was a very good production, directed by Roland Reese. It was first staged Upstairs at the Court, and then again at the ICA.

Hilly Elkins invited me to share in a production of Ibsen's *A Doll's House* which he had done in America with Claire Bloom as Nora. It had a very successful run in London at the Criterion. I also wanted to do a Peter Weiss play about Trotsky, but I could not cast it properly.

Then came two of the most critical events of my professional life, both of them centred on Vanessa Redgrave. Robert Shaw had written a play, *Cato Street*, about the Cato Street conspiracy of 1820, a radical plot to murder the British cabinet. Vanessa agreed to be in it. Originally, it was going to be done at the National. Robert had been offered a date in 1972 – this was 1971 – but was too impatient to wait, which caused much friction between him and Olivier, the Director of the National. It had been at Olivier's suggestion that much of the motivation had been given to Susan, the wife of Arthur Thistlewood the leader of the conspirators, in order to create a strong female lead. This was the part, of course, that appealed so strongly to Vanessa.

Robert took the play to the Young Vic. But as that theatre had, by intention, the lowest seat prices in London, and as there were some forty-five speaking parts, it had to be subsidised. Robert, Vanessa and I formed Thistlewood Productions as a management company. Our idea was to open at the Young Vic, then move to the West End, which was somewhat optimistic, considering the size of the cast.

Robert was a man of many different abilities. He was a major actor, a writer, and he had also been a director. I would have been against his directing *Cato Street*, as I am against any author directing his own work. Some people have done it, notably David Hare in England, but on the whole it is a bad idea. But of course in the theatre there are no rules! But, as it happened, we were not even to have him present as the author during rehearsals. He had signed to be in Pinter's *Old Times* in New York, directed by Peter Hall. The director we got, Peter Gill, has since proved to be one of the best in England. But it would have been much better for all of us, since Peter was quite young, the play complex and the leading lady very formidable, if Robert could have been around.

Inevitably, Peter Gill and Vanessa fell out. There were some memorable rows once rehearsals got under way. The play was over-long as well as intricate, with endless crowd scenes, and we were trying to get it together in three and a half weeks instead of six or seven which a play of this complexity required.

One of the few moments of light relief stemmed from a decision by Vanessa that in the massacre scene, the play's climax, she ought to have a child with her. It was another liberty with history, but effective. My son Joshua was the right age – about seven, then – so he was roped in. Once, he was late for rehearsal with thirty-five actors on stage waiting. As he walked in, Bob Hoskins led them in singing from *Dreamcoat*, 'Joshua, Joshua . . .' Joshua was to play a few more parts in the theatre and in films, but he has not yet decided whether he wants to act.

In the end Vanessa said she would not go on with Peter Gill. I was faced with the unenviable choice of him or her. She is an alarming opponent, especially when she zeroes in with those serious and beautiful blue eyes. But the production was undoubtedly in real trouble, and as part of the management as well as the star she held the most cards. Even if Gill had been right in his view of the production – which he probably was – he had to go.

Although no longer married to Vanessa, Tony Richardson was on very good terms with her. He was extremely helpful through all this, trying to persuade her that she should give Peter Gill more time, then trying to explain Vanessa's character to him. But to no avail. Vanessa had made up her mind.

When I broke the news to him, Peter blamed me. He sent me a very hurtful present – or rather he left it on the set of the Royal Court, where I had another play going on – the Don McCullin book of Vietnam war photographs. I was really distressed. He attributed much more power to me than I actually had in that ridiculous three-cornered committee.

To keep the disastrous momentum going, just before *Cato Street* opened the Pinter play closed in New York and Robert Shaw flew back, came to the theatre virtually straight from the airport, and proceeded to have a blazing row with everyone. But, despite his propensity for that kind of outburst, I emerged from the experience of *Cato Street* with a much greater admiration for Robert than I had previously held. He combined the actor's ability to deliver amusing stories with a high degree of seriousness and culture. He was a marvellously well-rounded man of whom I became deeply fond, fiery, excitable, opinionated, very easy to push over the edge.

One night, he and I were dining at the Savoy Grill and John Osborne and Jill Bennett were at a nearby table. Robert was married to Mary Ure, who had earlier been married to Osborne. Osborne invited us to join them for coffee, which was a bad mistake. In no time, the three of them were involved in a row which emptied the restaurant. Jill provided her share of ammunition for the fiery exchanges. I had seen her in action before. She in turn had been married to Willis Hall, who among his many other accomplishments did the English adaptation of *Chin Chin*. Once while visiting them I made some critical remark about her dog, and Jill picked up a huge stuffed leather pig and threw it at my head, knocking me out.

Cato Street was not a success, although Vanessa gave a fine performance. There was no question of moving it to the West End. It lost an enormous amount of money for the three of us. I was saddened. I had thought the Redgrave-Shaw-Gill combination would work. And perhaps if Robert had been there from the beginning it might have. Either he ought not to have taken *Old Times*, or he should have put off *Cato Street*. But I did not tell him that at the time. I did not appreciate how important his presence might be.

My regard for Tony Richardson had already proved quite costly. Just prior to *Cato Street* I presented and he directed *I, Claudius* at the Queen's Theatre, which provided a perfect illustration of how the wrong design can wreck a good play far more certainly than the right décor can save a bad one.

Even today there is no one in the theatre I respect more than Tony, but with *Claudius* everything was wrong except the actors and the adaptation by John Mortimer. David Warner was Claudius and he was wonderful, proving that good actors can shine out whatever directors make them do. John Crosby, then critic for the *Observer*, wrote, 'The set was a sort of football stadium, tiers of hard wooden seats, inconceivably ugly, having as much to do with ancient Rome as a supermarket. Why so many talented people got mixed up in this disaster is beyond moral comprehension.'

He was certainly right about how horrible it looked, which was strange considering what great taste Tony usually showed. I had had my doubts and I should have voiced them. If I had been less in awe of Tony I might have said something. And the radical concept did have a certain appeal to me. As it was, I strolled into the theatre after the interval on opening night and my heart sank at the sight of a lot of people I knew standing at the bar, in no hurry to go back in. One of them, a very well-known actor – who had not noticed the billing – asked me, 'Isn't this the biggest load of tripe you've ever seen?' He was very embarrassed later that night when somebody else said, 'Poor Michael White. What a disaster on his hands.'

Nonetheless, after the dust from *Cato Street* had settled, I did not hesitate when Tony Richardson suggested that we do *The Threepenny Opera*. Lucille Lortel had had it running in New York all the time I worked there. It was – still is – one of my favourite musicals. And, as well as some other wonderful ladies – Hermione Baddeley, Annie Ross, Barbara Windsor – we got Vanessa for it.

It was a terrific production staged as though in a fairground. *The Times* review read:

As Brecht has a black record in the commercial theatre, congratulations are due even at this late date to Michael White for risking a West End production of *The Threepenny Opera*. Heaven knows, it ought to run, if star casting, a masterly book and the best score in the history of musicals are any criterion for commercial success.

This might have been true, had we been able to get Vanessa to commit herself to a long engagement. But I had made a mistake I will never repeat. I agreed to have her in the show for only nine weeks. I knew at the time that it was foolish but I believed – wrongly, as I found to my cost – that Tony would be able to convince her to stay longer once we were running.

But there was little he or anyone else could do to alter Vanessa's course. She is certainly the most remarkable actress I have ever seen. But she is totally inflexible politically, believing that her politics must always come before the theatre. She even missed the dress rehearsal because she insisted on going to a peace demonstration in Ireland. When her eight weeks were up, she went.

Although we had been doing sell-out business, so much publicity had been built up around Vanessa – and she was wonderful in the part – that the box office just dropped like a stone once she had gone. It would have been far better to do it with somebody less talented who would have stayed. Now, I would never sign any actor on for less than six months, although more and more actors do not want to be tied up for long runs, I understand that. But with today's costs a producer just cannot afford such luxury.

I also presented Fujard's *Siswe Banzi Is Dead*, and *A Ride across Lake Constance*, a wonderful avant garde play written by Peter Hanke, the Austrian playwright. An amazing cast under Michael Rudman's direction took it into the Mayfair Theatre in December 1973 – Jenny Agutter, Faith Brook, Nigel Hawthorne, Nicky Henson, Alan Howard, Gayle Hunnicutt and Nicola Paget. Then there was *Snap*, a play about an embarrassing social malady, by Charles Lawrence who had written the funny play, *My Fat Friend*. Bill Gaskill directed it. *The Times* judgement was very canny:

It's an evening of bits and pieces. The plot of the play is that, after 16 years of fidelity, Ben has had a girl at a party and is now feeling rather poorly. There is a working class photographer and a model who turns English into mock Spanish and seems responsible for Ben's bout of el clappo.

Connie, his wife (Maggie Smith) takes an instant dislike to her. As soon as they're left alone Mr Lawrence manhandles them into an intimate relationship, so as to get his exposition across. It is the first of several such clumsy reversals.

Meanwhile, the plot forges ahead with secret trips to the clinic for Ben and Connie, where they both have farcical encounters. Connie's godmother descends in the shape of Elspeth March playing a stout lesbian, who gives her address as Radclyffe Hall, and subsequently mounts guard over both men after a mock rape scene, armed with a champagne bottle and a prize-winning dog.

The Times went on:

Those who see the production will be rewarded with the most extrava-
gant mannered performance by Maggie Smith, with nothing to support
her in the part of Connie. She creates laughter from her own vocabulary of bodily contortions and strangulated irony. Her timing is outrageous. When somebody asks her whether she bought her sumptuous
dressing-gown in a street market, there follows an immensely prolonged pause during which her face expresses all the crushing replies
she might make, before settling for Mr Lawrence's line, 'Something
like that.'
    For Miss Smith the show represents some kind of triumph, but it
is hard to understand how Mr Gaskill and Barry Ingham as the
agonised Ben became involved in it.

Irving Wardle, who wrote that notice, was right about Maggie Smith
(and, I must confess, about the play). She is the greatest light comedian
of our day. She has the ability to do things with an audience by her
timing and delivery that is magic to watch. She made a weak play into a
total sell-out, and the proof was that, when she left, business collapsed.
A great contemporary comic part has yet to be written for Maggie.   ·

As *Snap* showed, the star syndrome is very treacherous. Sometimes a
producer worries about a feeble play, he will 'star it up' and that will
change its prospects. I was still being led astray in this way as late as
1976, when I presented Poliakoff's *City Sugar* at the Shepherd's Bush
Theatre. In the lead at the Bush was a very good actor, John Shrapnel.
But I felt that, to move to the West End, we needed a 'name'. The fact
is that, if someone is very good in a part, the name you need is his.
Anyway, I cast Adam Faith, of whom I am immensely fond.

It was a very difficult play, particularly for someone who is not
thoroughly used to the stage. It had immensely long, almost stream-of-
consciousness speeches – the character is a D.J. (Tim Curry did it on
television later.) And, although Adam was good, he was not as convincing
as John had been, and the production was unfavourably compared to the
one at the Bush.

*

During most of this time I was living in Brunswick Gardens, just off
Kensington Church Street. Sarah was brilliant at finding marvellous
houses. We bought this one very cheaply because it was in an appalling
condition. But, renovated, it was a big, rather pretty, Edwardian house

with four floors and a huge living-room. We had had all our children by then and Sarah had stopped working, which I think was the beginning of the end of our married life.

It is a mistake for wives to give up working. Instead of having a separate life in the outside world to worry about, they just look after the children and the house all day. Dealing with purely domestic matters makes them exaggerate the importance of trivia to a depressing extent, particularly if they are not stupid and have already been active in business.

It could not have helped that I was incredibly busy in those early 1970s, working day and night, doing a lot of shows, always pre-occupied It must have been very irritating for Sarah. I tried to bring her into my professional life, but whenever we went to the theatre together everybody would talk to me rather than to her. It was hard for a strong, interesting person like Sarah to accept.

So things started to get difficult. Sarah spent more time away from London. We tried to have what was then being called an 'open' relationship. I have yet to see one work, although perhaps it might if the couple did not actually live together; what one does not know one might not mind.

I was very loath to split up the marriage. But Sarah met somebody else and went off to America. It was a fairly unhappy parting, very painful. I reacted very stupidly by selling the house and ended up in a rented one looking after three children, all at different schools.

The wounds of splitting up took a long time to heal. I was lucky to meet my next partner almost at the moment of finally separating from Sarah – in a way that set the tone of the slightly haphazard relationship. I had been going to take Richard Neville, of whom I had been a supporter during the Oz upheavals, to a big Eric Clapton concert at the Rainbow. He could not come but told me that an Australian girl called Lyndall Hobbs wanted badly to go. The name meant nothing to me.

I told Richard I had never been on a blind date (which was quite true). Trust me, he said. The result was that I turned up at Lyndall's flat in Langton Street and, because she was not ready, went into the Langton Gallery and bought a picture.

When she came down, I said, 'Look what I've just bought.' She thought that was incredibly flash, she told me later. It put her off. Anyway, we went off to the Clapton concert, and then we went to dinner and at the next table was Dudley Moore, with whom it transpired Lyndall had gone out in Australia.

Lyndall says she was surprised that I rang her again. But I did and we went out quite a bit. Then I was going skiing, and she was going to the Milan fashion shows with Gayle McKay, who was her best friend. I picked them up there and took them to St Moritz, where we did a lot of rocking and rolling in the rather staid nightclubs.

Richard Neville was slightly peeved when he discovered how far the relationship had developed, but he got over that. Lyndall was very different from Sarah – everything she thought and felt she expressed. Everything came out, no hidden resentments. If she was unhappy about something or someone she said so.

Australians, when they are energetic – and Lyndall is the most energetic person I have ever come across – combine the best of American and British qualities. They do not suffer from the class hang-ups of Britons nor from that kind of blandness Americans so often have. The first time I took her to a traditional English dinner, she refused to leave the table with the other women because she thought it was wrong for women to be split up from the men.

A rather old-fashioned word captures her style – madcap. When she was working as a television reporter for Channel 9 in Australia the programme went to do a story at a shark aquarium – Australians are obsessed with sharks. One of the cameramen said that it would speed up the story if she would jump into the tank. And she did – into a pool with twenty sharks. At heart she is a real Lois Lane, girl reporter. In England, at a fair in Wiltshire, a hot air balloon intrigued her. She threw herself into the basket as it took off, not knowing where it was going, or when it would be back. Once, when we were at the Derby, she said she wanted to take some pictures. I looked down from the grandstand to see that she had elbowed the pros aside and got into the closest position from which to snap the Queen.

So Lyndall is uninhibited, and sometimes annoys people. She is also warm-hearted, extremely fit, fiercely independent, incredibly hardworking and ambitious.

All that suited me very well. There was never any question of Lyndall not being ready to live her own life. Soon she was a whirlwind of activity, working for Thames TV news, writing magazine and newspaper articles and already thinking of making films. After a certain amount of time we started to live together. She was extremely good with the children. They liked her a lot and she them; they all became very good friends. But Lyndall was not interested in domestic life. We got engaged at one point but there did not seem any real point in that. I do not suppose we ever got disengaged, but we spend a lot of time apart, which in my view helps a relationship; makes a couple appreciate each other more when they are together.

It was just as well Lyndall did not have too many pre-occupations in 1973 when we met because a whole tribe of uninhibited characters was crowding into my life. *The Rocky Horror Show* was on the road.

The Rocky Horror Show, one of the truly remarkable cultural phenomena of our times, started, as had so many things, with Oscar Lewenstein who was then artistic director of the Royal Court. The Court would have liked to stage it but did not have enough money in their budget. They were looking for a West End management to pick it up.

The director was to be Jim Sharman, who had directed *Jesus Christ Superstar*. I had only talked to him at the first night party for a few minutes, but we remembered each other well. From what he told me about the concept I was interested. But I was also busy. Twice I had to cancel appointments to hear the *Rocky Horror* music – and music was all there was, the book was written during the rehearsals.

I dislike plays being read to me or scores being played to me. I prefer to take the material away and absorb it in my own time. When *Threepenny Opera* was in rehearsal, Charles Marowitz had invited me to a run-through of a play by Trevor Griffiths. It took place in a hall with the lights full on. We sat in chairs facing the actors. Every nuance on both sides could be seen. Trevor got the impression I did not like the play and took offence so badly that we were uncomfortable for years. But what I disliked was the situation into which I was put.

So I was not in the most receptive of moods when I had to turn up at Jim Sharman's flat in Chelsea one morning – morning! – to hear the *Rocky Horror Show* music for the first time. But the opening, pretty primitive rendition, just Richard O'Brien strumming a guitar and singing 'Science Fiction Double Feature', intrigued me immediately. Here was everything I had been waiting to hear celebrated in song – the 'B' movies I had always loved, old Hollywood cult figures like Leo G. Carroll and Fay Wray.

By the time I had heard three songs, I had also been given the story in a vague shape – Frank 'N Furter, the innocents in the castle. I was hooked. Of course I would put up the money. I knew that it could not fail to be an entertaining show, right in key with the period. I had no idea that Sharman would come up with one of the most brilliant musical productions of all time.

CHAPTER THIRTEEN

From 'Rocky Horror' to Dame Edna

Although *The Rocky Horror Show* is never less than terrific in any of its manifestations, it has never been better than during the first three weeks at the Royal Court. Many of my productions I have admired objectively, abstractly. I loved every minute of *Rocky Horror*, just as a couple of years later I was to love every minute – well, almost – of *Chorus Line*.

It is the only show I have ever done that I can watch time and time again – I must have seen it a hundred times. If the audience is particularly interesting it takes on a whole new flavour. And it is snappy; only an hour and twenty minutes, non-stop, no interval. Every three minutes you are being socked with another song or event. Everything about it works. *The Rocky Horror Show* is critic-proof.

On the opening night there was an audience of only about eighty people in the Theatre Upstairs. Vincent Price and Coral Browne sat behind me. The auditorium was banked up and the seating was unusual. This intimacy became a keynote of every stage production.

I had taken only a casual interest in the rehearsals – I think I looked in on only one – but when preview time arrived I was delighted to find that the show still managed to encapsulate so many things I found riveting. The features that had first appealed to me apart, I was fascinated by the sexual ambiguity. That play liberated a lot of people. Most people after all are not totally hetero – or homo – sexual, they drift to and fro across a borderline. All the dressing up, down and across had the effect of making it fun. Someone could be a transvestite without feeling an idiot. Only one episode is really sexual: where Frank gets off with Janet and then with the boy, Brad. Kids took this in their stride. My own, who were then about ten or younger, wanted to go again and again. *Rocky Horror* turned people into instant super-fans – it is still doing so.

Quite unrelated to my new life with Lyndall, I was being swamped by Australians. There was Jim Sharman in whom I saw many similarities to myself. Deep down he was very serious. He had directed all Patrick White's plays (and now runs the Adelaide Festival). But, highbrow though he might be, his father was a showman – Sharman's Circus – and it must have rubbed off. Jim was very self-confident; he knew exactly what to do once I had agreed to back *Rocky*.

There was Richard O'Brien who played Riff-Raff – and who had written the songs I first heard. Jim set him to writing the whole show, both words and music. But Richard Hartley, the arranger and a brilliant musician, had plenty left to do. *Rocky* was a mighty musical event as well as a spectacle.

The scenery was done by Brian Thompson and the costumes by Sue Blaine, one of the best costume designers in the world. Ten years later she was to do the National's *Guys and Dolls*, but both she and Brian had a hard time getting established. They might be all right for *The Rocky Horror Show*, was the view sadly typical of British attitudes, but not for, say, *Titus Andronicus*. Why should designers be judged differently from actors? If they were good, they would be good at everything.

But what Jim did most brilliantly of all was cast the show. To pick Tim Curry was an inspiration. With the whole world to choose from, he could not have done better than Julie Covington.

With word spreading speedily from the Royal Court, the question arose: should it move to the West End or – the great brainwave! – the Classic Cinema in King's Road? Even though it only had 200 seats? I cannot remember who first suggested the Classic but they were right, artistically speaking. It was the best space in London for *The Rocky Horror Show* and had the best atmosphere, even if it was no place to make money.

We had barely moved, amid incredible publicity – at the last night at the Court, Mick Jagger had been turned away – when some property man bought the Classic and said he was about to tear it down and put up an office block. So we had to spend all the money we had made, plus a lot more, moving to another Chelsea cinema, the Essoldo. (The Essoldo is now one of the Classic cinemas which is confusing.)

I made the mistake of not buying the Essoldo, which was offered to us. I have always been very nervous of owning property and never feel comfortable with people who deal in it. Though what we really should have done rather than transfer to the Essoldo – which still only had 400 seats – was to move to the West End then and there.

We would have made marvellous profits which we never earned from the stage show. Instead, everything was done to make the Essoldo wonderful. We ripped out fifty precious seats to put up a centre gangway for Tim Currie to make his entrance. There could not be a better example of putting the show first and money second.

We were not too worried about money, however, because we had begun to get a feel of the sort of freakish show that we had created. I could go on a Friday night and see people who had been there the previous Friday. It became a great pick-up spot, a place to meet, a big continuous party. The masked usherettes going round at the beginning pretending to frighten people melted individuals into a whole. Everyone would start talking to everyone else. The show's grip on the young was unshakeable.

Soon enough we started to receive offers from America but, as usual, from the wrong people. We all felt it would be better to open in Los Angeles, the home of the music business and more receptive to this freaky hit, we thought, than New York.

I had become extremely friendly with Hercules Belville, whom I had originally met as a result of that car crash after *The Connection*, and he told me about Lou Adler, whom he described as 'a very exciting and interesting' record-producer in Los Angeles. Adler was then living with Britt Ekland who, coincidentally, had seen the show in London and told him about it. I got a call from Elliot Roberts, who was then part-owner with Lou of the Roxy, a club on Sunset Strip which was a pivotal address in the rock-and-roll business. It was a great kick-off place; a lot of big bands made their Los Angeles début there, although it only had about 400 seats.

Next door to the Roxy was the Rainbow, a restaurant-cum-nightspot, and upstairs there was a club with the smallest membership in the world called On The Rocks, basically a place for Lou to entertain his friends. It might have only two or three people a night in it. When there was an 'event' on, it would have thirty.

Lou Adler does business in a very unusual way, although nearly everything he has touched has turned out well. He started out with Herb Alpert of Tijuana Brass – in fact he was Herb's insurance man. He went into business with Herb, and then set up his own record label, Ode. He produced many famous songs – and wrote some of them. His first movie, *Monterey Pop*, which he partly financed himself, became one of the biggest grossers of its year.

What appealed most to us, however, was that he and Elliot (who later dropped out) also managed a couple of big rock groups. We felt more and more that *Rocky Horror* should go to rock-and-roll people rather than to legitimate theatre. So off went Lyndall, Jim Sharman and I to Los Angeles.

It took about five days of hanging about until Lou was ready to see us. Most West Coast heavies seem to have the idea that they must assert their stature by imposing these ritual waits. Not appreciating this quaint local custom, we nearly upped and off. We were there to do business and nothing was getting done. But Los Angelenos are a little out of touch with the way things work in London or New York. They really only know their own town, with its satellites like Hawaii, Las Vegas and Aspen, where they make occasional brief forays, heavily escorted by other members of the tribe and their gofers.

It is very different from London where someone might be a farmer, but if demonstrably amusing would be welcome anywhere. People who are successful in California mix only with their own kind. Outsiders make them nervous. So does the thought of any way of life with which they are not conversant: a wide range. When those that I met at this time were not doing business their only diversion seemed to be basketball games. Otherwise they just sat around and smoked dope. Everything was ultra-casual. There was no making arrangements for dinner or lunch next week. In fact, they rarely ate real meals.

So it took me a while to appreciate that Lou, the epitome of laid-back Los Angeles, was a man of enormous charm. Nothing would get him out of jeans, and like most of his ilk he always looked the same to me, but in fact what he wore was readily recognisable to the discerning – boots from some place in Texas, hand-made, incredibly expensive hand-knitted sweaters decorated by an artist. His house at Malibu is very spectacular – which cannot be said for Malibu itself. It was packed with art déco chosen from around the world. He had an office in the old Chaplin studio, which had a wonderful atmosphere.

All business in California seemed to be done on the phone. In all the years I have now been dealing with Lou I do not believe I have ever had a letter from him. However we did get *The Rocky Horror Show* together, which would probably not have happened otherwise, and Lou and I became friends. He loaned me a two-seater Ferrari – there are not many of those around and even fewer owners so generous. But that is typical of Lou.

Once *Rocky Horror* was running at the Roxy, various film companies began to get interested. Finally, Lou negotiated a deal with 20th Century Fox, at a very low budget even for those days – $1,000,000. It was to be shot in London and billed as a joint presentation, Adler-White in

America and White-Adler in Britain. Lou was executive producer, I was producer. Title: *The Rocky Horror Picture Show*.

Everything looked fine. Then, ten days before we were due to start filming, there was a change of management at Fox. Peter Beale, then head of Fox in London, told me that the new board did not want to finance the film without meeting the director. They had suddenly realised what a weird property they had on their hands.

There was no way Jim Sharman could start a film in ten days time *and* go to Hollywood and explain what he was doing. But I would come over, I told Beale – Lou was already there – but if Fox did not want to do it after all that would be fine with us too.

Film companies often try to make new conditions in a deal at the last moment and, because a producer is at that stage committed and must have the money to start the film, he usually has to agree to whatever they want. But one of the great moments of my life had arrived. Lou and I were in a position to raise the entire million ourselves, so Fox could do what they liked.

So, on days before filming was due to start, Peter Beale and I flew out to Hollywood, and the next morning – Sunday – had a meeting round the swimming pool of a senior Fox executive, with everyone in tennis clothes. After several hours of discussion we got a bemused go-ahead. But, after we had been filming for a week or two, Alan Ladd Jnr came in as the new Head of Production and flew to London to have a look at what was going on.

Filming had begun in November 1975 – very cold weather – in the famous 'haunted house' that had been used for all the Hammer horror films, Oakley Court, next to Bray Studios in Berkshire. It is a wonderful building which has now been turned into a hotel, but was then in total disrepair. It had been used by General de Gaulle as a weekend home during World War II, and simply abandoned one day. There were documents and letters still in the desk drawers even though some forty films had been made there. There was no heat – indeed there were no windows – and the draughts were incredible. It was quite hard at 9 am to get a rock-and-roll number together.

In fact *Rocky Horror* was a tough film to make, particularly in six weeks, and it was not a particularly happy one. With so much work to do in such a short time, people get over-tired and argumentative. Heaven knows what Laddie, as everyone calls him, thought of it. He certainly looked extremely bewildered as we showed him round the sets. There has never been another film like *Rocky Horror Show*, and nothing could ever resemble the making of it.

All the people in the film were completely unknown, which is not so of many of them now: Meatloaf, who played Eddy, Susan Saradon, Barry Bostwick, who is now a big Broadway star ... Then there was Koo Stark, aged seventeen at the time, who got her Equity card through playing one of the Transylvanians. She is barely recognisable, because everyone in *Rocky Horror* was made up to look ugly. One of the principal charms of the film is that it is a homage to ugliness. Apart from Tim and Rocky, nobody is meant to look good, a factor that has given a lot of reassurance to those who are not among life's cutest numbers.

I had met Koo through the film *Emily*. Henry Herbert, the producer of that harmless frolic, and I were friends. We had owned horses together. I suggested her for *Rocky* and, while I would never say to a director that he had to have a particular person, she got a small part. It was the beginning of a close friendship which endured through all her other dramas.

Just as the *Rocky* express was working up to top speed it came off the rails with a jarring shudder on 16 March 1975, the night it hit Broadway. Lou, tired of the small-scale production that had run for nine months at the Roxy and determined to provide Fox with an appropriate launching pad for the *Picture Show*, moved it into the Belasco Theatre, a yawning dome of a place which he decked out as a cabaret. Perhaps he wanted to show that a boy from out West could take on the East Coast smarties on their own ground.

The show was hopelessly overstaged and the confusion of waiters serving drinks completely destroyed the invaluable quality of intimacy. Savaged by the critics, it closed after fifty performances, losing $400,000. Fox, as aghast as Lou himself, began to think again. *The Rocky Horror Picture Show* did well in Los Angeles where its audiences were mainly gay. But in other places hardly anyone came through the cinema doors. The big New York opening planned for Halowe'en was cancelled. A very sorry year was to pass until some rather sharp marketing men at Fox followed their noses around a few university towns and realised that they had a natural for the midnight movie circuit, one of the few growth areas of the 1970s where Hollywood was concerned.

A few courageous exhibitors went along with the idea and, as Stuart Samuels wrote in his 1983 study *Midnight Movies*, *TRHPS* soon became 'the king of midnight cult films'. It played for over six years – only at midnight – to 5,000 people a week in over two hundred theatres throughout America. And the audiences do not just sit there and watch. I had been living in New York in 1956 when *Rock Around the Clock* came out and I saw a packed cinema go completely ape, the audience dancing in the aisles, shouting and screaming. Nothing like that ever happened again at the movies until *TRHPS* was released.

The show has long since aroused the curiosity of sociology professors. A lengthy article in an American film magazine by a professor of sociology at UCLA investigated the reasons why people, having sat through films for fifty years in relative silence, were suddenly moved to turn this one into their own show. Someone else is preparing a learned treatise on the subject. The participation craze dawned slowly. It was quite a while after the film's release when it became apparent that something quite unprecedented was going on.

I took Sam Spiegel to see *TRHPS* at the Eighth Street Playhouse in New York, now its spiritual home. He was as astounded as he had ever been in fifty years of cinema-going. At 8th Street or indeed anywhere else it is shown in America, the queue to go in has become part of the show. People take on the identity of the character they feel most in sympathy with. There will be five Columbias, eight Frank 'N Furters, countless Janets.

The action starts with the wedding scene at the beginning. Showers of rice wash across the cinema. The audience know every line spoken on the screen and all the songs. Ritual comments are choroused, the thrust of them being that Brad is a jerk and Frank 'N Furter – Tim Curry – is the hero.

Whenever a character does a song on the screen, all the clones out front get up and do it too. When Brad and Janet have a flat tyre he says, 'I should have mended the spare', and the entire audience shouts, 'Arsehole!' When Brad and Janet get out in the rain the audience raise newspapers over their heads. Then, when they arrive at the castle and Richard O'Brien's face shows in the top window, the audience light candles. When Riff-Raff introduces her as Janet Veiss instead of Weiss, everyone shouts, '*Veiss!*'

Anyone who did not know what was going on would think the whole place was on some weird trip. Which is why the film goes on going on. First-timers are called 'Virgins' by the seasoned fans. And there are always new ones coming along. Some kids go a hundred times and more.

It took quite a while for Fox to realise that all this was happening. But then it spread like crazy. Apart from Eighth Street, Tiffany's in Los Angeles and Austin, Texas are the main centres. Tiffany's, right on Sunset Strip, has screenings at midnight and two a.m. The shows are messy for theatre managements, the rice and other debris involves much cleaning out. But *TRHPS* fans do not rip up seats or destroy the cinema, they just have massive fun.

Pretty soon, of course, there was a fan-club. It is run by Sal Piro, a former scripture teacher, who puts out a magazine, postcards, bulletins, organises weekends. *Rocky* changed his life as much as it did those of the actors.

Tim Curry brought great wit and attractiveness to *Rocky Horror* both on stage and screen. Of course he is completely different off-stage, very low-key, modest, unflamboyant. On the few occasions he has gone to *Rocky Horror* conventions in America – they take place regularly – the fans have been very disappointed to see him in corduroys and shirts. They wanted him in transvestite gear. Whenever I go to a screening in the USA now the fans even ask for *my* autograph.

Rocky was the first film I had produced that was financed without an investment from me, so I was not at risk. But it must be one of the most successful films ever made. Look at the figures. The first year it took $25,000 at the box office and the second year $100,000. But the third year it took $4 *million*, the fourth year $5 million and the same in the sixth year. All of it at midnight screenings, apart from year one. Perhaps the ultimate accolade was a scene in Alan Parker's film *Fame*, in which two of the student characters go to a midnight screening of *The Rocky Horror Show*. When the fans go into 'Touch me, Touch me, I Want To Be Dirty', the girl takes her blouse off and does a dance in her bra.

*

Even beyond *Rocky Horror*, my Australian connections kept multiplying. I had first seen Barry Humphries perform in 1966, when he came to London and appeared at the Fortune. He did not go over very well, but it gave a foretaste of what was to come. Practise can make perfect. Barry's success is the proof of it.

He came back to London because of Lyndall. She had interviewed him often when she was a TV reporter in Australia and he was still plain Edna Everage – not Dame. He was drinking a lot then, and hanging around art galleries – he painted, and we liked a lot of the same paintings; I thought he was a bit over the top. But Lyndall was a great fan of his, and she was forever urging me to do something about him. So I agreed to present him in *Housewife Superstar*.

We got Brian Thompson, the designer of *Rocky Horror Show*, to do a very cheap but wonderful environment which extended right outside the theatre. Fake foliage was spattered with wonderful Sydney tabloid headlines: *Woman Eats Shark . . . Mother Gives Birth in Lift*.

We had the cream – and the foam – of the Aussie world at the first night, with curtain up at eleven p.m., which made for a wonderful atmosphere. Barry was absolutely brilliant. The show was one to which people could go night after night – and I often did. Personally, I would like all theatre to start at ten or eleven p.m. – even midnight.

Barry handles an audience better than any performer I know. I think the gag where he takes the coloured hankies and waves them at the front row of the audience and says, 'Oh, we've got a little foreigner here, a little ethnic person,' is simply brilliant. 'This is the first thing she's reacted to in the entire show,' he goes on. 'It must be the colour . . . Now she's laughing, now we've made her happy.' It is such a simple joke, but he does it brilliantly. It shows amazing control.

Barry had gone on the wagon by then which made a lot of difference to his life. As a performer he was highly organised, punctual, punctilious, terrific eye for detail, knew exactly what he wanted in his costumes, wigs, jewellery. He needs a lot of people to help achieve his effects, although the concepts are all his own.

I came to like Barry as much offstage as I adored the Dame's performance. He became a friend of mine as much as Lyndall's, and marvellously entertaining at any time. Every night was Barry Humphries Night while he was on form, nothing was too much trouble for him. I realised I had not really known him at all earlier – which made what happened subsequently all the more upsetting.

Superstar was a total triumph. For a publicity stunt, we got Edna down to Royal Ascot in the largest hat ever seen, and many similar things were devised for the media. I did not make that much money because I had kept the prices down too low, something I have done far too often. Then it moved to the Globe for another six weeks, still an unqualified hit, different wonderful things happening every night.

When the run ended Barry said he would like to introduce Dame Edna to New York. I thought America might be ready for him. *Monty Python* was catching on well over there and so was the *Rocky Horror Show*, although few of the fans would know of its Anglo-Australian origins. I found a New York producer to present *Housewife Superstar* – to manage it, that is – and agreed to finance it myself. Then we made a disastrous error – although not as big a one as going to New York in the first place. We booked Theatre 84, way over on the West Side beyond 10th Avenue. The notice in the *New York Times* was appalling. It cost a quarter to get cross-town, it said, in effect. Don't spend the quarter, never mind the price of the ticket.

Stupidly, because I knew New York quite well enough to see that this meant death – Dame Edna was not *Oh! Calcutta!* – I did not simply say, Well, it hasn't worked, we close tomorrow night. Instead, I thought of what failure would do to Barry's prestige in London. I resolved to keep it on for five weeks, even if it was losing money. But one always under-estimates the cost of a failing production. That one-man show cost me $80,000.

The next thing I knew was that an agent named Fred Bestell arrived from Sydney saying that he wanted to discuss Barry's next London season. I was intrigued to realise that he seemed to think I was something of a newcomer to show business. But, in any case, I never heard anything more from either him or Barry. Then it was announced that Dame Edna would shortly be appearing at the Piccadilly. But without a management.

Now, I happen to think that a performer is wrong to decide that, having become a big star, he does not need anybody to manage him. It is extremely dangerous for an artist to do everything for himself even if it means a bit more money coming in. The show can never be seen objectively. But if that is what a star wants he has a perfect right to it. It is not a matter of principle I am complaining about. It is the money.

I felt Barry had an obligation to allow me to continue to present him so that I could try to recoup what I had lost in New York. But, if he did not want me to, then he should have told me so himself. I was so furious I did something I had never done before. I sued him for breach of contract, claiming that there was a verbal understanding between us.

I think I might well have won my case on the evidence – certainly I would have won in New York. It would have been understood that I would not have kept the show on there without a reasonable purpose – to get Barry back to London where he belonged with as little damage as possible to his standing.

As it happened the solo run at the Piccadilly was immensely successful. I did not go on with the suit – how could I stay angry with anyone so talented? But I did not speak to Barry for a long time and I still consider myself something of a goodie by casting him in a leading role in the film *Shock Treatment*.

CHAPTER FOURTEEN

'Chorus Line'

It is always interesting to see how a particular actor will respond to the offer of a script. Some seem to take an imperious pleasure in dismissing a play out of hand. Others go to great lengths to show that they have weighed it up and analysed its prospects. This letter from John Gielgud is a sparkling specimen of the second category.

Thank you very much for sending me the play. I enjoyed the dialogue immensely, which surprised me, as I have tried to read one of his books, and been unable to get through it.

But I fear this is really not a play. There is simply no central focal point, and one does not know who to be interested in out of the different couples. Also the dialogue, clever as it is, is really 1930 it seems to me, and those kind of characters belong to the Evelyn Waugh period, and not today at all. This would, I fear, complicate the acting of the play, and above all it is really only a series of sketches, and I think by the end of the evening one would have got very tired of everyone speaking the same way. It is a pity, as there is so much that is original, and indeed brilliant and funny in the whole thing. When one first reads it one feels extremely excited about it, but the more one studies the script, the more one comes to the regretful conclusion that it is too slight and repetitive. It needs some sort of situations to hold it together, and except for the short episode of the fake suicide in the last act, nothing really happens at all. Perhaps with perfect casting and a tiny theatre, like the Arts, it might be possible to make an amusing thing of it, but I am a bit dubious myself.

Although actors understandably detest auditions even more than I do –

not that anyone would dare suggest one to Sir John – the experience of them leaves an indelible impression in every theatrical memory. Which was why *A Chorus Line*, which I brought to London in 1976, was, apart from its public appeal, instantly seen to be the show business show to end them all. And that was before its run took a twist that would have made a show business show plot in itself – the sacking of Elizabeth Seal, after she had been chosen as lead in the British company, and her replacement by Donna McKechnie who was also the wife of the director Michael Bennett. Pure soap opera.

It may be that English actors in particular take badly to auditions. Certainly, I have frequently been amazed when an actor I know (and know to be good) comes on and does a really sloppy thing for an American director who does not know any more about him than what he can see. On a very busy day for a musical, one might be seeing 200 people a day – they come on, sing, go off. They feel like a sack of potatoes; I feel unhappy and uncomfortable. But what is so often wrong is that they simply have not done enough homework. Most actors do not even bother to dress for a part. If you are trying for a part in a play about terrorists in Italy, in my opinion, you should project the ambience – not come on in a city suit. You should dress and look as if you have thought about what you are auditioning for.

When we were doing *Two Gentlemen of Verona* I was sitting in a complete slump, with the American author's team, and a man came on and did a little routine that lasted four minutes – 'Simon and His Dancing Bear' – which was so outstanding and brilliant that even the blasé stage crew stopped everything and watched. That was Tommy Tune who has since become a very successful choreographer as well as a star. He had obviously spent time thinking out something that would show off all his talents. Unfortunately he still didn't get the part, as he was American and couldn't get a work permit.

Long before it became a Broadway hit, I had heard about *Chorus Line* through Joe Papp who first produced it in New York. I saw it very early on, when it was in the Public Theatre. The opening was the best I had ever seen for a musical, an overwhelming theatrical experience. The first ten minutes alone shook me. There was a great strong story immediately. At the end of the opening number you really knew exactly what was happening: these were dancers hoping to get a job in a musical. The choreography of that first number was dazzling, and the song is now played at every theatrical gathering (together with *There's No Business Like* ...). It sums up the anguish every actor understands.

166

I never had any doubts at all about *Chorus Line* for London, although plenty of people did. I always feel that the British like strong performances and real dancing and this show had them in a way that is rarely seen outside the ballet. In addition the individual stories were very good and there were half a dozen show-stopping songs.

Making one of my celebrated instant judgements I negotiated with Bernie Gersten, Joe Papp's trusted associate, and I did not, I must admit, make a deal to be proud of. One thing that I did decide on was absolutely correct, however. We had to bring an American company to Britain. We could not take over the company that was by then appearing on Broadway, because it was just getting into its stride. A new company would have to be formed, with perhaps one or two key people from the original group. Foolishly, I agreed that the new company would be able to play Toronto en route, a production for which I paid without getting a share of the Canadian proceeds. I went to Toronto for the opening and the company were marvellous to behold. But, instead of immediately recouping £40,000 of the £200,000 I had raised in Britain, all I got was the pleasure of seeing a great production come together.

I now had a far more pressing matter to worry about. I knew that, if the show was a hit in London, I was very soon going to have to start raising an English company. Equity was only ready to allow the American cast to play for six months in Britain.

It had not been difficult to get a second company together in America. Or indeed a third and a fourth. Papp and Michael Bennett already had feelers out by the time I signed because it was obvious the show would go on tour. When auditioning, they had seen a lot of good people they had not had room for in the original cast. In America an actor must sing or dance if he and she is to be offered many jobs. In England a lot of very good actors do not do either.

But Canada was such a success that my worries were temporarily submerged in the excitement that grew and grew as the London opening neared. We had Drury Lane, the best theatre in London for this musical. We had pretty strong advance publicity. I knew at the very least that we would do a lot of American tourist trade. Even though the show was on Broadway it was such a hot ticket that only a few non-New Yorkers would have been able to see it.

And the first night was totally unforgettable. *Chorus Line* was tailor-made for a professional audience, and we had managed to get every showbiz pro in town there. Everybody in the business had heard about it and wanted to go. I will never forget coming out of the stage door afterwards and seeing about fifty people standing round. They all yelled

167

and cheered. It was marvellously exciting – and a long way from *The Connection*.

Almost immediately, though, Michael Bennett and I had to face up to getting a British cast together. Most people doubted that we could do it. But we thought we could find one to equal the Americans, particularly if we had enough time in which to train them. I got on very well with Michael. I had never done anything with him before. He had been the choreographer on Hal Prince shows and this was his first solo. We discovered that we were both perfectionists, determined to bring it off.

The auditions we held were an eerie reflection of the show itself. A lot of actors complained about the toughness. Yet many of those who came – and went – said they learned more from trying out for Michael than they had ever learnt in an English dance class. He knew exactly what to say to achieve results and how to say it.

We saw hundreds and hundreds of people, usually ten at a time. Grateful kids and often disgruntled ones; a lot who thought they were wonderful but were not and did not like making the discovery. It cost over £100,000 to replace the American cast, an unprecedented sum, partly spent on long, long practice time. We had virtually to re-teach the British dancers to dance.

When we had finished, the chorus and smaller parts were very good, if not quite as good as the American company had been. But we had not been able to settle on anyone for the female lead, Cassie. It was a role that required immense 'dance presence' and top-flight physical ability. There was a solo dance, in particular, that went on for six or seven minutes, making highly concentrated demands on talent.

Two promising understudies, Petra Siniawski and Jennie Lyons, were keen to have a chance at it. On the other hand, rightly or wrongly, if a name could do as well why not have her? Our search for an established star narrowed down to Elizabeth Seal. I made the decision. We were sitting in the company manager's office and Michael finally asked me, 'It's time for decisions. Who shall we go with?' And I said, 'I think Elizabeth.' He said, 'Fine, that's it.'

Fine it was not. I had misgivings even then for, at the age of forty-two, Elizabeth was in for a hard time in that demanding part. Only through an enormous amount of hard work was she likely to pull it off. She would have to get into immaculate trim and stay that way.

A couple of weeks before the new company went in, there was a party at Robert Fox's place. About 1.30 a.m. I found myself brooding over Elizabeth's presence there, wondering if she ought not to have been home in bed. Soon I became aware that Michael too was nervous about

168

my choice of Elizabeth. It had been wrong. I had to admit it and I had to fire her – and quickly.

Looking back on all of this, I do not think we could have done otherwise. But I do think we could have softened the blow. In our haste we must have seemed quite heartless. On the other hand we had very little time and we thought we were doing the least painful thing.

There are several ways of firing people and I am very bad at all of them. I hate doing it and normally it takes me ages to get around to it. But, with time running out, the only method seemed to be swift amputation. Elizabeth was paid off.

Understandably perhaps, she did not feel like going quietly, which I still think was a mistake on her part. My advice to any actor who is fired, even if it is unjustifiable, would be to shut up about it and fade away. Why draw it to the public's attention? It was certainly the cause of endless trouble for us because Michael Bennett and I had both come to feel that to get the new show on – which was now only about ten days away – we should bring over from New York Donna McKechnie who had starred in the original production; and who, at that point, was married to Michael.

I told Elizabeth that it was up to her what she said publicly, but why not say that she was not feeling well or make some other excuse? But she obviously felt very aggrieved and decided to fight. The press had a marvellous time. We came out as terrible monsters: Michael, the American villain, getting rid of our British star to get his wife into the show – as if Donna needed the job!

We assured Equity that we were quite happy to put an English girl in if we could find one who could deal with the part – and learn it in time. They agreed that this might be asking a lot of anyone.

I realised why people come to hate the press. Wherever we went and whatever we did, they were lying in wait. One day Michael, Donna and I came out of the theatre and five or six photographers pursued us. We went down an alley to escape them, and came to a brick wall. We had to fight our way back through them. Michael said: 'Screw this, I'm leaving, I can't stand these people. Close the show, I don't care what it costs, I'll pay.'

He meant it. It was a serious threat to the production and at that time we had not made much money. We had got back our £300,000 production costs, and made less than £100,000, which had already been spent in replacing the cast.

So I went round to the Berkeley Hotel where he was staying and pleaded with him. We drank a lot of vodka and got tearful and maudlin, and very reluctantly he agreed to go on with the show. He did not mind being criticised, but he hated the slurs on his wife, and the inference that he would have fired somebody to advance her.

The show did go on, of course, and eventually ran for two and a half years. It was the third longest running show at the Lane after *My Fair Lady* and *South Pacific*. It might have run longer, but we felt it was too sophisticated to be staged anywhere in Britain outside London.

I got a lot of ridiculous hate mail over the Elizabeth Seal episode, much of it from actors. And Equity got hundreds of telephone calls, saying, you must not let those Americans come over here with their Broadway ruthlessness. My view is that the British theatre could often do with just a bit more 'ruthlessness', if that is what it is. The show is the baby, after all, and if the baby is sick, you must do whatever is necessary to keep it alive. There are times when you must decide which is the more important – and do it.

CHAPTER FIFTEEN

Movies

For as long as I can remember I have always loved film. In my teens, on a rainy summer holiday near Lausanne, I went to the cinema almost every day. In the course of eight weeks I saw sixty-eight films. An amusing reminder of this is the diary I kept, in which I wrote a critique of each film I saw and recorded my rather strong prejudices. I liked then, and still do, the big performance, and I think that this is also what audiences enjoy most. My tastes lie between the serious and the silly. Here at random and without much thought are some films I really liked: *Citizen Kane*, *The Girl Can't Help It*, *Slightly Scarlett*, *Napoleon*, *Imitation of Life*, *Jailhouse Rock*, *Wild Strawberries*, *Le Règle du Jeu*, *Battleship Potemkin*, *Zéro de Conduite*, *Belle de Jour*, *Beach Party* and *Seven Samurai*. This split of interests is indicated in the films and shows I have produced.

John Goldstone was doing an apprenticeship in films with Joe Janni at the same time I was with Peter Daubeny and it was he who, on a number of occasions, suggested that I go into film production. It was curious that the project he brought to me was one that involved many people who ten years before had been involved in *Cambridge Circus*. In the decade since, they had created the brightest programme on television, *Monty Python*. They now hoped to make a film, *Monty Python and the Holy Grail*; they wanted it to be made as an independent production and approached friends in the industry for the finance. John had already read the script and strongly recommended it to me. I came in as co-financier.

It was budgeted at £220,000, which was low even for 1973. This was a deliberate decision so as to avoid clearing with the major film companies who are filled with opinionated people who frequently change the original idea of a film. I feel the most successful films arise from one person having an idea and carrying it through. Films that are individualistic are often difficult to finance. The Pythons, having had complete freedom on television, wanted to maintain it in the cinema, and the only way to do this was with private money. The script for *The Holy Grail* was excellent.

We were reasonably certain the film would do well in England but its success in America was a pleasant surprise to us all, as the Pythons were known only to a smallish cult audience. However, the day *The Holy Grail* opened in New York, at 11.30 a.m., there were several hundred young people waiting outside the cinema. Don Rugoff, the American distributor for the film, was an eccentric and amusing character and he had decided that he would give a coconut shell to everyone who came to the film on that first day. So there were these hundreds of coconuts on Third Avenue, a phenomenon which in turn caused all the passers-by to stop and look. It was an excellent and cheap publicity stunt that worked. *The Holy Grail* is a film that does not date and as a result has had continued success at the box office.

One of the curious aspects of the film, which does not get publicised, is how much money is taken away by the various people between the producer and the box office. In the theatre, four days after the end of each week you receive a cheque from the theatre owner with a detailed statement of where the money that has been withheld has gone, namely the rent, the staff, the heating, the lighting, etc. Whereas, in the cinema, it can take six to nine months before it reaches a producer. This is because the cinema takes a considerable bite out of box office receipts and then the distributor takes off his costs including advertising and general publicity and a portion of his office overheads. By the time the money paid to the box office reaches the producer, a great many chunks have been taken out. It is misleading when members of the public who are not in the film business read 'Film takes 20 million dollars': little do they realise that 10 million of that can have just vanished into exploiting it and distributing it. Generally, a film has to take four times what it cost in order just to recoup. *Holy Grail* stayed for long periods in small cinemas and therefore the costs of distribution and publicity were not so great, and as a result the returns to the investor were much better than on most films.

The role of the investor in the cinema is not very clear-cut. In the first few films where I was involved as an investor I did very little except make general observations on the rough cut and try to help with the publicity campaign. The Pythons, being very self-contained and self-assured by this time, needed little help, and I just smoothed over various small problems.

172

Monty Python and the Holy Grail was directed by two people, which was something of an oddity, Terry Jones and Terry Gilliam. Gilliam had done the inimitable graphics for the *Monty Python* television shows and then wrote an original script called *Jabberwocky*. On this film John Goldstone, Sandy Lieberson, who was then David Puttnam's partner, and I were all involved. I had raised a substantial part of the budget when an investor who was in for almost a third of the cost pulled out. Sandy and John were terribly worried and asked me to up my investment, which at the time was impossible. Bernard Delfont, whom I had known for a number of years through the theatre, had just become chief executive of EMI and I approached him for the missing investment of £200,000. We had an amiable lunch at the Café Royal and it was agreed that EMI would come in. (It was EMI who had distributed *Holy Grail* in the UK and seen how well it had done.) A few days later I received the standard thirty- to forty-page contract from EMI's lawyers; it had the curious addition of the provision of a personal guarantee. We were now hours away from starting to film and, though normally in business I would not undertake to give a personal guarantee, I agreed as it was too late to withdraw. After the first year, *Jabberwocky* had not recouped its cost and EMI duly called in their guarantee. Fortunately *Jabberwocky* went on to make money, but only after a long period.

Generally, the fewer films you invest in the greater the risk and vice versa. If a company has fifteen to twenty films a year being released, the chances are that several of them will do well enough to pick up losses from the less successful. Today, if one can afford to wait long enough, a film can generally make its money back. This is because of the various safety nets that have been created; video, cable in the USA, and now satellite. It may take six or seven years but this means that a film that does not have box office success has a second chance before being ditched. A lot of studios must regret having sold off in the Sixties their library of old films to television for what was a comparatively small amount of money.

The next project in film came from an idea of Henry Herbert's. He wanted to set up a fund by which films could be financed and he had found the perfect vehicle for raising the money. These were a couple of odd gentlemen with luxurious offices in Mayfair who worked out that, if you had sufficient capital, you could use the interest from the capital to make films and not really be at risk. It sounded too good to be true! However, they were not prepared to go ahead with the scheme unless we paid for the legal costs in advance. Their lawyers were very expensive but the rule of 'you can't make without investing' seemed in this instance correct. We had a series of funny meetings, and on occasions when we visited their offices waiting to see them were some extremely high-powered people including the chairman of a major public company and the trade delegation of an African nation. We seemed in good company but of course, once we had put the money in their hands, they vanished. The only consolation was that a few years later we were asked by the fraud squad if we would give evidence against them and, from what the detective told us, we got off relatively lightly. Some very important and influential people round the world were ripped off for considerably larger sums of money.

Meanwhile, I was looking for a musical film that would somehow reflect the activity and excitement that was taking place in England at the time. Davina Belling approached me (she had worked for me in the past before going on to be a successful film producer with Clive Parsons). The idea they brought to me was one which immediately appealed. *Rude Boy* was a low-budget film featuring The Clash; it was about a boy who devotes himself to following them around as a groupie or ligger as they were then called. The film reflected the desperation of the rootless unemployed and their ways of coping with a life that appeared to have little future. *Rude Boy* was shot in black and white and has a very cold-blooded atmosphere. However, there were problems with the film before it was finished. In order to incorporate the story and a dozen songs or more, the film had to be made much longer than originally anticipated, and as a consequence we went considerably over budget. The Clash, like all brilliant and creative people, had very clear ideas of how they wanted to be seen and this also caused problems. The director was Jack Hazan who had directed the excellent film *The Big Splash* about David Hockney, but to deal with the civilised artistic world was a much easier task than coping with one of the angriest rock groups around.

A lot of film and music people felt very positive about *Rude Boy* and several American critics thought it was the best film about contemporary England they had seen. Certainly in New York, when it opened, week one broke the box office record for the cinema, week two did all right, but by the third week nobody wanted to see it. The film did not get a cult following and we were unable to release the album, all of which was somewhat disappointing.

But I still felt that another musical was worth trying and in 1980 I embarked upon *Urgh A Music War*. I wanted to make a film about the new wave without a story, simply non-stop music. I was in Los Angeles and went to see David Picker who was now at Lorimar Films and who as head of United Artists in England in the Sixties had been responsible

174

for some of our best films. I then tried to engage Jonathan Demme, one of the American directors I admire most, to direct the film. However, we did not manage that and, when David Picker agreed to distribute, time was short.

He asked me how much it was going to cost, and I said – mistakenly – that I could deliver it for $1½ million. There were the inevitable discussions about details on the contract, but he and I had accepted that figure, and I was to be stuck with it.

Gil Freisen of A & M Records suggested Miles Copeland, the manager of The Police, and of IRS records as a partner, saying that he knew as much about new music as anybody around. Which indeed he did. So I co-opted Miles and his brother Ian. Miles suggested Derek Burbidge, who had done a lot of music films and videos, as director. Lyndall became deeply involved too.

The idea was to make a comprehensive and encyclopaedic production. But my hankering for perfection led me into an error of judgement. Instead of bringing each band – and we filmed fifty – to either Los Angeles or London, and shoot a couple of days on each, I wanted each band shot on location. This was, at least financially, somewhat insane because a band is a band whether it is playing at CB-GB's in New York or the Lyceum in London. But we flew a crew of seventeen wherever the bands were from London to Los Angeles, to New York, to the South of France.

We ended up with eight hours of edited material, and had to discard twenty-two bands whom we had paid, filmed, processed, mixed. Eventually the film went out at 100 minutes, because in America that is the length distributors prefer.

Then, no sooner had we delivered the film, than David Picker left Lorimar. It was the old story. Nobody there was really into the project the way he was. Lorimar then sold it to Filmways, a distribution company in the process of going bust. The movie was eighteen months old before it opened in Los Angeles so I was hardly surprised that it did not do very well.

We were unfortunate in London, too, when we opened – an IRA bomb went off in the Wimpy bar next to the cinema on the second day. However, some critics liked the film, and it received an interested reception in the trades; it was extremely well made – almost too well. Some of the groups we filmed, then unknown, became successful: The Police, Joan Jett, The Gogo's, The Human League.

Historically, it is very important. But *Urgh* was also a breakthrough in terms of getting something of that size together and doing it well. On some films I have done nothing but organise the finance and offer some advice. On *Urgh* I had far more to do every day than I cared for. It was easily the most difficult production I had ever taken on. Having to deal with each band, the manager, the record company, the music publishers and all their lawyers, was a nightmare. It soon became the thickest file in the office.

I am determined not to waste that experience. I still think *Urgh* was a good concept and, had it been released when it was delivered to the distributor, I think it would have done well. The relationship between music and films fascinates me still. I would like to have another crack at something similar on video and get it out within three months.

Lorimar showed *Urgh* at the Cannes Film Festival. There was a party at a huge nightclub called Studio Circus, during which I was asked to judge the best-dressed couple contest. Suddenly I spotted Gary Glitter whom I like a lot. He hardly qualified but because he was a friend I cheated and gave him third prize. Film festivals are, as everyone complains, circuses. But the advantage of Cannes is that it does bring together in one place hundreds of people in the film industry who might otherwise never meet each other. A great deal of business gets done there. And, if anyone actually wants to look at the films, there are always plenty of intriguing ones.

Polyester, the first 'smellie', came my way at Cannes. It had a script by John Waters, who was the first serious director deliberately to set out to explore the murky and uncharted territories of bad taste, and was to star Tab Hunter and a 300-pound transvestite called Divine. The film was only going to cost $300,000. John was as suave and elegant as a South American diplomat; slender, immaculate and incredibly knowledgeable about film. Gross and outrageous though his movies may be, his home town of Baltimore, where they are usually made, celebrates him as a local hero.

I was happy becoming a partner in *Polyester*. But I did not think the smells were necessary. I fought – but lost – against the card that members of the audience scratched to release the odours. When the film came out, and much was made of this gimmick in the reviews, everybody said, 'See? You were wrong.' But I still do not think the film needed the smells. Besides, the cards cost 40 or 50 cents each, which added to the distribution costs.

Polyester did handsomely in America but it was very disappointing in Europe in terms of box office. The trouble was that people liked Waters' earlier work, but he, being himself beyond shockability, felt he had to go farther and farther out to get an effect. But not everyone enjoys such rude shocks as *Polyester* provided. It was too crazy for middle-of-the-road people and not crazy enough for the fans, though I think it is another film that will travel on.

I was beginning to feel like the tortoise of the film business, involved as I always seemed to be with productions that might not do well on first release but held great promise for the future. Well, at least some of them did. Before *Polyester* I had produced, with Andy Braunsberg and John Goldstone, a comedy version of *The Hound of the Baskervilles*. The cast was a classic line-up of the late '70s: Dudley Moore, Peter Cook, Spike Milligan, Hugh Griffiths, Joan Greenwood, Denholm Elliott, Irene Handl. The director was Paul Morrissey, who directed most of the Andy Warhol films and who was fascinated by English comedies like the *Carry On* series.

Disaster struck this promising enterprise half-way through. Paul got hepatitis. We were faced with several choices and unerringly made the wrong one. The insurance company was ready either to pay all our costs up to that point so we could just walk away, or it would pay the daily costs until Paul recovered. We could have let Pete and Dud take over the film and finish it in their own incomparabe fashion. So it was not for want of options that Andy Braunsberg, John Goldstone and I then made absolutely the worst decision, which was to wait for Paul to get better. The actors wanted to get the film finished and the insurance people were fretting, so Paul went back to work after only a few weeks, which was too soon for him to have completely recovered. It is an unfortunate fact that it takes a long time to get over hepatitis, and a sick director meant an ailing film.

Hound was released but, as they say in Hollywood, it didn't open. It died everywhere, in spite of the appeal of the terrific cast. I like to think it would have turned out differently if Paul had not fallen ill. But perhaps the marriage between off-beat New York sophistication and the spirit of *Carry On* would not have been a happy one. Anyway, even after *10* and *Arthur* made Dudley Moore a big star, *Hound* still didn't do any business.

Malcolm McLaren, who created The Sex Pistols in the mid-'70s, is one of the most remarkable creative people in music, but he is a notoriously difficult man to deal with. We shared an adventure when The Pistols were at the height of their fame. Malcolm had thought up the idea of getting Russ Meyer, the Hollywood maverick who has built a prosperous career on filming huge female bosoms, to direct a movie starring The Pistols to be called *Who Killed Bambi?* John Goldstone approached Fox and they were interested. But that soon foundered. Princess Grace of Monaco had just joined the Fox board and the company was having a board meeting in Monte Carlo to mark the involvement. Alan Ladd Jr had liked the project. But, when he arrived in Monte Carlo among the gala dinners and black tie affairs, Laddie found the atmosphere a little too refined to mention anything so vulgar as Meyer and a pack of punks. So the Fox board never got to hear of *Bambi*.

Meanwhile, Russ Meyer had begun his first day's filming – in the spirit, presumably, in which he intended to continue – by ordering a deer to be shot in Richmond Park. His film crew promptly went on strike. The deer had been due to be culled anyway, but it was too much for their animal-loving English sensitivities. We set out to try to raise the money elsewhere. We had a meeting with Richard Branson of Virgin Records, the Pistols' label. There were about eighteen lawyers present, which was eighteen too many for me save for my friend Barry Shaw who over the years has helped me with many difficult legal entanglements. It showed that matters were out of control. So, at that point, we cancelled the whole thing. Some time later my brilliant producer Jeremy Thomas got the project going again, this time with Julian Temple as director. They made a marvellous and remarkable film which was released as *The Great Rock and Roll Swindle*. But Russ Meyer's *Bambi* with the Sex Pistols would have been unique.

Since the runaway success of *TRHPS* was by now staring everyone in the face, it seemed sensible to try out a sequel. So another film with the same team, *Shock Treatment*, was scripted. Again we were negotiating with Fox. Again there was a change of management right in the middle of things and Sherry Lansing was installed as the first woman in charge of a studio. But Sherry did not want *Shock Treatment*. So we went into long discussions with Paramount – I sat in Los Angeles for nine weeks trying to make a deal with them while Lou Adler, with whom I was a partner, was directing a film in Canada. He had set things in motion but I did all the negotiating – and got nowhere. Then much later – in the middle of the Cannes Film Festival – Sherry changed her mind and said yes. Tim Hampton had by then taken over as head of production for Fox in Europe and he was also keen on *Shock Treatment*.

But, after all that, the results were disappointing; though the film has a great soundtrack, it just did not take off, not even in Australia, possibly because Tim Curry was not in it and it was not a real sequel to *TRHPS*.

My reputation for speedy decision-making got a boost when Wally Shawn came looking for $125,000 to make the film of his play *My Dinner with André*. Peggy Ramsay had urged me to go and see it when it was on at the Royal Court in 1980, saying that Louis Malle wanted to film it. I knew Wally, who also acted in it (with André Gregory as the only other performer), through his involvement with Joe Papp. He had also written a play I liked which I had seen in London at the ICA.

I found *André* absolutely fascinating. Wally, Peter Eyre and I had dinner in an Italian trattoria to talk about it and, the next day, Wally came to see me in the office to ask for the money.

'Sure,' I said. Then he said, 'What else do I have to do?' I said, 'Nothing.' He could not believe it was that easy. But I had made up my mind.

When I was next in New York it was plain that Wally had been dining out on the story. Lillian Ross said to me, 'I heard about you, you're the man who got Wally Shawn out of your office in ten minutes when he expected to be there for days.' And *My Dinner with André* turned out to be a winner, much to everyone else's surprise, and it ran for over a year in one theatre in New York.

A film with a slightly similar title, *Eating Raoul*, which was a big hit in America, led me into testing my confidence as a moviemaker. I was asked to come in on it by Mark Forstatter and Paul Bartel, but I did not want Paul to play the lead. Donning the role of the heavy producer I said I would finance or partly finance the film if somebody else played the husband, the main part. They refused, I withdrew and they went on to success without me.

More swift decisions were called for with *Moonlighting*, the drama about Polish exiles starring Jeremy Irons. I came back from a trip to Australia about the middle of January 1982 and went to play tennis on a Friday with Jerzy Skolimowsky. He told me about the plot of the film he wanted to make. It was to be about a group of Polish workers stranded in Britain while back in Poland Solidarity was being crushed. He was speaking from experience. He had recently sat out Poland's ordeal in London himself. He thought he could do something on film that would capture his emotions about what had happened in his homeland, the depression, isolation, impotence he had felt.

I read his script, which was extremely simple in construction, yet full of unspoken eloquence.

We met at my house on the Sunday and walked around the garden for an hour talking. Britain's new TV channel, Channel 4, had offered to put up half the money. On Monday I went to the bank and borrowed the necessary £300,000, and we started filming a couple of weeks later. In May that year *Moonlighting* was awarded a special prize at the Cannes Film Festival and later the *Evening Standard* Award as best British film of 1982.

Then there was *Ploughman's Lunch*, in which Richard Eyre directs

Tim Curry and Jonathan Pryce in a love story about a TV political commentator. Alexander Walker, the distinguished critic, called it the best British film for ten years.

Low-budget led, logically enough, I suppose, to no-budget. Hercules Belville and Blaine Novak, who wrote the script, first came up with the proposal for *Strangers Kiss* which was being finished out in Los Angeles at the same time that *Ploughman's Lunch* was being screened at Cannes. I had been on holiday in Long Island in the summer of 1982 when he rang to say that he had a Hollywood film lined up in which all the participants had agreed to work for nothing until the film was completed and sold to a distributor. Then they would be paid according to the number of points that their notional salary represented.

The idea of deferment was not new in itself. It was by no means unknown for a star or a director to forgo part of their salary, to help along a limited budget. But this was an astonishing break-through, which, if it worked, could revolutionise film financing. Everyone – all the actors, the director, designers, cameramen, grips, right down to the caterers – was ready to take a chance along with the backers. All that would have to be paid for was film stock, transport, office costs, telephones, light and heat – the essentials.

Hercules was raring to go because all the people willing to participate were, miraculously, available and ready. Now. We raised $140,000 to finance the project that, without the deferments, would have cost $2,250,000. *Strangers Kiss* is a love story set, appropriately, around the making of a film back in the 1950s. And it was made in a marvellous spirit by everyone involved. Not only did we make a fine movie but we made a little bit of Hollywood history as well.

CHAPTER SIXTEEN

'I'

Every impresario knows that the masks that form the traditional trademark of the theatre do not represent drama and tragedy at all. They stand for success and failure. I do like to think however that my failures have always had a certain style. They have certainly improved in scale.

I first met Vladimir Forgency and Caroline Roboh – and therefore the origins of the spectacular débâcle of *I* – in 1981 through Sabrina Guinness. They were friends of hers over from Paris who explained at dinner that they were looking for an English producer to handle a show they wanted to put on in London, a theatre cabaret in the grand European style.

Caroline was only twenty-four, dark, attractive, intelligent, rather ethereal. Vladimir was in his late thirties, very lively, enthusiastic. They planned to shape the show around an Italian actor-illusionist-magician, Arturo Brachetti. They had already raised the money.

Caroline was an actress and she had also directed a film with Arturo, called *Clementine Tango*, which Vladimir had produced. Vladimir is of Polish origin, but has lived in France all his life and been involved in a lot of productions there. Since neither of them was without some experience in the theatre the result of my collaboration with them was all the more disillusioning.

I liked both of them and I liked the idea. But I declined to become involved at that stage. I was concentrating on film production, and I knew that putting something on which required knowledge of something like catering, about which I was ignorant, would involve a great deal of work and trouble. I am extremely particular about food. I could all too easily see people I knew coming up to me and saying, 'We went to your place last night. We didn't like the chicken. The waiter was rude.' I did not care for that.

So I said no thanks and suggested a couple of people who might help. Then I met Caroline and Vladimir again seven or eight months later. They were very depressed. They had spent a lot of money sitting around in London and they had still not found a publicist or a stage manager, let alone a theatre. Feeling rather sorry for them, I said, 'Look, I won't produce the show since you seem to know what you want to do' – and they seemed to. 'But I will help you out by *presenting* the show.' That, I knew, would assure them at least of a theatre.

I said I would also find them a publicist, an ad agency, production manager – in other words, I would guide them. But I made it quite clear that I could not be around all the time and that I would only take limited responsibility. In return they were to pay me a token fee and a very small percentage of the profits.

But of course *I* did begin to take up more time than I imagined it would, because there were a great many things of which Caroline and Vladimir were ignorant, or that they were not getting done. I had been given the impression that the show they had in mind had already been staged somewhere and that they were going to transplant it, with suitable modifications, to London.

My first tremor of nervousness was brought on by the realisation that, nearly a year after our first discussion, they did not have anything except Arturo Brachetti and a good idea. They were still looking for a choreographer and a composer. 'Aren't you doing *Flick Flack*?' – the show in which Arturo was a great hit in Germany and Austria – I asked. 'We don't own that,' they said.

But both of them were immensely industrious and busy and finally, between us, we got all the elements together; the composer, the book writer, a cast, interesting people to do the choreography – Derek Deane and Graham Fletcher from the Royal Ballet.

Caroline and Vladimir were besotted by an Italian designer, Pierre Simonini, who was going to do both sets and costumes – and indeed they showed me drawings which were absolutely beautiful. In the event, the designs were one of the most difficult areas.

After months of negotiation we leased from Ian Albery the Piccadilly Theatre which was perfectly situated. We took it from the first of January 1982, even though the show would not open until April. We were fortunate with architects and builders and in no time it looked absolutely magnificent.

Because the eating and drinking arrangements were an entirely new factor, and because there could be no question of an out-of-town try-out which would be normal for a brand new musical, I wanted to be sure we would be able to have more than the usual number of run-throughs to get the show right and the waiter serivce, which would be an integral part of the evening, working smoothly; so that, by the time we came to the previews, the first of which was set for 6 March, we would be in impeccable shape.

The idea was that patrons could dine before the show, watch it, and afterwards the theatre would become a nightclub with one cabaret star spot at midnight.

We spent nearly £750,000 transforming an ordinary theatre into a glowing jewel of a cabaret. If things did not work out we had to put it back the way it was.

But at this stage everything looked great. Vladimir reported that the rehearsals were going well. Any misgivings I had were no worse than I might have on any show. Invariably, one wakes up some morning or another thinking, Oh dear, this is a terrible mistake.

In the early days I went down to the rehearsal rooms in Hammersmith a few times and it all looked in pretty good order. To whatever criticism I had, Vladimir understandably said, Listen, this number is meaningless without the sets and costumes, the lighting, the tricks, the magic. I was well aware that a musical in preparation, more than any other kind of show, is like an unfinished painting. Or, indeed, like an unfinished film. It is impossible to judge whether it is good or bad, too many elements are missing. With a musical, the moment of truth is the dress rehearsal.

The Piccadilly alone was soon going to cost up to £10,000 a week. Some time before this David Astor had become the show's co-producer, so I said to him, categorically, 'We're going in for anything up to £2 million. Are you sure the money is okay?' Because, if it was not, I knew that anybody who was owed anything would be coming to me, because I was the only person involved who was known in the London theatre.

The money, it seemed, was the one thing we did not have to worry about. But there were soon plenty of other problems. In spite of all the discussions and plans, the scenery was running late and the costumes even later. The first worrying noises were coming from the rehearsal rooms in Hammersmith. Ken Grant, the stage manager, who was very experienced and had worked for me before, and some of the actors were not happy with the linking dialogue. But that was nothing major. Still, by the end of February we were three or four weeks behind schedule. We had to postpone the first previews.

Now, I was worried. I said I was not going to go to see any more rehearsals. But as soon as possible I wanted to see the show from A to Z with scenery, costumes and lighting. I was not the director or the producer. But my name was on the bill, and what if I did not like what was going to come out of Hammersmith? A lot of other people were looking forward to the first night, for Peter Thompson had done brilliantly at getting publicity. A huge burst of media attention had been keyed to our opening date, now 16 March, a Wednesday. It was to be a charity gala with tickets at £50 and Princess Anne in attendance.

I saw the first complete run-through at the theatre on 8 March. There were plenty of good things. For instance David Rappaport, the dwarf who played the Master of Ceremonies, was never better. But there were also glaring things wrong. The show was at least twice as long as it should have been. And, disconcertingly, not much of it seemed to make any sense.

Only a few of the costumes were ready. Quite a lot of the scenery had finally arrived. But everything had been rushed, and the backcloths which had been folded damp were wrinkled and looked awful. But that was not the worst of it. The Simonini sets would have looked marvellous in, say, Covent Garden, where the front rows of the stalls are at least fifty feet from the stage. But they were completely unsuitable for the kind of atmosphere we were trying to create. The nearest seats would be close enough for the customers to see the seams in the huge, overwhelming drapes. So there was already a major problem. The sets had cost £300,000.

It took a while to absorb what we had been shown. I asked to see another run-through on the Thursday, after a lot of cuts had been made. But the wigs had not arrived by then, so I agreed to wait until they were ready.

In the meantime it became very clear that the problems with the script were major. The story line had not been too clear to begin with, and trying to put the show together in French as well as English caused havoc. The hatchet job done in such haste on the script had not helped. Ian Albery had seen what was going on and wrote me a friendly warning note, which was sent to Vladimir and David as well, saying that unless we put in an English director we were headed for trouble. He suggested Peter Coe who had directed many large shows.

We had already decided that at the very least the show must have a firm directing hand. In addition to Coe I rang Jonathan Lynn with whom I had worked happily on *What the Butler Saw*. On Friday, 11 March, he sat in the back of the stalls with us – Peter Coe could not get there that night – and watched a dress rehearsal that was little short of a travesty.

Arturo, who is a brilliant performer, came across very badly. He was so exhausted, worried and depressed that even his set pieces, which we knew he did well, were not working properly. Half-way through I said to Jonathan, on whom I was depending to speak as a friend, 'Well?' 'I hate to say it,' he replied, 'but there's nothing I can do to save this show and I don't think there's anything you or anyone else could possibly do either. If I were you . . . '

'I know,' I said. 'Don't open.'

Jonathan put into words what I had felt deep down for days. It was not just a question of somebody coming in and saying, All right, you guys, lets get these choruses together, sing that song this way and cut that number. The show in its present form and state was hopeless.

Nonetheless, the decision I made that night was simply to postpone the opening. I still nursed a wispy hope that, when Peter Coe saw it on the Monday, he might come up with some magic solution.

We put up notice for the back stage and front of house staff, the waiters and waitresses, the orchestra, the chefs, the barmen. They would add £25,000 a week to our losses and it was evident that, whatever happened, we would not be opening in under three or four weeks. We also put up notice for the actors, which was slightly premature although we felt that, if a director did come in, he might want to change a lot of things – and people.

It was a dreadful weekend. The media had got hold of several versions of what was going on. Princess Anne did not receive any of the letters sent by Buckingham Palace to three different places where she was supposed to be over the weekend. She first heard of the postponement on the radio on the Monday evening which, understandably, was annoying.

There were a lot of phone calls and dramas, culminating in David Rappaport's decision to leave the cast, whatever happened. On the Friday he had rewritten his script and read it straight from the page, which had not improved the performance.

By Sunday night, Peter Thompson and I were unnerved to the point of hysteria. On the telephone to each other we were gripped by fits of giggles.

Peter had been vehement in his dislike of the show and said to me, after the first run-through, 'Get some rock and roll groups in.' He was the first person to see that it was a disaster and had not hesitated to say so, something which not everyone in his place might have done. His frankness is one of the reasons I like him so much.

One constructive move was made. Vladimir telephoned his friend

Jean-Marie Rivière in Paris to ask if he would be prepared to put his spectacular and highly successful show into the Piccadilly, incorporating Arturo and as many of the cast as he possibly could.

On the Monday night, then, we had Peter Coe, his agent Michael Linnet, a friend of mine who was also Richard O'Brien's agent, Jean-Marie Rivière, with a choreographer he had brought along, David Astor who had invited his wife and his brother-in-law, and Una Mary Parker who had organised the doomed charity.

It was unbearable. At the end, Peter Coe gave us a cutting analysis. 'It is not simply that the show fails of itself as a show,' he said, 'but when people come somewhere like this they will be expecting a certain *kind* of event. With all these French and Italian names on the bill they are entitled to expect something on European lines. This could be *anything*.'

It would be out of the question, said Peter, to come in and do anything with the show as it was. It needed a complete rethink.

After he had gone I could see that Vladimir hoped Jean-Marie would be more optimistic. He was not. His Paris show was complete and committed to its present run. But he did say that it might be possible for him to gather together an entirely new show along the lines of his previous successes.

So it was on that Monday we decided we could not open *I* at all. With each successive day, all the bad things I had felt myself had been confirmed by others. The magnificent, and expensive, posters came down.

To begin with, the cancellation had aroused astonishing interest – right on the button, Peter Thompson had delivered a wave of publicity timed for the original opening date. A week earlier, magazines and papers all carried upbeat pieces on the great new cabaret. On Tuesday I went on a peak-hour TV programme and broke the news in an interview with Michael Barratt.

'*I* regrettably will not be seen by the London theatre-goers or anyone else, because the truth of the matter is that the show, in my view and that of my associates, is not good enough to open. This has never happened to me in twenty-odd years of putting on shows, and it's not something that's very pleasant. But there's never any point in doing something if you know in your heart you're in the wrong. It's much better to admit it and start it again.'

Barratt was taken aback.

'Can I just make sure that I heard all right there? You are saying this show will not go on, at all, in any form.'

Me: 'Not as envisaged.'

Barratt: 'This comes as a shock to me, I must say.'

Me: 'It is a shock and, as I said, it's a very unpleasant situation.'

Barratt: 'David Rappaport says the thing has got progressively worse, whatever attempts were made to get it better.'

I had heard quite enough from Mr Rappaport by then, but decided to hold my peace. Instead, I explained:

'That quite often happens in the theatre, or in any enterprise. When things start to go wrong, they snowball, and they get totally out of hand. For instance, David's performance at the first rehearsal was wonderful, and as he got depressed and demoralised, naturally it got worse. But the truth is – I was thinking about it on the way here – I can't think of anyone really since Orson Welles who's directed and starred and brought it off. And that's the nub of the problem.'

I was referring to Arturo of course. I was not trying to blame him. I felt sorry for him. He was only twenty-three and he had been working non-stop for half a year or more taking voice lessons, going to the gym, dancing. He is a very agreeable, intelligent, talented person. But he obviously needed somebody to direct both him and the show. If you are on stage, how can you see what things look like from the stalls? Which is what a director is supposed to be doing above all. The whole concept was wrong and he had suffered as much as anyone in consequence. With hindsight it was obviously mad for Arturo both to have starred and directed, and all of us involved were guilty of allowing him to do it. Jean-Marie, who had worked with Arturo, said that the effort of trying to combine the two functions seemed to have drained him of talent as though it had been squeezed out of him in a press.

Some of the responsibility for the fiasco had to go to Caroline and Vladimir of course. They were childish and unrealistic in their enthusiasm and their blithe conviction that it would all be all right on the night. They had never been involved in anything on this scale. Also, there is a vast difference between what might be acceptable as a theatrical performance even in Paris, as against London.

Had we in fact opened *I* that week, I think we would have sold out for two months, no matter how awful the show had been. There was such interest in it, that I think people would have come just to be able to say how bad it had been. I went to a grand dinner a few days after my announcement and somebody came up and said, 'You've done it again – what a brilliant publicity coup. When can I get my tickets for the opening night?' A lot of people really thought that the whole shambles was a great publicity stunt. Oh, that it had been!

We asked the charity what they had expected to get out of the gala evening, and sent them a cheque for the amount, over £5,000. On the night we were supposed to open, a policewoman arrived at the Piccadilly, saying she had been assigned to sit out the evening in the Ladies as security for Princess Anne. Ken Grant, who was still sorting out the wreckage, told her what had happened. 'I've had my instructions from Buckingham Palace,' she said. 'And, until they're revoked from Buckingham Palace, I'm going to do what I've been told.' So off she went to the Ladies. She was the only person in the theatre that night.

In a disaster of such magnitude, naturally the performers' unions showed an interest. Equity sent down the head of its Variety Department, Archie McMillan, to see if his members were being protected. David Astor and I went to a meeting. The actors were saying things like, Why didn't you see what was happening? I asked, 'Why didn't any of you come to me when there was still time to do something? You're all saying now you knew weeks ago that we were in trouble. Why didn't a deputation come and say, "We're very worried about the show, can you demand a run-through now, see it, do something?"'

The cast were incredibly depressed. They had worked extremely hard for nine weeks and at the end of the day nothing – except that for a number of weeks they had been on full salary.

Look at Broadway this season, I said. Four or five major musical flops opened and closed in days. None of the people involved in *those* wanted that to happen. Would you rather have opened *I* and read in the *Guardian* and *The Times* in detail how awful the whole thing was?

In the end they all said, No, we knew we couldn't open. That was really the bottom line – knowing that the critics, unless they all went collectively mad, would have slated the show and all of us.

There is no doubt that where I went wrong was in allowing myself to believe that a lot of the show had already been tried out. I was not working directly on *I*. I was acting, in a way, as an old-fashioned impressario, presenting something that someone else had produced. Or was supposed to have produced.

Equity said that, if the show went on again, they wanted to be sure that Michael White himself participated more closely. Had I this time, they said, the calamity would probably not have happened. This was flattering, no doubt. But to the outside world it must seem as though I failed badly. My name after all was on the show.

People had come along before and said, All we want is your name, you don't need to do a thing. But I knew from experience – and *I* proved it again – that, if you have a name which means something in the theatre, it is you who are held responsible if anything goes wrong.

The most exceptional aspect of the entire drama of *I* was that there was no discord between Arturo, Vladimir, Caroline, David or myself, or any disagreement with Ian Albery who had been extremely constructive and helpful. No 'I-told-you-so', no recriminations. Nobody looked for a scape-goat, although it might have been tempting to seek one in poor Arturo.

A few days after Jean-Marie returned to Paris, he said he would be willing to get a new show together, and off went Vladimir to Geneva to get another half a million pounds. Over Easter, Vladimir and I flew to see Jean-Marie. He lives, when not in Paris, on an island in the Caribbean. Talking to him in his simple but comfortable seaside house I was made firmly aware that here was a man steeped in the world of high entertainment who knew exactly what he wished to do at the Piccadilly.

As well as bringing in new acts, some from Paris, a thought I heartily welcomed, Jean-Marie was determined to have an orchestra that could be seen. One of the many things wrong with *I*, everyone agreed, was that the orchestra of about fifteen musicians was out of sight beneath the stage apron, heard but not seen.

Jean-Marie insisted, rightly of course, that the sight of live musicians is an essential element of cabaret. The entrance of the conductor, the first stroke of his baton, turns that particular atmosphere on in a great anticipatory gush. I could see, however, that this might be problematical. The conversion of the Piccadilly was complete. There was no room left for a new orchestra pit and no money to spend on making one. No problem, said Jean-Marie. He would settle for an orchestra of, say, seven, for whom space *could* be found. And much of the music would be provided by tapes. Many of his numbers were only practicable, in any case, with taped accompaniment.

Ever since the collapse of *I*, I had been under pressure from associates and advisers to break my connection with its originators. I had been reluctant to do so, however. I was fond of Caroline and Vladimir and I did not want to undermine their efforts to start anew, by publicly stepping off the deck of the sinking ship. However, I had an inkling that Jean-Marie's strategy – and he was adamant, no tapes, no show – might make it impossible for me to continue.

Back in London, David Astor and I went to see the Musicians' Union and my misgivings were confirmed. No tapes. All the music must be live. That we still planned to have a midnight show in which another seven or eight musicians would be employed made no difference.

As a foreigner who was not a member of the Society of West End Producers, Vladimir was in quite a strong position. Musicians' Union disputes are often so arcane that they are not automatically supported by Equity or by the backstage unions. There would be nothing to prevent him from using tapes and, since British musicians would not be allowed to work in the theatre, he could import those he needed from Paris.

My position was very different. If the MU decided to 'black' me personally because of my association with the show, my other two musical productions in which their members were employed, *Pirates* and *Annie*, could be black-balled.

It was an honourable parting. I wished Caroline and Vladimir luck and urged them – not for the first time – to forget about calling their second effort *Y*.

They deserved to succeed. London could do with the kind of place we had tried to turn the Piccadilly into. Their first failure – all right, our first failure – had to be seen in proportion. The same week that the roof fell in on *I* to the tune of £1.5 million, British Rail were scrapping the Advanced Passenger Train. That cost £40 million. People make mistakes.

For a week after we put up the shutters at the Piccadilly I was terribly depressed at the waste of time and money. I could have done ten plays and a musical for what had been spent on *I*. Or a motion picture. But that would be like asking a man, Why do you want a Rolls Royce when you could buy twenty Minis?

Now, a year later, the show *Y* has done well, and is heading for Broadway – and Arturo personally received rave reviews and was hailed as a star.

*

What next? In the theatre my biggest production for some time, *On Your Toes*, with some gold-plated theatrical names, music by Richard Rodgers, lyrics by Lorenz Hart, book and direction by George Abbott, the liveliest ninety-six-year-old in the theatre or for that matter anywhere else, and choreography by Georges Balanchine, has opened to great acclaim.

Some years ago Peter Richardson came to see me for backing a comedy club in Soho featuring The Comic Strip. Since then there have been thirteen half-hour films for Channel Four, including a few gems like *Five Go Mad In Dorset, Gino, Bad News Tour, Susie*, and lots of others – for The Comic Strip is a new group of young comedians, not Oxbridge, but street smart and very funny. Now we're planning a feature film.

Then there's James Fox's book set in Kenya, *White Mischief*, and the John Masters thriller, *The Deceivers*, set in the India of the 1820s. And now the 'phone is ringing and it must be someone with a marvellous idea for a play? A film? A musical? And certainly lots more fun.

190

Index

191